Rethinking Human Security

Moufida Goucha and John Crowley

T0374712

Blackwell Publishing was acquired by John Wiley & Sons in February 2007. Blackwell's publishing program has been merged with Wiley's global Scientific, Technical and Medical business to form Wiley-Blackwell.

Registered Office
John Wiley & Sons Ltd, The Atrium, Southern Gate, Chichester, West Sussex, PO19 8SQ, United Kingdom

Editorial Offices
350 Main Street, Malden, MA 02148-5020, USA
9600 Garsington Road, Oxford, OX4 2DQ, UK
The Atrium, Southern Gate, Chichester, West Sussex, PO19 8SQ, UK

For details of our global editorial offices, for customer services, and for information about how to apply for permission to reuse the copyright material in this book please see our website at www.wiley.com/wiley-blackwell.

The rights of Moufida Goucha and John Crowley to be identified as the editors of this work has been asserted in accordance with the Copyright, Designs and Patents Act 1988.

Library of Congress Cataloging in Publication Data applied for

ISBN 978-1-4051-9263-7

A catalogue record for this book is available from the British Library.

Set in 10 on 12 points, Times by Macmillan India
Printed in Singapore by C.O.S. Printers Pte Ltd

International Social Science Journal

Rethinking Human Security

Moufida Goucha and John Crowley

Abstracts

Human security and human rights interaction

Wolfgang Benedek

This contribution analyses the interaction of human rights and human security. First, the author explains the emergence and conceptualisation of human security. By taking into account the actions on both research and policy levels and the human security initiatives by international organisations, such as UNESCO, by governments, NGOs and academia, the contribution sheds light on the potential of a multilayered and multiplayer approach to human security. In a second step the author identifies the interrelation and interdependence of human security and human rights. The results of this more theoretical part are then empirically tested in a case study on the interaction of human security and human rights, with a particular focus on the implementation of a human security approach to the right of education. Further, the contribution identifies human security-related best practices. The conclusion argues that, in light of the interdependence of human rights and human security a more holistic and integrative approach is necessary. Their international dimension needs to be complemented by a local focus on human security and human rights. An important step towards this goal is the integration, by states, of human security in national human rights learning curricula.

Conceptualising the environmental dimension of human security in the UN

Hans Günter Brauch

Peace and security are goals of the UN Charter. In 2005, Kofi Annan addressed three pillars of human security: freedom from want, freedom from fear and freedom to live in dignity. This chapter examines two conceptual discussions on human and environmental security in the social sciences and in the UN system, and considers conceptual linkages for a people-centred environmental security concept and the environmental dimension of human security. It assesses the environmental challenges for human security posed by climate change, desertification, water, and natural hazards. It concludes that natural hazards pose manifold threats, challenges, vulnerabilities and risks for human, environmental, national and international security. Addressing environmental dangers to security requires a combination of strategic instruments and policies to reduce the vulnerability to hazards and the risks for affected societal groups. This requires a dual strategy for dealing with the short-term situational impact of extreme weather events and natural hazards and long-term structural impacts of global environmental change.

The ethical challenges of human security in the age of globalisation

J. Peter Burgess

The moral innovation of human security is also its terrible Achilles' heel. In a world of globalisation, where the values of the global view are imposed upon most people with the force of necessity, the concerns of individuals resist global action. At the very moment when individual concerns are put on the agenda, the possibility for achieving anything local is nearly erased by individual weakness in a world of massive collective interests. What can the particular interests of individuality make claim to in such a strong environment of universality? The aim of this chapter is to discuss the ethical dimensions of the concept of human security in a principled discussion of ethics and international relations. It starts with the evolution of the concept of human security, its use in international policy and its philosophical history. It ends with a discussion of the paradoxes of different philosophical positions with respect to the concept.

Building the agenda of human security: policy and practice within the Human Security Network

Keith Krause

The Human Security Network (HSN) represented an innovative attempt at flexible multilateralism, working with a small group of like-minded states. This article traces its origins and evolution, in particular, in the campaign to ban anti-personnel land mines) and examines the process of developing and implementing policy-in and beyond the HSN. The HSN struggled to develop a coherent and focused human security agenda and distinguished itself somewhat from other international efforts to define human security. In several different areas (like small arms, the "responsibility to protect" and the civilian protection agenda) the HSN can be shown to have been at the genesis of several concrete initiatives. It has been somewhat less successful at institutionalising its interactions, and in embedding a vision of human security in the foreign policies of participating states. Finally, the article explains how a full appreciation of the impact of the HSN requires examining not just its formal diplomatic and political efforts (which have had limited results), but its broader contribution (along with many other actors) to the setting of the human security agenda worldwide.

Gender aspects of human security

Ghada Moussa

The chapter deals with the gender dimensions in human security through focusing on the relationship between gender and human security, first manifested in international declarations and conventions, and subsequently evolving in world women conferences. It aims at analysing the various gender aspects in its relation to different human security dimensions. Gender equality is influenced and affected by many social institutions: the state, the market, the family (kinship) and the community. Human security also takes gender aspects. The author focuses on the dimensions in human security that influence gender equality. These are violence as a threat to human security and negative influences in achieving gender equality, the needs approach, poverty alleviation and considering women as among the most vulnerable groups in the society. Raising the capabilities of women is essential in achieving gender equality, thus security and participation is needed to guarantee equality and to realise gender equality.

Basic elements of a policy framework for human security

Paul Oquist

The species *Homo sapiens sapiens* is the unit of analysis and action for human security defined as risk reduction and expansion and realisation of potential. In this chapter the history of our existence is explored, as well as the conditions for human existence, prior extinctions and current threats of extinction, including the human impact on the environment and the continued high levels of violence in human relations in an era of nuclear weapons. Many of the very same factors that contributed to our success as a species, especially our transformative capabilities, are now contributing to the destruction of life. The values, ethics and morality of existence and extinction are examined as a foundation for a culturally, historically and ethically based integrated, holistic human security policy framework. Successes and failures in international human security policy are analysed, as well as the advantages of the proposed framework, for which concepts, levels of application and tentative policy areas are outlined. The objectives are to support the humanisation of economics and politics, as well as pointing out which values are dysfunctional for survival, to contribute to the equilibriums that maintains human existence and life on Earth, as well as to discontinue policies and practices that lead to mass extinctions, including our own.

The uncertain future of human security in the UN

Taylor Owen

Since its original articulation in the 1994 Human Development Report, the concept of human security has been widely used to understand and address post-Cold War threats to international peace and security. However, a review of policy documents using the concept in the United Nations (UN) system finds that human security is at risk of disappearing from the organisational landscape. I argue that this is a result of three interrelated problems with the way human security has been used–the failure to distinguish clearly between the concept and practice of human development and of human security, a lack of differentiation between human rights and human security and a lack of attention to the perils of conceptual overstretch. Two possible solutions are discussed. First, a narrow definition of human security as freedom from organised violence is reviewed and critiqued. Second, a threshold-based conceptualisation of threats to human security is defined and used to address the three problems with the use of human security in the UN system. The chapter concludes that the narrow definition of human security is unnecessarily restrictive, leaving out too many relevant threats, and that the UN system is uniquely positioned to actualise a broad threshold-based conceptualisation.

Rethinking human security

Pierre Sané

Since the early 1990s the concept of human security has been the focus of many debates in the UN system, in international and regional organisations and governments of different regions, as well as in the academic and intellectual fields. Indeed, with the end of the Cold War, the world became aware of the multiplication of non-military threats to security, be it at the international, regional, national or local levels. A great deal of theoretical and practical effort has been made to identify the most suitable modalities to deal with these threats given the compounded impact of intra-state conflicts, degradation of the environment, worsening of extreme poverty, spreading of pandemics and political exploitation of cultural and ethnic differences, particularly on the most vulnerable populations.

Needless to say, human security, given its multidimensional approach in tackling various threat and risks, is still a controversial and debated concept both in the UN and the academic world. But against that background, it is essential not to forget that the most important starting point for understanding human security is simply its focus on the human being, for human security is a concept that puts at centre stage the protection and dignity of the individual human person. Thus, the emphasis on human rights is essential to a conceptual differentiation between the notion of global security and human security.

The difference between these two concepts could lie in three areas. First, the difference is between a focus on human need (comprehensive security) rather than human rights (human security). Second, while comprehensive security tries to answer to the question "which threats to security?" the central question of human security is "whose security?" Third, while the political element of comprehensive security focuses on order and stability, human security is closely linked to justice and emancipation.

While supporters of human security defend its focus on individuals, some critics can complain about the broadness and vagueness of the concept. A debate over the exact definition and scope of human security still persists, as the concept can be, and has been, understood in a variety of ways. There is still thus a lot to be done in understanding and refining the notion of human security in all its perspectives and, beyond this, in disseminating it in the various regions of the world where it could be useful for the relevant actors.

The present work addresses major issues – in their interlinkages with human security – such as the human rights and human security nexus, gender aspects of human security, ethical challenges related to human security, environmental dimension of human security, the human security agenda developed by the Human Security Network, the ontological approach to human security, or the ongoing debates on this matter in the UN. The variety of these topics illustrates the wide scope of human security itself and could lead, it is hoped, to refreshing thoughts on this concept.

Rethinking human security finds its origin in a high-level working meeting held at UNESCO headquarters on 12–13 December 2005. This gathering was attended by 15 international experts, by representatives of the member states belonging to the Human Security Network, by representatives of various intergovernmental regional organisations (Organization of American States (OAS), League of Arab States (LAS), Organisation for Security and Cooperation in Europe), by the UN University and by UNESCO member states. The main objectives of the meeting were to review existing international human security initiatives and their follow-up, as well as to debate and share different points of view on the outline of a major UNESCO publication on human security, focusing on the Organisation's specific interdisciplinary contribution to human security, which has been published earlier this year (UNESCO 2008).

Indeed, over the past six years UNESCO has strived to foster research and action with a view to promoting human security, on the basis of the First international meeting of directors of peace research and training institutions convened by UNESCO in November 2000, on the theme "What agenda for human security in the twenty-first century?" In their final recommendations, the participants pointed out that human security can be considered

[a] paradigm in the making, for ensuring both a better knowledge of the rapidly evolving large-scale risks and threats that can have a major impact on individuals and populations, and a strengthened mobilisation of the wide array of actors actually involved in participative policy formulation in the various fields it encompasses today.

As such it is an adequate framework for

■ accelerating the transition from past restrictive notions of security tending to identify it solely with defence issues, to a much more comprehensive, multidimensional concept based on the respect of all human rights and democratic principles
■ contributing to sustainable development and especially to the eradication of extreme poverty, which is a denial of all human rights
■ reinforcing the prevention at the root of different forms of violence, discrimination, conflict and internal strife that are taking a heavy toll on mainly civilian populations in all regions of the world without exception
■ providing a unifying theme for multilateral action to the benefit of the populations most affected by partial and interrelated insecurities (UNESCO 2001, p.113)

In 2001 human security was embedded into UNESCO's Medium-term strategy for 2002–2007, under strategic objective 5, "Improving human security by better management of the

environment and social change". This strategic objective is closely linked to the Organisation's contribution to the eradication of poverty, in particular extreme poverty, to the promotion of human rights, to the implementation of the United Nations Declaration and Programme of Action on a Culture of Peace, as well as to the International Decade for a Culture of Peace and Non-Violence for the Children of the World (2001–2010) for which UNESCO is lead agency.

With a view to opening new perspectives for focused research, adequate training and the preparation of pilot projects, and to further consolidate public policy and public awareness on human security issues, UNESCO activities have been aimed so far at emphasising three important elements needed to translate the concept of human security into action:

■ developing a solid ethical foundation based on shared values that lead to the commitment to protect human dignity, which lies at the very core of human security.
■ buttressing that ethical dimension by putting existing and new normative instruments at the service of human security, in particular by ensuring the full implementation of the instruments relating to the protection of human rights
■ reinforcing the educational and training component by better articulating and clarifying all the ongoing efforts that focus on issues such as education for peace and sustainable development, training in human rights and enlarging the democratic agenda to human security issues.

In the chapters in this monograph – for which I would like to express my deepest gratitude to their authors, each focusing on a specific dimension of human security – it is our hope that we will move towards a better integration and mainstreaming of human security, keeping in mind the needs of the most vulnerable populations and responding to both a conceptual and a practical imperative.

Human security and human rights interaction

Wolfgang Benedek

Introduction

This chapter analyses the interaction of human rights and human security, based on a study that includes analysis and recommendations on the interaction of human security and human rights.[1] Part I focuses on the development of the concept of human security and addresses the institutionalisation of human security and the impact of human security in selected international forums. Part II analyses the interrelatedness and interdependence of human security and human rights. Part III contains a case study investigating the potential of a human security approach to selected human rights in the fields of culture and education, and in particular human rights education. Part IV addresses best practices with human security backgrounds. Finally, the conclusion (Part V) draws attention to the main arguments raised and future developments to be considered.

Wolfgang Benedek, Professor of International Law and the Law of International Organisations at the University of Graz; Director of the European Training and Research Centre for Human Rights and Democracy; Chair of World University Service (WUS) Austria. Publications in the field of regional human rights systems, human security, women and human rights, terrorism and human rights, globalisation and human rights, human rights education, international economic organisations and global governance, international civil society, information society and human rights. Email: wolfgang.benedek@uni-graz.at

The concept of human security

Human security is a new paradigm for the development of the international legal order (Benedek 2004, p.176). It can be seen as a notion or a construct that brings into focus, and provides answers for, the question of "how we can place the security of the individual on the same level as the security of the state" (Oberleitner 2005a, p.197). Thus, human security is conducive to a post-Westphalian conception of states that requires a new approach to notions central to international law, such as state sovereignty, peace and threats. By going beyond the traditional concept of the nation-state whose problems stop at state borders, the concept of human security aims at enfranchising the global citizen.

This enfranchisement is the core content of human security and its connecting point to the concept of human development, which, in turn, is in a triangular relationship with human rights and human security (Tadjbakhsh and Chenoy 2007, p. 51). Yet the concept of human security still fluctuates between a political agenda, a new research category and an all too universalistic, theoretical concept without a clear definition. As far as human security per se is concerned, international lawyers agree to disagree. The ideas that underpin human security, however, have numerous historical forebears. Among them is US President Franklin Roosevelt, who included "freedom from want" and "freedom from fear" among his four fundamental freedoms (Benedek 2005, p.26). The coalescence of conceptual equivocality and the lack of definitional clarity make it necessary to develop a coherent and cogent conceptualisation of human security.

Conceptualising a catchphrase

Although numerous reports from 1982 onwards laid the groundwork for the conceptual development of human security, it was the 1994 UNDP *Human development report* that created and shaped human security. Subsequent reports are discussed in Brauch and Owens in this volume. However, more than a decade after the *Human development report* introduced the concept of human security, the *Human development report* 2005 noted that there was still no consensus as to whether the threats that individual needs protection from are primarily violent, or whether it means something more than safety from violent threats. Arguably, "the two concepts are complementary rather than contradictory" (Human Security Centre 2005, p.viii). An integration of non-violent threats into the purview of human security can be very far-reaching, as exemplified by the Japanese approach, which includes development concerns (Bosold and Werthes 2005, pp.84–101). A UNESCO study (UNESCO 2005, pp.93–94) identifies as threats to human security a wide range of vulnerabilities. Some of these have been outlined by the present UN High Commissioner for Human Rights, Louise Arbour (2005).

Faced with this multitude of possible threats, authors have identified three approaches to human security. The first, a rights-based approach anchored in rule of law and treaty-based solutions to human security, believes that new human rights norms and convergent national standards can be developed by international institutions. The second, humanitarian conception of human security, according to which the "safety of peoples" is the paramount objective, links human security to preventive and post-conflict peace-building. The third, sustainable human development, view draws on the 1994 UNDP *Human development report*'s distinction of seven main threats.

The international debate (see Burgess and Owen 2004, pp.345–387) on conceptualising human security in international law is instructive. Conceptualisations developed by international scholars include human security as a "new organising principle of international relations" and the natural step (Oberleitner 2005a, p.198) towards an individual-centred approach in international law. This approach is based, on the one hand, on the conviction that states are responsible for the individual and, on the other hand, that individuals are responsible for violating international human rights and humanitarian law.

This trend is shown by institutions such as the International Criminal Court and the two International Criminal Tribunals in The Hague and Arusha (Benedek 2005, p.31). Despite debate, some international lawyers and states, still doubt the usefulness of the concept of human security while, nevertheless, acknowledging its integrative role (Oberleitner 2005, p.187). Although human security has experienced many conceptualisations it should be asked whether the "Canadian approach" to human security is really so different from the "Japanese approach"? Is there really one human security vis-à-vis conflicts, and a different one vis-à-vis development; one human security focusing on civil and political rights, and a different one focusing on economic, social and cultural rights? Is there one human security that emphasises first generation rights, and another one that emphasises second (and third) generation rights? The answer is clear: just as with human rights, human security is indivisible. While freedom from fear and freedom from want aptly describe aspects of human security, the concept remains undivided. States should not choose to concentrate on certain aspects of human security while ignoring others.

Defining human security

A broad variety of ideas has been expressed as to possible ways of expressing of human security. Taking into account the different definitions offered by Annan (1998), Axworthy (1997), Oberleitner (2005a) and Sen (2000), further study towards a common understanding of human security seems indispensable. In order to shorten the process of defining human security and thus enabling the international community to start focusing on discussing the de facto or de jure implications in international law of human security-related concerns and human security-oriented measures, attention should be drawn to a holistic definition proposed by Taylor Owen. After lamenting that human security "has no clear theoretical grounding" (Owen 2004, p.374), Owen proposed a "threshold definition" (2004, p.382), encompassing aspects mentioned by the Commission on Human Security 2002 report and the threats to human security pointed out by the 1994 UNDP *Human development report*: "human security is the protection of the vital core of all human lives from critical and pervasive environmental, economic, food, health, personal and political threats" (UNDP 1994, p.383).

Since threats to life, health and safety are, essentially, threats to human dignity, this definition can further be simplified. A succinct definition of human security is useful and necessary, and, while running the danger of semantically closing the door on the manifold concepts embraced by the concept of human security, can better focus the academic (and practical) debate on the essential aspects of human security. Thus human security, in this study, is understood to mean the security of people against threats to human dignity.

Revisiting security: the impact of the evolving understanding of security on human security

The important enrichment of the notion of security in international law by an individual dimension has been instrumental in paving the conceptual way forward for human security. States have started accepting responsibility for the global citizen. Before the evolution of human security, national security was often founded in an absolute reading of national sovereignty and equated with the security of the regime in power, protected by the military (UNESCO 2000, p.101). The international community's commitment to provide for peace not only between but also within states, and by a new interpretation of sovereignty, has put an end to this.

The new concept of security is widely accepted, especially as the UN Charter links the concept of peace with that of security (Oberleitner 2002, p.8). Insecurity is no longer attributed primarily to outside aggression (UNESCO 1997, p.147). Fundamental concepts of international law such as territorial integrity and humanitarian interventions (Axworthy 2004, p.348) have been re-evaluated. The narrow

state-centred approach to security has ignored the position of the individual in international law and jeopardised human security (Møller 2002, pp.48–49). Faced with different conceptions of threats to security there is an acute need to develop an individual-centred approach.

The impact of human security on international law

From repositioning the individual as an actor, and not just a factor, in international law to influencing UN reform, the emerging concept of human security has had a noticeable impact on international law. While the relevance of human security for the UN reform is still debated, critics have voiced concerns over the wooliness of human security literature (Mack 2004, p.366) and have expressed doubts as to its usefulness (Oberleitner 2005a, p.187). These points need to be addressed, as does the impact of human security on selected international issues of concern.

The concept of human security and UN reform

Human security is closely linked with UN institutional reform. New institutions such as an enlarged Security Council with a membership that is more representative of the international community, are more likely to take human security-related considerations into account (Benedek 2005, p.32; Kettemann 2007, pp.98–101; Ramcharan 2002, p.21). These include reforms suggested in 2003 by UN Secretary-General Annan (2004) and introduced a new security consensus to answer the new threats to security that surface internationally. Furthermore, at numerous points the High-level Panel emphasises the dichotomy between "state security" and "human security", (Annan 2004, p.165), such as when states are asked to determine whether the threat to "state or human security [is] ... sufficiently clear and serious, to justify prima facie the use of military force" (Annan 2004, p.207).

In the 2005 report entitled *In larger freedom: towards development, security and human rights for all* (Annan 2005); see Brauch and Owen in this volume, Kofi Annan took up many of the issues and recommendations formulated in 2004. While underscoring many of the ideas associated with human security in parts of his report, Kofi Annan expressly mentions "human security" only once (Annan 2005, p.133). This can be taken as an indication of the existing reservations from a few states about the use of the concept in the UN (Benedek 2006a). They seem to be afraid that, through the concept of human security, the concept of humanitarian intervention could be introduced into the UN through the back door. However, this concern is unjustified.

The UN World Summit, held at the 60th anniversary of the UN in September 2005, was marked primarily by a plenary meeting of the heads of states and governments of UN members from 14–16 September. The 2005 *World summit outcome* document that was accepted consensually by the states present is probably the most important step yet, on the UN level, towards institutionalising human security by finding common ground for a definition of the concept. The paragraph on human security reads in full (UN 2005, 143):

We stress the right of people to live in freedom and dignity, free from poverty and despair. We recognize that all individuals, in particular vulnerable people, are entitled to freedom from fear and freedom from want, with an equal opportunity to enjoy all their rights and fully develop their human potential. To this end, we commit ourselves to discussing and defining the notion of human security in the General Assembly.

In 2008 the General Assembly took its commitment seriously and organised a thematic debate on human security in May.

Between wooliness and usefulness: the relevance of human security in international law

The UN's commitment to human security notwithstanding, critics have voiced doubts about human security as being a concept that is too universalistic to be meaningfully reflected in practice. Critique on the concept of human security concentrates mainly on two aspects: the individual-oriented approach, and the difficulty of prioritising political action, as discussed by Brauch in this volume. Other authors (Takur 2004, p.348) point out that states alone cannot counter the globalised threats of today. While some (Acharya 2004, p.355) see human security as an answer to the globalisation of international

policy, others (Hampson 2004, p.350) praise it as a tool that gives a voice to marginalised groups. There is therefore a need to scientifically evaluate the potential of human security by identifying the international law basis of human security and the legal implications of the concept.

The normative influence of human security on international law

Despite the non-binding nature of these reports, declarations and outcome documents, human security has had a considerable impact on international law. Some authors have underlined that human security poses a manifold challenge to international law and the law and practice of international organisations (Oberleitner 2005a, p.197). Others stress that the human security concept sets out to "strengthen the rule of law in international relations" (Benedek 2005, p.34) and to support the development of public international law and multilateral diplomacy.

Introducing human security as a structural principle in international normative processes has already resulted in procedural changes in drafting international norms. Human security stands for an involvement of individuals in developing new international normative instruments. This will lead to a better reflection of the "balance between the concepts of state sovereignty and concern for the individual" (Oberleitner 2002, p.26). The human security approach to international law is "holistic instead of sectoral", "participative instead of exclusive" and "preventive instead of reactive" (Benedek 2005, p.35, translation by the author).

Through enhanced civil society and non-governmental organisation (NGO) participation, as well as a renewed focus on the individual as a bearer of rights (and obligations) – and, accordingly, an actor in international law – the creation of numerous human rights treaties has been influenced by non-state actors (see, for example, Alston 2005). A wide range of treaties that have been particularly influenced by the new role of the individual in light of human security considerations are listed by Oberleitner (2002, p.26, 2005a, p.195) and Benedek (2005, p.34).

Furthermore, human security has engendered "normative changes in the international legal order" (Oberleitner 2005a, p.185). These include a stronger focus on the legitimacy of humanitarian interventions and an individual-oriented approach to UN reform (Oberleitner 2005a, p.197). Enhancing the role of human security will lead to a broader understanding of security (Oberleitner 2002, p.8). It can be argued that human security inspires a growing body of law that provides "international humanitarian standards to challenge the supremacy of national states sovereignty" (Axworthy 2004, p.348).

This new human security conditionality of sovereignty implies that states must "serve and support the people from which [they] draw [their] legitimacy" (Newman 2004, pp.358–359). Human security can be considered as a unifying concept of international law, bridging the conceptual divides and providing solutions to different fields of international law such as human rights law, humanitarian law and anti-terrorism law (Oberleitner 2005a, p.197).

Institutionalising human security: ensuring compatibility and coherence

Since 1994 the concept of human security has grown in importance. International organisations, government bodies, states – in frameworks such as the Human Security Network (HSN) – and research institutions have emphasised human security. Inter-institutional cooperation, promoted, for example, by organisations such as the Canadian Consortium on Human Security, ensures compatibility and coherence. The central actor in the human security field International organisations is the Human Security Unit at the UN Secretariat's Office for the Coordination of Humanitarian Affairs. Other specialist bodies are found in the United Nations Development Programme (UNDP), United Nations Educational, Scientific and Cultural Organisation (UNESCO) and the United Nations Centre for Regional Development (UNCRD).

Governments, affiliated and independent organisations

Fourteen UN member states involved with human security constitute the HSN. The Canadian Department of Foreign Affairs and International Trade and the Ministry of Foreign Affairs of Japan have dedicated specific websites to human security, among other states. Finally, the Canadian Human Security Gateway offers rich resources on human security.

Research institutions

Among the research institutions that have made interesting contributions to the conceptual development of human security are the Canadian Consortium on Human Security. Others are based at Oxford, Oslo, Graz and Paris in Europe, Pittsburgh, Harvard, British Columbia, Simon Fraser and Tufts universities.

NGOs and civil society associations

NGOs and civil society in general play a major role in the study of, and advocacy on, human security concerns. NGOs are involved in practically all human security issues. Their expertise is recognised by the HSN when it invites NGOs to its expert or Ministerial meetings. Among the NGOs focusing on human security are Action Aid International, Center for Humanitarian Dialogue, Ford Foundation, International Peace Academy, African Human Security Initiative and the Aga Khan Development Network. In this context the People's Movement on Human Rights Education needs particular mention. It has helped the HSN to identify and formulate the relationship between human security, human development and human rights since 1999.

More than 1,000 NGOs were involved in the International Campaign to Ban Landmines (a network of today more than 1,400 NGOs), leading to the 1997 UN Convention on the prohibition of the use, stockpiling, production and transfer or anti-personnel mines and on their destruction. In 2004 the Nairobi Summit on a Mine-Free World adopted the Plan of action 2005–2009 containing numerous commitments for speedy implementation of the Convention securing the right to life and to health (UN 2004). In a similar way NGOs collaborate with interested states and international organisations to establish better control of small arms and light weapons.

Human security journals

Among the international legal journals dealing with human security are *Security Dialogue* and the _Journal of Peace Research_. There are on-line publications such as the _Human Security Bulletin_ (Benedek and Ketterman 2008) and daily updates on news relating to human security are provided by _Human Security News_. European journals focusing on human security include _Human Security Perspectives_ and the _HUMSEC Journal_.

Human security and selected international forums

Different international actors have responded to the challenges to international law posed by the emerging concept of human security in different ways. Two of these are notable for their success and their scope: an inter-state cooperation promoting human security, the HSN, and the regional approach followed by UNESCO.

Cooperation for human security: the case of the HSN

Starting from the presumption that "human security has become both a new measure of global security and a new agenda for global action", the HSN was initially a bilateral cooperation between Canada and Norway, and was joined by Austria in elaborating the 1997 Convention on anti-personnel mines. From its inception the HSN aimed at promoting the new concept of security focused on people and on forming an informal and flexible coalition of like-minded countries (UNESCO 2000, p.83). The HSN identifies certain topics of collective concern that are then targeted together. It has so far played "a catalytic role by bringing to international attention new and emerging issues" (Fodha 2002, p.17) such as the role of non-state actors and the repositioning of the individual.

The HSN has regular ministerial meetings and yearly changing presidencies that prioritise different aspects of human security. It also seeks to provide for the coalescence of strategies aimed at reducing fear and want. The main issues on the agenda of the HSN are strengthening multilateral institutions, especially with regard to the reform of the Commission on Human Rights, respect for human rights and fundamental freedoms, equality for women and men, girls and boys as core issues of human security and conflict prevention. These are also interlinked

with human rights development, including a focus on human rights education and strengthening the international humanitarian system, among many other areas of concern.

Human security and UNESCO

The research inspired by UNESCO and its initiatives have more than once changed the sociology of conflicts and international security. It has made an essential contributory role to security studies from the 1950s onwards by exploring the socio-economic causes of conflicts (UNESCO 1998a). UNESCO reports and proceedings from 1996 onwards focus on the shift in international security thinking (UNESCO 1997, 1998b, 2002). In 2004 UNESCO included the improvement of human security as a strategic objective in its strategy.

By better management of the environment and social change, UNESCO has set out to preserve and enhance human security today (UNESCO 2004d, p.93). The organisation is committed to bringing about "genuine human security" (UNESCO 2004d, p.5) and coping with the "manifold risks and menaces within UNESCO's spheres of competence" (UNESCO 2004d, p.94). It has focused on the challenges of hemispheric security (UNESCO 2003a, p.2) and the advantages of the regional approach to human security.

Human security and human rights interaction

Although human rights and the concept of human security are interrelated, interdependent and mutually reinforcing (Benedek 2006a, p.98), they should not be used interchangeably (Oberleitner 2005b, p.605). Human security is unthinkable without human rights and inconceivable without its impact on sustainable development (UNESCO 2004d, p.5). A secure environment is a prerequisite for enjoying human rights. Living conditions that violate human dignity make people prone to violations of human rights. Denying the potential of human development is a violation of human rights and provokes human insecurity (see Ramcharan 2002, pp.31 and 51). The relationship of human security and human rights, however, is not that straightforward (for a comprehensive discussion, see Benedek and Kettemann 2008).

Human dignity as the common source

The "extensive overlap" (Tadjbakhsh and Chenoy 2007, p.123) of human security, human rights and human development is due to their common source: human dignity. The growing "universalisation of the values and principles enshrined in the 'Universal declaration of human rights' (UDHR) as well as the "development of international law as it relates to the protection of the individual" (UNESCO 2004d, p.61) have greatly influenced human rights law. Both developments can be explained by focusing on what an influential international human rights lawyer wrote on the core of human rights: they are "essentially a manifestation of human dignity" (Nowak 2003, p.1). This focus on human dignity has already been reflected in the preamble to the 1948 UDHR (UN 1948).

A recent confirmation of this relationship can be found in the results of a survey of the International Rescue Committee on the Democratic Republic of Congo, which shows that, out of 3.9 million people who have died since the beginning of the conflict in 1998, less then two per cent of the deaths are directly linked to the violence. Most resulted from indirect causes, such as limited access to health care (International Rescue Committee 2006).

Human dignity is also a fundamental concept of human security. The relevance of human dignity was highlighted, once again, in the UN "Millennium declaration". The 150 heads of state and government that adopted it recognised that, "in addition to our separate responsibilities to our individual societies, we have a collective responsibility to uphold the principles of *human dignity*, equality and equity at the global level" (UN 2000).

Aspects of the interrelatedness of human security and human rights

Similarities that count

One of the seven core aspects of human security, as enumerated by the UNDP *Human development report* (1994), namely, political security, was understood to include individuals' freedom to exercise their basic human rights. This link between human rights and human security is resilient (Benedek et al. 2002, p.15) and the concepts are intertwined, interrelated, mutually reinforcing and contingent upon each other. Since the focus of human security and the bearer of human rights is the individual, both share some of the same concerns. The importance of the concept of security, too, is similar: aspects of the security of individuals (their personal security (UN 1948) and social security (UN 1948 are human rights by and of themselves).

International documents such as the UDHR, the UN Covenants on economic, social and cultural rights, and the UN Covenant on civil and political rights, as well as regional human rights instruments, refer to security as a human right (Benedek et al. 2002, p.16). Further research is needed to reach a fuller understanding of how the Declaration's and the Covenants' concepts of "security" relate to human security. With the new centrality of the individual in international law, normative foundations such as Article 3 of the UDHR, pursuant to which "everyone has the right to life, liberty and the security of person", will have to be interpreted with a focus on human security.

Conversely, existing understandings of human rights can help define the concept of human security (Ramcharan, 2002, p.10). Since human rights lie at the core of human security, they provide a "sound conceptual and normative foundation" for human security and ensure that it is an "operational concept firmly rooted in international law" (Benedek et al. 2002, p.16). To many, the best way to achieve human security is through the full and holistic realisation of all human rights (Benedek 2004, p.179).

The state cannot opt out from fulfilling its human rights obligations with regard to the interaction between human security and economic, social and cultural rights, although it is permitted to meet them in a gradual, progressive way, depending its ability. The Social Watch report of 2004, with the title *Fear and want, obstacles to human security*, showing how failures to ensure economic, social and cultural rights can result in problems to human security, reinforces the fact that human security and human rights depend on each other (Instituto del Tercer Mundo 2004).

These similarities are seen in the Lysøen Agenda of 1999 (UNESCO 2002, p.86), in the principles underlying the HSN and in Annan (2004). In contemporary times the importance of human rights in the human security discourse varies, as shown in UNESCO documents. The term "human rights" appears 72 times in a UNESCO report on Latin America and the Caribbean, 76 times in a similar report on East Asia, but are only 28 times in a shorter study on human security in the Arab states. This leads us to ask whether the interrelationship of human security and human rights is less important in Arab states than in similar frameworks elsewhere.

Differences that matter

Although human security and human rights are deeply interconnected, differences, however, exist. While human rights violations occur all too often, the concept of human rights itself is not questioned. Yet there are still authors who question the necessity of the concept of human security. Human rights entitle and oblige but human security is a holistic political concept, generally without justiciable obligations. Faced with a multitude of different threats, human security allows for and, indeed, necessitates prioritisation. Prioritising one human right over another, however, is accepted only in rare cases and, whereas international law provides for the protection of human rights, the advancement of human security is secured by international cooperation (Benedek 2004, p.179).

The dilemma is obvious: "the more human rights are integrated as a normative backbone into human security, the clearer ... the concept becomes, while at the same time its distinctive character as a new approach to ensuring human dignity wanes and gives way to a repackaged form of human rights" (Oberleitner 2005b, p.598). It should therefore be noted that while human rights provide a point of reference for human security, the terms should not be used interchangeably. Three main arguments must be taken into account by those who argue for bridging the divide between human security and human rights:

human security may dilute the legal character of human rights; human security seems to allow for choosing one

right over the other on the grounds of their value for "security" and thus "securitises" human rights; and human security could invite governments to defy human rights obligations under the pretext of guaranteeing human security instead. (Oberleitner 2005b, p.606)

Thus, not only should human security and human rights not be merged, the legally binding character of human rights and the political character of human security need to be distinguished. However, human security concerns are increasingly translated into legal obligations through international conventions and protocols. Human rights, too, translate human security needs into legal obligations. In light of this, the interrelationship of human security and human rights and the potential for their mutual reinforcement need to be explored.

Enriching the human rights discourse

The human rights discourse can be enriched by human security. Fodha (2002, p.13) notes "like human rights, human security is indivisible; like human rights, human security must also be universal". A human security approach enables the international community to deal with threats in a way that cannot be provided by an exclusive focus on human rights and human security-based strategies can deal with threats that are not accommodated by human rights concerns (Oberleitner 2005b, p.601). Among these are earthquakes, hurricanes, landslides, economic downturns or drug abuse.

However, these threats, and threats such as crime and disease as well, which some authors see in the category of threats not related to human rights, often raise serious human rights issues (Owen 2004, p.23). Yet they differ insofar as the source of the threat is concerned. The threats mentioned above do not stem from the state but from non-state actors (criminal groups, economic realities or nature), which either are not or cannot be sufficiently bound by international human rights law. As it takes a people-centred approach, human security is not concerned about the source of the threat (however, see Nowak 2003, pp.51–56).

Human security can also operate as a warning mechanism for human rights violations. High crime rates can be considered a violation of human security before they amount to human rights violations. On the other hand, human rights violations are reliable indicators of threats to human security, and monitoring them is therefore essential in order to prevent the threats. In addition, a holistic concept of human security might stimulate the human rights discourse and help overcome outdated divisions between first, second and third generation rights (Oberleitner 2005b, p.602). Only a few absolute human rights exist; most human rights have "relative validity", and interfering with them is considered a violations only when this cannot be justified (among them are torture, slavery, the recognition as a person before the law and the freedom of conscience (Nowak 2003, p.57). Many human rights instruments allow states to derogate these mechanisms in cases of public emergency, thereby unilaterally setting aside human rights. In these cases, human security, however, may be the last vestige for human dignity left (Oberleitner 2005b, p.602).

Using human security in human rights discourses may lead to a new understanding of possible exceptions to the use of force in international law. Applying human security considerations as a guiding light in the context of humanitarian interventions might lead to giving moral reasons for intervention to the intervener. Thus, human security interventions would reflect a "sense of transnational responsibility for the fate of a 'global citizen'", signifying "a new era in international politics" in which human security would take precedence over the protection of national sovereignty (Schnabel 2001, p.143).

Indeed, with this focus on human dignity as the ultimate yardstick of the legitimacy of interventions, human security might lead to a better understanding and enhanced recognition of the doctrine of humanitarian interventions (cf. Ramcharan 2002, p.21) and the "responsibility to protect". Finally, the potential of "human security interventions" can be measured.

A case study: human security and (human rights) education

Human security is closely linked to human rights education (Benedek 2004, p.180). Furthermore, receiving information on one's rights is a human right: the right to know one's rights. The relationship between human security and education is explored below.

The relationship between the right to education and human security

This relationship between education and human security has been recognised since the inception of the concept of human security (UNESCO 2004d, p.169). To facilitate a human security approach to education, UNESCO has undertaken regional studies on ways of promoting human security in educational frameworks. Experts have concluded that "basic education for all ... must be placed high on the human security agenda" (UNESCO 2000, p.138). It provides the basis for the Plan of Action for the first phase 2005–2007 of the World Programme for Human Rights Education, which focuses on a rights-based approach to education in primary and secondary schools. The interaction of the right to education with human security is particularly relevant when there is discrimination and inequality in access to educational opportunities, which may have ethnic, religious, social or cultural reasons.

Human rights education on the school curriculum promotes human security (UNESCO 2003b, p.86) by raising awareness towards one's own rights and the rights of others. An international workshop on human security and human rights education in Austria in 2000 explored the relationship between human security, human development and human rights education and learning and concluded that human rights education and learning were "indispensable operational development strategies" (Benedek et al. 2002, p.45) towards human security. International bodies such as the HSN were expressly asked to lead the current efforts of human rights education and learning "to higher levels of political awareness, cultural visibility and more comprehensive forms of co-responsibility" (Benedek et al. 2002, p.47).

During its presidency of the HSN in 2003 Austria identified political initiatives directed towards acquiring a worldwide culture of human rights through human rights education. Under Austrian auspices the 2003 HSN ministerial meeting in Graz therefore prepared a "Declaration of principles on human rights education" (HSN, 2003), and a manual on understanding human rights (Benedek 2006b; Benedek and Nikolova-Krees 2003) which was intended to be used globally for human rights training. The holistic approach of the meeting included civil society participation, and cooperation with national human rights centres, international organisations and NGOs. The Manual on human rights education, *Understanding human rights*, has so far been translated into 14 languages so far, with the assistance of members of the HSN and international organisations. The manual is used from Kabul to Beijing and from Sarajevo to Moscow by diverse target groups ranging from peacekeepers to journalists and from ministry officials to students.

Prioritising human rights education

The Graz Declaration reaffirms Article 26 of the UDHR, which states that "education shall be directed to the full development of the human personality and to the strengthening of respect for human rights and fundamental freedoms". Representatives of HSN member states assembled in Graz adopted a number of principles of human rights education, namely, reinforcing human security through human rights education, and seeing the promotion of human rights as an integral part of human security. Second, HSN members stated that the right to know one's human rights was "part of the human dignity of each individual". Indeed, the HSN affirmed "that Human Rights Education and Learning is an imperative for the promotion and protection as well as the full enjoyment of all human rights" (HSN, 2003, para. 6).

Next, HSN members sought to strengthen society and empower the individual and the members were asked to respect diversity, and find new methods for teaching and learning human rights (HSN, 2003, para. 15). Lastly, states were reminded to acknowledge that they bear the "main responsibility" to ensure the promotion of human rights education in public institutions on all levels from the executive and legislative level to local levels (HSN, 2003, para. 18). This required disseminating knowledge about human rights and encouraging its incorporation into education on all levels. It also involved creating instruments and networks for reviewing, systematising and disseminating experiences and materials on human rights education in collaboration with other organisations.

Human security, human rights and best practices

While human security is a subject of intense debate in academia, its practical dimension should not be overlooked. Promoting human security today "requires an enhanced exchange of best experiences, practices and initiatives in the fields of research, training, mobilisation and policy formulation" (UNESCO 2000, p.113). Many projects undertaken by international organisations, governmental organisations or research institutions in the fields of human rights and, in particular, human rights education have a human security dimension. The most promising way to learn is by studying successful examples of integrating human security into human rights projects that have already been completed. The best practice approach will enable the concept to acquire further scientific status.

Other organisation have been involved in similar exercises, For example, UNICEF has sent child rights advisors to work with UN peace-keeping forces in Sierra Leone, in order to strengthen peace-keepers' awareness of children's rights. An example of a best practices approach is a book on human rights education that included selected best practices (Benedek et al. 2002, pp.35–39).

Conclusion

The interrelationship and interdependence of human rights and human security are apparent. The two concepts are mutually reinforcing, and, like human rights, human security has become an international concern, which cannot be diluted by reference to the principle of non-interference. The uneasiness of certain states with the concept in the UN might be true for weak states that fear for their sovereignty, or states that neglect the human security of their citizens. But human security does not mean to weaken the state, and may very well strengthen or rebuild the "failed state" or those in post-conflict situations.

On the international level, human security and human rights interact meaningfully and multidimensionally. Human security, understood as a comprehensive concept encompassing more than the absence of violent conflict, is conducive to an environment where "each individual has opportunities and choices to fulfil his or her own potential" (Commission on Human Security 2003, p.4). The human security approach can broaden our conception of peace and security, and redefine and refine our approach to the realisation of all human rights for all. It accepts that providing security includes enabling economic development, securing social justice, providing environmental protection and guaranteeing democratisation, disarmament and respect for human rights and the rule of law (Annan 1999). Human security has broadened our understanding of threats to the individual. As a new category of threats has emerged (armed aggression, nuclear attack, terrorist threat or attempted destabilisation carefully prepared by some adversary) (Annan 1999) it needs as much attention as the threats to the human right to life.

The debate on human security and international law has not yet drawn to a close. The concept has been acclaimed for its integrative impact in numerous international normative processes. It can be convincingly argued that the international legal order and its greatest organisational realisation, the UN, are not limited to ensuring cooperation and avoiding situations endangering the maintenance of international peace and security. As Kofi Annan put it, "[o]ur guiding light must be the needs and hopes of peoples everywhere" (Annan 2005).

The solemn commitment by UN member states to refine the definition of human security at the most important international forum in 2005 is an important step for the conceptual debate on human security and human rights in international law. It is now up to the General Assembly to fulfil the task entrusted to it by UN members, i.e. to "discuss and define the notion of human security" (UN 2005). The thematic debate on human security on 22 May 2008 is a step in the right direction. It is hoped that a consensus can be reached on what states consider human security concerns and what they do not. Academic research and debate should diligently research human security issues in order to ensure that the decision is an informed one. In this connection, UNESCO can facilitate research and provide the forum for debate.

International law is dynamic, and human security is a concept in motion, growing, as it should, with newly emerging human needs and international threats. It can thus be maintained that "the traditional, narrow perception of security [that] leaves out the most elementary and legitimate concerns of ordinary people regarding security in their daily lives"(International Commission on Intervention and State Sovereignty [ICISS] 2001) is no longer internationally accepted. In this context, a more holistic and integrative approach is needed that embraces scientific communities and interest groups. This would include the communities involved with human rights, humanitarian law, transitional justice, crime prevention, peace, development and human security per se.

Human rights education and learning are of increasing importance. The right to know one's rights is essential in order to enable the individual to claim his rightful position. States are nonetheless responsible, with necessary support from civil society and non-state actors, for integrating human security in national human rights learning curricula. From President Roosevelt's "four freedoms" to the 2005 World Summit's commitments, proponents of human security have succeeded in enriching international law by a structural idea that has the potential to increase worldwide recognition of the pivotal role of individuals in international law and, in the words of the former UN Secretary-General, "to perfect the triangle of development, freedom and peace" (Annan 2005).

Notes

1. The author would like to thank Matthias C. Kettemann for his research support.

Conceptualising the environmental dimension of human security in the UN

Hans Günter Brauch

Introduction

This chapter has two aims:

- to examine the two separate conceptual discussions on human and environmental security in the social sciences and in the UN system and to consider conceptual linkages with regard to a "people-centred" environmental security concept and the environmental dimension of human security
- to assess environmental challenges for human security with regard to challenges posed by climate change, desertification, water, and natural hazards.

Conceptualising environmental and human security

Peace and security have been key goals of the UN and of the League of Nations from the outset. In contemporary understanding the three prerequisites of eternal peace are democratic governance, Kantian (1795a, 1795b) an international organisation with a collective security system and human rights that combine the three levels of analysis: the human being, the state and the international system. Both the League of Nations (1919) and the Charter of the UN (1945) aimed at international cooperation and "to achieve international peace and security".

Hans Günter Brauch is chairman of Peace Research and European Security Studies (AFES-PRESS), teaches at the Free University of Berlin, is Fellow at the UNU-EHS, editor of the HEXAGON series with Springer and lead editor of *Security and environment in the Mediterranean* (2003), *Globalisation and environmental challenges: reconceptualising security in the 21st century* (2009), *Facing global environmental change: environmental, human, energy, food, health and water security concepts* (2008) and *Coping with global environmental change, disasters and security* (2009). Email: brauch@afes-press.de

A survey of UN statements indicates that a fundamental shift has occurred in thinking on security since earliest times when it was focused on nation-states and military security. In 2005 Annan (2005) said that the UN's three key goals were security, development and human rights. He structured this report around three pillars of an emerging human security concept: freedom from want (a shared vision of development), freedom from fear (a vision of collective security) and freedom to live in dignity (under the rule of law, human rights and democracy). Kofi Annan recommended member states to "integrate the principles of sustainable development into country policies and programmes and reverse the loss of environmental resources". He acknowledged that "our efforts to defeat poverty and pursue sustainable development will be in vain if environmental degradation and natural resource depletion continue unabated" and noted the significance of desertification, biodiversity and climate change, as well as natural disasters in these efforts (Annan 2000).

Against the background of a conceptual innovation in response to the fundamental global contextual change, this study addresses the following questions:

- How has human security been conceptualised, both as a declaratory goal and as an operational concept in the UN system since 1990?

■ How have water, food and health security been conceptualised in the UN, and in the scientific and in the political realm (Bogardi and Brauch 2005; Brauch 2004, 2005a, 2005b, 2006a, 2006b).

■ How have environmental security dangers and concerns (threats, challenges, vulnerabilities and risks) been conceptualised?

■ What are the key environmental challenges for humankind in the twenty-first century posed by climate change, desertification and water stress, and how have these new security dangers and concerns affected the environmental dimension of human security?

Conceptualising human security in the UN system

Despite the shift in the object of security between the League's Covenant and the UN charter from nation-states to peoples, the UN system overall has remained state-centred, with the exception of its human rights activities and work on refugees and migrants. Gradually, however, the narrow, state-centred focus on peace and international security in the UN Charter during the Cold War has widened and deepened as economic, societal and environmental dimensions have been added to the classic diplomatic and military dimension of security (Buzan et al. 1998; Wæver et al. 2008). These five dimensions are still addressed primarily from a state-centred perspective. However, the United Nations Development Programme's (UNDP) *Human development report* (1994) has urged a "human-centred" approach, supplementing these five national security dimensions with seven human security dimensions of economic, food, health, environmental, personal, community and political insecurity (UNDP 1994; Schott 2009).

Narrow security concept in the UN charter

Of the four key concepts of the "conceptual quartet" – peace, security, development and environment – only the first two, "international peace and security" were used, but in the UN Charter the terms "international security" and "security" are never used alone (Wolfrum 1994, p.50). The UN Charter saw collective security as primarily directed against the illegal use of force within the group of states. (Wolfrum 1994, p.51).

Although the UN Charter did not define its key goals of peace and international security,they were different from the new concept of national security that emerged in the USA during World War II (Yergin 1977).

During the Cold War the idea of collective self-defence prevailed while collective security was paralysed (Brauch et al. 1998) but after 1990, NATO and the EU emerged as key security institutions. Since 1990 the UN Security Council has enlarged its view of humanitarian intervention and environmental and human security:

Today's threats recognize no national boundaries, are connected, and must be addressed at the global and regional as well as the national levels. No State, no matter how powerful, can by its own efforts alone make itself invulnerable to today's threats.... What is needed is nothing less than a new consensus. ... we all share responsibility for each other's security. (Annan 2004).

The Panel distinguished six clusters of threats, ranging from economic and social threats to environmental degradation and transnational organised crime. Thus, for the first time environmental degradation was included as a threat. The Panel points to the lack of effective governance structures to deal with climate change, deforestation and desertification, as well as to the inadequate "implementation and enforcement" of regional and global treaties. Two of the 101 recommendations of the Panel deal with environmental issues, with renewable energy sources and with the Kyoto Protocol. Although the Panel mentions "human security" several times, its main focus remained on the "state" as the cause and as a key actor in dealing primarily with military and societal threats.

The Secretary-General's report, *In larger freedom* (Annan 2005), was organised around three pillars of human security: "freedom from want, freedom from fear, and freedom to live in dignity, while the term human security was mentioned only once. The Millennium Declaration reaffirmed the commitment of all nations to the rule of law as the all-important framework for advancing human security and prosperity. It noted, however, that "in many places, governments and individuals continue to violate the rule of law, often without consequences for them but with deadly consequences for the weak and the vulnerable."

Development and environment as new tasks of the UN

In 1945 "development" and "the environment" were not yet perceived as major policy issues. However, the term was sometimes used, as when the UN is mandated to promote "conditions of economic and social progress and development". In 1948 the UN General Assembly asked the Secretary-General to organise teams of experts "to assist developing countries in building capacities to help themselves" which ultimately led in 1965 to the UN Development Programme (UNDP) that has become the lead UN agency for development (Kaul 2002, pp. 70–71).

The UN in 1972 endorsed the Action Plan for the Human Environment and established the first global organisation on environmental issues, the UN Environment Programme (UNEP). In 1989 the General Assembly convened a UN Conference on Environment and Development (UNCED) in June 1992 in Rio de Janeiro, and approved the mandate for the UN "Convention to combat desertification" that was adopted in 1994 (Wolfrum 1994a, p. 775). In 2002 at the UN Summit on Sustainable Development (UNSSD), the "Johannesburg declaration on sustainable development" and the "Johannesburg plan of implementation" were adopted, in which the states committed themselves to achieve the Millennium development goals (MDGs) (UN 2000).

Conceptual quartet: peace, security, development and environment

Since 1965 and 1973 UNDP and UNEP have become the main actors in the UN system to promote the new global agenda focusing on development and the environment. All four goals – peace and international security

addressed in the UN Charter, together with later conceptual developments – have now formed a conceptual quartet of key policy goals that have become an object of the global debate of "reconceptualising security" in relationship with the other three goals of "peace", "development" and the "environment" (Brauch 2008a).

On each of the four key goals of the contemporary UN systems, highly specialised research programmes have emerged in the social and human sciences with their own theories, methods and communication media and networks, often with relatively little exchange between each other. John Herz (1950) developed the term "security dilemma" to explain the interaction between fear and the arms competition during the Cold War.

A new concept, "the survival dilemma" has been coined (Brauch 2008c) to refer to the difficult choices that confront individuals, families, clans or villages with a high degree of social vulnerability in response to environmental stress, natural hazards, wars and complex emergencies. Such extreme events often pose, for the most vulnerable, three "no-win" options: to die, to be forced to move out and migrate or to struggle for their own and their families' survival.

Reconceptualisation of security as a social science concept since 1990

As a social science concept, security is ambiguous and elastic in its meaning. Wolfers (1962) pointed to two sides of the security concept: "Security, in an *objective sense*, measures the absence of threats to acquired values, in a *subjective sense*, the absence of fear that such values will be attacked". For social constructivists security is "what actors make of it" (Wendt 1992), thus adding an intersubjective meaning.

In the UN system at least three different security concepts coexist. The Hobbesian concept focuses on the political and military dimension of national security. The extended Grotian concept aims at "cooperative security" that includes economic, societal and environmental security dimensions and the "human security" approach that been promoted by the Human Security Network (HSN), the Commission on Human Security (CHS 2003) and by the Secretary-General (Annan 2005).

Since 1990 not only has the scope of "securitisation" (Wæver 1997, 2008) changed, but so has its reference from a national to a human-centred security concept, both in the UN system (UNDP 1994; UNESCO 1997, 1998a, 1998b, 2001, 2003c, 2004a, 2004b, 2004c, 2005; United Nations University [UNU] 2000, 2002, 2003; United Nations University Institute for Environment and Human Security [UNU-EHS] 2004, 2005), and in the academic (peace-focused) security community.

Since 1990 a fundamental and expanded reconceptualisation of security has gradually emerged (Abdus Sabur 2003, 2009; Buzan et al. 1998; Brauch 2005a; Brauch et al. 2008, 2009a), at least in European security discourses. Møller (2001, 2003) distinguished between national security and three expanded concepts of societal, human and environmental security. Oswald (2001, 2004, 2008a, 2009) suggested combining human, gender and environmental security (HUGE) in an integrated concept.

Ullman (1983), Mathews (1989) and Myers (1989a, 1994) added environmental concerns to the US national security agenda. The Global Environmental Change and Human Security Project (GECHS) (1999) shifted the focus to the linkages between global environmental change and human security, and Bogardi (2004) and Brauch (2003a, 2005a, 2005c) suggested focusing the human security discourse on its environmental dimension (Bogardi and Brauch 2005).

Concepts of human security

The human security concept used by UNDP (1994) triggered a global and ongoing scientific debate, while the academic debate on environmental security influenced the policy agenda of several international organisations. Since then, human security has been referred to as a level of analysis, as a human-centred perspective (Annan 2001) and as an encompassing concept (UNDP 1994). The first approach addresses the individuals affected by environmental stress and its outcomes, the second approach uses a normative orientation and the third combines the seven dimensions and five levels of a widened security concept. The first approach is too narrow for political relevance, while the third is too wide for analytical use (Mack 2004). The

second position, of a people-centred human security concept, comes closest to Kofi Annan's (2001) political perspective and the approach of GECHS (1999).

UN Secretary-General Kofi Annan (2001) pointed to three building blocks of the human security concept. The proposed fourth pillar, "freedom from hazard impacts" (Brauch 2005a), builds on his previous remarks.

For the security studies community, the state remains the major reference object that must be secured, while both human security visions deal with the protection of the individual or citizen. Mack (2004) noted that a major shortcoming of the state-centred security paradigm is that it cannot deal with threats to the individual emanating from the state, and it cannot explain state collapse.

In the academic human security debate, no common definition on human security has emerged after 12 years and the human security concept has remained controversial. While many have rejected the human security concept, authors with a Grotian or Kantian, liberal and constructivist perspective and those from peace research have rallied behind it. However, some proponents are critical of such a wide concept as freedom from want (Krause 2004; Mack 2004), and have argued instead for "pragmatism, conceptual clarity, and analytic rigour" (Owen 2004, p.375).

Many authors of a forum in *Security Dialogue* (2004) supported a wide agenda that includes freedom from fear and from want. Human security as an analytical and theoretical tool differs from human security as a political mandate. Uvin (2004, 2008) uses the concept to bridge the fields of humanitarian relief, development assistance, human rights advocacy and conflict resolution (Owen 2004).

To overcome the dispute between the proponents of a narrow and a wide human security concept, Owen (2004) suggested combining the wide UNDP (1994) definition with a threshold-based approach "that limits threats by their severity rather than their cause". After 10 years of debate in the social and human sciences, the conceptual human security discourse remains inconclusive, and the human security definition used depends on the approach, the preferences and agenda of the respective author.

Human security concepts in different regions

The UNDP Report (1994) triggered a global conceptual and operational debate among social scientists in all parts of the globe, which has resulted in four pillars of a wide human security concept.

Four pillars of the human security concept

Since 1994 human security has been used as an encompassing concept that shifted the focus from the nation-state to a human-centred perspective (Annan 2001) and deals with the protection of the individual or citizen. The notion of human security as freedom from want was promoted by Japan (Shinoda 2009) and the notion of human security as freedom from fear was promoted by Canada, Norway and members of the HSN (Dedring 2008). Kofi Annan (2005) added a third pillar, freedom to live in dignity. Bogardi and Brauch (2005) have since proposed a fourth pillar, freedom from hazard impacts (Brauch 2005a, 2006a, 2006b, 2008b). These four conceptual pillars of a wider human security concept are briefly reviewed below.

The first human security pillar: UNDP and freedom from want

Human security, according to the UNDP (1994, p.23), means "safety from such chronic threats as hunger, disease, and repression" and "protection from sudden and hurtful disruption in the patterns of daily life". Human security is an "integrative concept" that requires the understanding "that development must involve all people". The UNDP considered seven main dimensions of human security through sustainable human development: economic, food, health, environmental, personal, community and political security.

Global human security deals with global environmental challenges, such as "land degradation, deforestation and the emission of greenhouse gases". The UNDP argued that "the real threats to human security" in the twenty-first century will arise from the actions of people and take many forms, such as unchecked population growth, disparities in economic opportunities, environmental degradation and international terrorism. In the scientific debate this conceptualisation of human security has remained controversial and "no major analytic empirical study has used UNDP's conceptual framework to actually study the war/development/governance nexus" (Mack 2004, p.50).

The second human security pillar: UNESCO and freedom from fear

UNESCO's medium-term strategy for 2002–2007 proposed "improving human security by better management of the environment and social change" and to address "the need to prevent conflicts at their source and the needs of the most vulnerable populations". This strategy aims at the elaboration of integrated approaches to human security at the regional, sub-regional and national levels.

The third human security pillar: Kofi Annan and freedom to live in dignity

In his report *In larger freedom*, Kofi Annan (2005) re-introduced into the human security dialogue a legal dimension that has also been on the agenda of the human security network. He reminded the member states of their commitment in the Millennium Declaration "to spare no effort to promote democracy and strengthen the rule of law, as well as respect for all internationally recognised human rights and fundamental freedoms".

The fourth human security pillar: freedom from hazard impact

Two institutions have addressed environmental challenges from a human security perspective: GECHS, a project of the International Human Dimensions Programme (IHDP) that is associated with UNESCO's science programmes, and the UNU-EHS. UNU-EHS is to develop the environmental dimension of human security further.

From this perspective human security is closely related to vulnerability. Vulnerability comes about by poverty, disease and the lack of (economic) options and it is characterised by weak governance and underdeveloped infrastructure (UN General Assembly 2004). Both environmental and man-made hazards may expose vulnerability. Vulnerable communities are particularly at risk to both creeping deterioration of their existence and the rapid impact of extreme events. These hazards have generally worsened over the years. Since 1950 the frequency and magnitude of natural hazards and their economic consequences have grown (Intergovernmental Panel on Climate Change (IPCC) 2001a; Munich Re 2006; UNDP 2004; United Nations International Strategy for Disaster Reduction (UNISDR) 2002, 2004) and the exposure of the poor to extreme weather events and subsequent disasters may delay development for decades.

Human security focuses on threats that endanger the lives and livelihoods of individuals and communities. Safeguarding and improving human security requires a new approach that would require a better understanding of social, political, institutional, economic, cultural, technological and environmental variables. These stressors amplify the impacts of environmental change. While man-made and natural hazards cannot be prevented, their impact can be reduced. "Freedom from hazard impact" implies that people can mobilise their resources to address sustainable development goals, rather than having to remain in the vicious cycle of the survival dilemma.

Human security as freedom from hazard impact is achieved when people who are vulnerable to environmental hazards and disasters that are often intensified by other associated societal threats (poverty), challenges (food insecurity), vulnerabilities and risks (improper housing in flood-prone and coastal areas) are better warned of impending hazards, and are protected against these impacts and are empowered to prepare themselves for them.

Dimensions, sectors and pillars of human security

The UNDP Report (1994), Buzan et al. (1998) and Wæver et al. (2008) all referred to an "environmental dimension", but differed its focus. The UNDP Report (1994) included the concepts of food and health security but excluded water security.

So far, the "environmental dimension of human security has not yet been included on the agenda of the HSN. Natural hazards and their impacts have been on the agenda of UNDP, UNEP, the Office for the Co-ordination of Humanitarian Affairs and the United Nations International Strategy for Disaster Reduction (UNISDR), but they have not yet been conceptualised as specific human security threats, challenges, vulnerabilities and risks (Brauch 2005a). Gender concerns have been addressed in UN General Assembly Resolution 1325 and they have also been promoted by several HSN countries.

Conceptualising environmental security in the UN system

As this author has analysed the development of the scientific and the political debate on environmental security elsewhere (Brauch 2003a, 2003b, 2004, 2005, 2006a, 2006a), a brief summary of these arguments will be sufficient here. After a brief review of global environmental change as an object of scientific analysis, the scientific debate on environmental security is assessed below. Following this the environment is analysed as a new policy task of the UN, with its three milestones since Stockholm (1972) to the earth summits in Rio de Janeiro (UNCED 1992) and Johannesburg (UNSSD 2002), and the new environmental security threats and challenges.

Global environmental change as an object of scientific analysis

During the Cold War environmental concerns were not perceived as security problems. The environmental debate has gradually evolved since the 1950s and, since the 1970s, it has focused on human-induced perturbations in the environment. According to Munn (2002, p.xi), "changes greater than humankind has experienced in its history are in progress and are likely to accelerate". Dealing with future environmental trajectories requires mapping "a broad range of future environmental trajectories" for future changes that could be far greater than those experienced in the last millennia (Munn 2002, p.xii).

The human dimension of global environmental change covers both the contribution and the adaptation of societies to these changes. These processes pose many social, cultural, economic, ethical and even spiritual questions, such as our motivations for saving and our and responsibility to the environment.

Global environmental change deals with changes in nature and society that have affected humankind as a whole and will increasingly affect human beings, who are both a cause of this change and often also the victim. However, those who have caused it and those who are most vulnerable to and affected by it are not always identical.

More recently, Steffen et al. (2004, p.1) have argued that a global perspective on the interactions between environmental change and human societies has evolved. This led to an awareness of two aspects of earth system functioning: "that the earth is a single system within which the biosphere is an active, essential component; that human activities are now so pervasive and profound in their consequences that they affect the earth at a global scale in complex, interactive and apparently accelerating ways".

Organisations, networks and programmes on global environmental change

Since the 1990s a global environmental change research community has rallied around coordinated scientific projects, sensitising policy-makers and the public alike. These programmes emerged in the framework of the International Council of Science, a non-governmental organisation representing 101 scientific bodies and 27 scientific unions.

The International Social Science Council, a non-profit scientific organisation lists in its mission statement these three main areas of its attention: globality, transdisciplinarity and attention to policy issues. It has conducted five international scientific programmes dealing with both issues of human and environmental security:)

Several UNESCO programmes have dealt with hazards, and UNESCO has been involved in several related collaborative initiatives.

At the Kobe conference (2005) UNESCO published a report of 93 cases of good practice in disaster reduction. The activities listed in the report have lead to a global disaster reduction education campaign (UNISDR) launched in 2006 by UNESCO and UNISDR.

Scientific perspectives and model on nature-human interactions

In the social sciences the analysis of global environmental change and the human-nature relationship is polarised between epistemological idealism and realism (Glaeser 2002, pp.11–24), or between social constructivism and neo-realism. The neo-idealist orientation has highlighted the uncertainty of scientific knowledge and claims. At least three standpoints exist on environmental issues, including a pessimistic or neo-Malthusian view and an optimistic or Cornucopian one that believes that an increase in knowledge, and breakthroughs in science and technology can cope with these challenges. These two positions have dominated the environmental debate since the Club of Rome's *Limits of growth* (Meadows et al. 1972, 1992). Homer-Dixon (1999, pp.28–46) distinguished among neo-Malthusians economic optimists and distributionists. Brauch (2002a, 2003a) opted for a third perspective of an equity-oriented pragmatist.

The position of the UN system may be described as that of Grotian pragmatism, in security terms, and as an equity-oriented pragmatic environmental perspective, where cooperation matters and is needed to solve problems.

The complex interaction between processes in the ecosphere and anthroposphere have been visualised by Brauch (2002a, 2003a, 2005a, 2008b) in a survival hexagon (Figure 1) of three resource challenges – air, land and water – and three social challenges – human population, urban systems and rural systems. These six factors may interact in different ways and contribute to environmental scarcity of soil, water and food that, in turn, intensify environmental

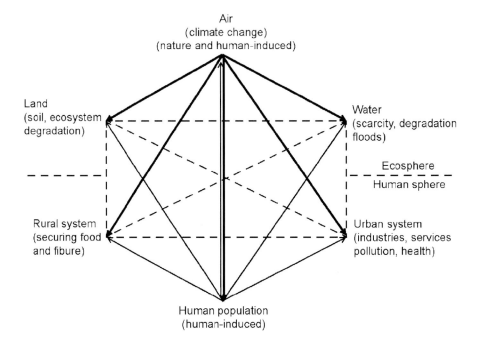

direct impact of nature and human-induced "root cause": climate change on five factors

direct impact of human-induced "root cause": population on five factors

- — ➔ complex interaction among four structural factors: land, water, urban and rural systems

FIGURE 1: Survival hexagon of six resource and social factors after Brauch (2005, p.15).

degradation. In specific contexts they result in environmental stress that may lead to conflictual outcomes that occur nearly exclusively at the national level. Whether environmental stress results in extreme and potentially violent outcomes depends on the national political process and on how knowledge is used for adaptation and mitigation purposes, as well as on the structures of governance.

These six factors contribute to global environmental change and represent the pressure in an elaborated pressure-response model that goes beyond the narrow scope of related models that have been used, such as the pressure-state-response" model by OECD (1993, 1994, 1998, 1999, 2000, 2001a, 2001b).

The six pressure points of global environmental change represented by the hexagon contribute to environmental scarcity and degradation that often interact negatively and result in environmental stress. Both environmental stress and the direct link between climate change and extreme weather events have increased the number, intensity and economic damage of weather-related natural hazards (IPCC 2001a, 2007a, 2007b). Climate change may increase the probability and intensity of extreme weather events and thus increase internal displacements, transboundary and even intercontinental migration.

The PEISOR model (Figure 2) goes beyond these models, and its six components stand for:

- P (pressure). The six drivers of global environmental change of the survival hexagon
- E (effects). The linear, non-linear or chaotic interactions of the factors of the hexagon for

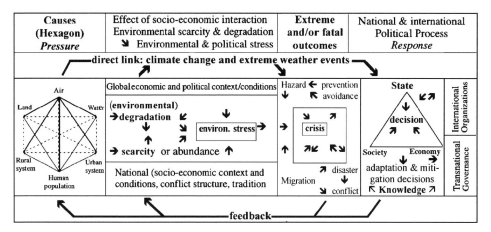

FIGURE 2: PEISOR model on causes and outcomes of environmental stress and hazards.
Source: Brauch 2003: 126; 2005: 16; 2005a: 16; 2008c.

environmental scarcity, degradation and stress

- I (impact). The extreme or fatal outcomes of human-induced natural hazards
- SO (societal outcomes)
- R (response)

The interaction between the state, the economy and society will differ, as will the role of knowledge and scientific innovations to enhance the national coping capacities. Whether these natural hazards result in disasters depends partly on environmental (external) vulnerability, but also on social (internal) vulnerability (Bohle 2002), that is, on the resilience of the people affected, on their protection and empowerment, and on their early warning and degree of disaster preparedness, as well as on their own coping capacities and that of their societies, business and governments.

Extreme societal outcomes may force people to give up their traditional livelihoods and migrate to the towns or the slums of major cities, or in some cases, overseas to the North. The response of the process on many political levels may also contribute to the severity of the societal and political outcomes and on whether they can be solved or result in local and domestic protests or, in the most extreme cases, in small-scale violence. Environmentally or hazard-induced migration has thus become a human security challenge as well as a challenge to regions in Europe and to national security. Migration has become a major security challenge for EU inter-governmental

policies, both in justice and home affairs, but also in common foreign and security policies.

Addressing the complex root causes may help to avoid future environmental conflicts. If these efforts fail, environmental stress and hazards may affect ongoing domestic conflicts, or trigger a chain of events that may result in extreme cases in violent conflicts, within or between countries, if their economic survival is at stake. Such conflicts, whether internal or at the international level may be caused by a complex interaction of inputs and processes.

Both hazards and migration interact and may contribute to domestic crises that may escalate to different forms of low-level violence. The nature-induced and human-induced factors of global environmental change may intensify ethnic, religious or political conflicts and may raise the need for peacemaking. Four different socio-economic scenarios of the complex interplay of these structural causes are domestic societal conflicts, resource and border conflicts (Klare 2001), regional violence and the militarisation of non-military causes of conflicts.

In many developing countries internal displacement has often been a first step towards transboundary migration, for example, from Bangladesh to India. But no violent conflict has so far been caused by environmental degradation alone. The question is whether these processes pose new threats and challenges for human security and survival (Brauch 2005a) and how these challenges be proactively addressed to reduce their impact.

With the Rio (1992) and Johannesburg (2002) summits, problems of climate change, biodiversity and desertification were added to the policy agenda. But the implementation strategies for sustainable development fell well behind the declaratory policy statements, such as the Agenda 21 or the Millennium Goals and the Johannesburg Plan of Action.

Scientific debate on environmental security

The fundamental changes in the international political order and the emergence of new wars (Kaldor 1999; Kaldor and Vashee 1997; Münkler 2002, 2005) resulted in new hard security threats, soft (environmental) security challenges and new vulnerabilities that are perceived and interpreted differently, depending on the policy-maker and the analyst. Against many of these soft security challenges no military defence is possible, but the military can assist in early warning and in a speedy and well-organised response. Many security challenges (such as the tsunami of 26 December 2004 and the hurricanes in 2005 in the Gulf of Mexico) do not discriminate between powerful and poor countries, although rich countries have better means to adapt and to mitigate their effects.

The increasing acknowledgement of these new global challenges have led to the progressive securitisation of global and regional environmental security issues. Environmental and ecological security have added new dangers to the national security agendas that legitimate new military missions and political tasks.

Since the 1970s global environmental change has become a new research field in both the natural and social sciences. According to Dalby (2002a) and Brauch (2003a), the research on environmental security evolved in three stages:

Phase I: In the 1970s and 1980s research on the environmental impact of wars was closely linked to the pioneering work of Arthur H. Westing and conceptual contributions by others.
Phase II: During the 1990s two comprehensive empirical environmental conflict research projects were conducted by the Toronto Group and the Bern-Zürich Group.
Phase III: Since the mid-1990s, partly in reaction to the work of both research teams,

comparative studies and conceptual deepening were launched by different research teams.

According to Dalby (2002b, p.96), "environmental security discussions can now move to a fourth stage of synthesis and reconceptualisation". Brauch (2003a, 2005a, 2005b) suggested that a fourth phase of research on human and environmental security and peace (HESP) should combine natural and human structural factors, based on the expertise of the natural and social sciences.

During the three research phases outlined above, the issues of environmental scarcity, degradation and stress, as well as their possible socio-political consequences, were put on the social and natural science research agenda and also on the political agenda of governments and international organisations. However, most social science studies of environmental security 1990 have ignored, the contributions of natural science research, and vice versa.

In 2007 the UN Security Council for the first time addressed climate change as a security issue. In an attempt to securitise climate change UK Foreign Secretary Margaret Beckett stressed that "what makes wars start – fights over water, changing patterns of rainfall, fights over food production, land use." But representatives of China, Russia, Qatar, Indonesia and South Africa argued that the Security Council was not the place for concrete action.

The climate change issue was discussed at the G8 meetings in August 2005 and in June 2007, where the G8 agreed to set a global goal for emissions reductions.

The UNDP also took up the relationship between human development and climate change in its *Human Development Report 2007* in November, suggesting that climate change poses major obstacles to progress in meeting MDGs and maintaining progress raising the HDI.

From a human security perspective, climate change was addressed by the GECHS programme of IHDP in June 2005 and it was the focus of the Greek Presidency of the HSN (2007–2008). The activities and the results have been analysed in detail elsewhere (Fuentes *et al.* 2009; Brauch 2009). There is now a need to move towards a fourth phase of research on environment and security linkages that builds on the available evidence and tries to overcome its shortcomings. The ultimate goal of a fourth phase of research on HESP is to induce policy-makers to accept new paradigms leading to proactive environmental initiatives and behaviour (Brauch 2002a, 2003b, 2003c, 2005a; Dalby et al. 2009).

The environment: a new task for the UN

In its political declaration and plan of implementation the UNSSD in Johannesburg (2002) referred to food security, but environmental and human security were not included. Later Kofi Annan (2003) pointed to the potential threats posed by environmental problems and suggested that the UN system should "build additional capacity to analyse and address potential threats of conflicts emanating from international natural resource disparities". After this initial success some countries opposed the signing of protocols with specific legal obligations: the *Kyoto protocol on climate change* (1997) and the *Cartagena protocol on biosafety* (2000).

The Organisation for Security and Cooperation in Europe (OSCE) has dealt with security risks from environmental stress. Among the non-traditional security risks confronting OSCE countries in central, eastern and southeastern Europe, the Caucasus, central Asia and other parts of the former Soviet Union are transboundary pollution, the shortage of drinking water, the disposal of radioactive waste and the reduction of human losses in man-made disasters and natural catastrophes.

The (OECD) has also addressed the linkages between development, environment and conflicts in several policy statements, such as "Development assistance, peace and development co-operation of the 21st century" (OECD, DAC 1997). The EU has pursued two strategies for environmental security: integrating environmental goals into all sectoral policies (Cardiff process), stressing conflict prevention and management in international organisations and specific regions. At the Barcelona European Council in March 2002 a sustainable development strategy was adopted that emphasised the integration of environmental concerns into sectoral policies. The European Council in Sevilla (June 2002) approved a conflict-prevention programme that aimed both at short-term prevention and at the root causes of conflict. The European Council meeting in Thessaloniki in June 2003 approved a green strategy for the EU (Brauch 2003a).

UNEP has been active in three areas: its disaster management branch, its ozone action programme, and its post conflict assessment branch (Haavisto 2003).

- UNEP's division of early warning and assessment launched an environment and conflict prevention initiative in 2004. It provides policy-relevant environmental data and information for decision-making on sustainable development.

For UNEP major milestones for the promotion of environmental issues that may be relevant for environmental security since 2000 have been:

- the *Malmö declaration of the first global ministerial forum on environment* (2000)
- the Millennium Declaration where environmental sustainability was adopted as a MDG (2000)
- the UNSSD in Johannesburg (2002)
- the *Millennium ecosystem assessment* (2005)
- the *World summit outcome* document

In 2002 OSCE, UNEP and UNDP launched a joint initiative to promote the use of environmental management as a strategy for reducing insecurity in south-eastern Europe and in the Caucasus. The results were presented to the 5th Ministerial Conference in Kiev in May 2003 where an environmental strategy was adopted for the countries of Eastern Europe, the Caucasus and central Asia. After Kiev, the Joint Environment Security (ENVSEC) initiative has focused on vulnerability assessment and on monitoring environment and security linkages, policy development and implementation and institutional development, capacity building and advocacy.

Environmental security threats and challenges

With changes in the understanding of security, the related concepts of security threats and challenges have also changed. But even in specific communities, such as of the hazard community, no agreement exists as to what vulnerability and risk mean, and what has to be protected.

The emergence of environmental and ecological security concepts

Both policy-oriented scientists and conceptually oriented policy-makers have focused on the complex linkages and interdependencies between environmental risks and challenges and their impacts on security. Because both security and the environment are relatively elastic concepts, it has been easy "to establish or challenge linkages between both terms" (Matthew 2000, p.36).

From a peace research perspective, Brock (1991, p.408) pointed to several linkages between peace and the environment. These are environmental depletion, ecological cooperation, using military means to enforce environmental standards, and a healthy environment as an integral part of a comprehensive security. He categorised them into four types of possible linkages: causal, instrumental, definitional and normative. Brock criticised untenable generalisations that environmental scarcities lead to violent conflict. He argued "for a broader analysis of environmental change in its relationship with economic and political change".

For Dyer (2002, pp.67–81), environmental security "should take account of the spatial and the temporal span of environmental change". In contrast, Matthew (1997, pp.71–90) argued "that a concise narrowly focused, and systematic definition would benefit policy, research, and environmental rescue (Matthew 1997, p.17). By integrating other ideas and concerns under world order concepts environmental security becomes

a component of a more general approach to the theory and practice of world politics that emphasises the significance of the ways in which social and ecological systems interact. Matthew (1997, p.89)

Matthew also argued that environmental research made pioneering contributions to understanding the shifting sources of violence and changing requirements of security. He suggested a broader approach should be taken on the ecological dimensions of violent conflict

and national and human security than making simple causal arguments about scarcity and conflict, building "on the remarkable achievements of the entire environmental security field" (Matthew 2002, p.120). These different definitions and assumptions on outcomes illustrate the lack of scientific consistency and consensus on the concept of environmental security.

Initially, the key contributions to the environmental security debate were made by scholars in North America, central and northern Europe and the South Pacific.

It was initially perceived with suspicion by diplomats from developing countries. Some are concerned that states in the North may try to dictate the patterns of natural resource usage, development priorities and population policies to the South. The elite in certain countries may find changing past social bargains for environmental reasons to be a larger threat to state security than the environmental destruction itself.

In several developing countries an academic debate has started on environmental and human security. In October 2000 Rajendra K. Pachauri (2000), director of the Tata Energy and Resources Institute in New Delhi and present chairman of the IPCC, defined "environmental security" as the minimisation of environmental damage and the promotion of sustainable development, with a focus on transboundary dimensions. For Pachauri poverty refers to the people's lack of control over their living conditions. In his view many other factors, such as lacking property rights, unsustainable resource exploitation, restricted access to resources such as fuel, the impact of science and technology, global economic factors and national economic policies, strengthen the cycle between environmental degradation and poverty. More recently the debate on environmental security has spread in Africa, Asia and Latin America, and many different conceptualisations have been offered by scholars in the South (Brauch et al. 2009b).

The environment as a new threat to national security

One of the pioneers of environmental security studies, Arthur Westing (1988, pp.257–264), pointed to both the military impact on the environment and to environmental factors such as territorial, shared or extra-territorial resources that require mechanisms for the non-violent resolution of resource conflicts. The former Norwegian foreign minister Holst (1989, pp.123–128) saw three relationships between conflict and environment: environmental deterioration as a consequence, cause and contribution to armed conflict.

Both aspects of the environmental impacts of military activities and of wars, and of the environment as a cause or contributing factor to hazards, migration, crises and, in the most extreme case, also to conflicts have posed threats, challenges, vulnerabilities and risks that have been increasingly conceptualised, since the late 1980s, as dangers to human security.

When the Cold War ended two influential articles by Mathews (1989) and Myers (1989a, 1989b) summarised the US debate on the widening security concept: "First there was a need to redefine security and to include a new range of threats. ... Second, there was an acceptance that the object of security was no longer simply the state", but ranged to levels above and below it" (Lonergan 2002, pp.270–271).

Norman Myers (1989a, pp.23–41) pointed to several environmental factors (soil erosion, ozone layer, climate change) as legitimate causes for international concern that may have repercussions for US security policy. He warned (1996, pp.20–21) that if the environmental foundations are depleted, "the nation's economy will eventually decline, its social fabric will deteriorate, and its political structure will become destabilised. The outcome is all too likely to be conflict, whether in the form of disorder and insurrection within a nation or tensions and hostilities with other nations".

Myers (1996, p.22) noted, among the environmental factors contributing to conflict: population growth; ozone layer depletion and global warming; mass extinction of species and, as a direct consequence, environmental refugees. These concerns had a conceptual impact on the US defence and security policy during the Clinton Administration but they were discontinued by the Bush Administration.

Environmental security agenda as an object of securitisation

Simultaneously, the Copenhagen School has widened the scope of the security concept since 1990 from a constructivist perspective. According to Buzan et al. (1990) it "concerns the maintenance of the local and the planetary biosphere as the essential support system on which all human enterprises depend". Buzan et al. noted that:

The scientific agenda underpins securitising moves, whereas the political agenda is about three areas: (1) state and public awareness of issues on the scientific agenda ... (2) the acceptance of political responsibility for dealing with these issues; and (3) the political management questions that arise. (Buzan et al. 1998, p.72)

On the scientific environmental agenda the disruption of ecosystems, energy problems and population problems are often included, along with food and economic problems and civil strife (Buzan et al. 1998, pp.74–75). For the Copenhagen School the state and the society remained major focus of securitisation, while Buzan (2002, 2004) remained sceptical towards the human security concept.

Environmental security issues as new causes of conflicts

At the centre of the second empirical phase of the debate on environmental security have been many case studies conducted by two research teams in Toronto (Homer-Dixon 1991, 1994, 1999, 2000) and in Zürich and Berne (Bächler and Spillmann 1996, 1996a, 2002), that focused on the linkages between environmental stress and extreme outcomes: societal crises and domestic or international conflicts and cooperation. While these case studies focused primarily on environmental scarcity (as grievance), other, more recent, studies have argued that resource abundance, or greed, has been a major cause of the new wars by local warlords (Bannon and Collier 2003; Brauch 2007b; Collier 2000, Collier et al. 2003; Conca and Dabelko 2002; Diehl et al. 2001, Gleditsch 2003).

On the eco-demographic contexts of emerging new conflict constellations in developing countries the American political scientist John Gerard Ruggie (1998, pp.155–171) argued that part of a population may experience "institutional barriers long before they encounter absolute physical scarcity", which may result in population pressures spilling over into international conflict. (1998, p.163) Ruggie argues that social turmoil from rapid urbanisation may result from the "insufficient capacity on the part of the cities to service such large increments of population in so short a time", concluding that, unlike in the past, the "interplay between socio-economic forces and biophysical factors have reached a planetary scale".

The British historian Paul Kennedy (2000, pp.239–245) stated that environmental pressures "could produce threats to human well-being and social stability" and that, if the projected effects of climate change are accurate, "then mankind will face atmospheric turbulences and environmental hazards in the future that will cause distress. But on regional and local levels this environmental damage could result in unrest and migration, often combined with violence. He argued that the new global challenges could bring some societies to worrying thresholds and thus could become threats to national and international stability.

Developing the environmental dimension of human security

The concepts of environmental security and human security have developed in parallel, both in the scientific discourses and in international organisations, with little thematic interaction. During the first three research phases the debates on environmental security were primarily state-centred or focused on the international organisations involved. The states and regions were of primary concern, and not the people. Although in the initial UNDP report (1994) environmental security was conceived as one of seven components of human security, but the HSN and most academic analysts have so far focused primarily on freedom from fear or from want, excluding environmental issues from their agenda.

What poses an environmental threat, challenge, vulnerability or risk to human security, that is to the individual human being or to humankind, depends on whether a wide or a narrow concept is chosen, focusing only on one or on all of the four pillars of human security.

Towards a people-centred environmental security concept

Barnett (2001, p.127) considered a "human-centred environmental security concept" justified on moral and pragmatic grounds "because addressing the welfare of the most disadvantaged means addressing many of the future sources of environmental degradation". For Barnett (2001, p.129), "environmental security is the process of minimising environmental insecurity", and has humans as the major focus of security. With this definition, he "seeks to treat the underlying causes that create environmental degradation". In his view, environmental security requires nation-states to "act domestically and in concert to curb global, regional and local processes that generate environmental degradation and human insecurity". His concepts draw on ecology and hazard theory, with the key notions of risk, vulnerability and resilience.

Najam (2003a, 2003b) proposed an environment and security discussion around two sources of insecurity (violent conflict and social eruption), and focuses the analysis on state-centred and society-centred activities. He suggests that the outcomes of this insecurity include interstate war, civil strife and human insecurity (as a society-centred social disruption).

Developing the environmental dimension of human security

The UNDP report (1994, p.22) argued that, for ordinary people in developing countries, security "symbolised protection from the threat of disease, hunger, unemployment, crime, social conflict, political repression and environmental hazards". For the UNDP, human security is "a concern with human life and dignity" that must focus on four essential characteristics: human security is a universal concern with interdependent components; it is easier to ensure by prevention than later intervention and it is people-centred. Human security, in this view, means "safety from such chronic threats as hunger, disease and repression" and "hurtful disruptions in the patterns of daily life". Among the threats to human security, the UNDP (1994, pp.28–30) lists environmental security as one of seven components.

Besides these local environmental threats to human security, the UNDP Report (1994, p.34) also refers to several global challenges where environmental threats are one of the clearest examples. For the UNDP (1994, p.34), the real threats to human security in the twenty-first century are the results of human activities. It lists environmental degradation among seven key threats to security, noting that "most forms of environmental degradation have their most severe impact locally". "[A]s habitats are fragmented, altered or destroyed, they lose their ability to provide ecosystem services – water purification, soil regeneration, watershed protection, temperature regulation, nutrient and waste recycling and atmospheric maintenance" (UNDP 1994, p.36).

Inspired by this comprehensive coverage of the local and global features of the environmental dimension of human security, the IHDP project on GECHS has made the relationships between global environmental change and human security its primary research question. The GECHS Science Plan (Lonergan et al. 1999) argued that the environmental changes affect human security include natural disasters, cumulative changes or slow-onset changes, accidental disruptions or industrial accidents, development projects and conflict and warfare.

GECHS recent activities include two workshops on Human Security and Climate Change (2005) and on Climate Change and Poverty. The Science–Policy–Practitioner Interface (2006). While the first workshop served to formulate a research agenda, the second discussed climate–poverty links relevant to mainstreaming adaptation to climate change in official development assistance.

A major conceptual and policy task for UNU-EHS (2004) is to contribute to developing the environmental dimension of human security (Brauch 2005a, 2005b) and to freedom from hazard impact (Bogardi and Brauch 2005). UNU-EHS needs to help efforts at all levels in building capacity for early warning, developing

vulnerability indicators and vulnerability mapping to reduce fatalities, primarily in developing countries. Much conceptual work on the links between environmental and human security, and on the environmental dimension of human security, is still needed.

International organisations need to incorporate a human security perspective into their environmental security initiatives. The work of the HSN also needs to include an environmental security dimension. As a scientific forum UNU-EHS can support the UN system through building human capacity towards freedom from hazard impact.

A fourth human security pillar: freedom from hazard impact

While man-made and natural hazards cannot be prevented, their impact can be reduced by early warning measures and better disaster preparedness. Human security in this pillar is achieved when people who are vulnerable to hazards are better protected against these impacts and can effectively prepare themselves to cope with the survival dilemma. To be free from hazard impact needs four different types of hazard-specific policies in case of:

Slow-onset hazards
Rising sea levels and temperature increases due to climate change require long-term strategies to reduce greenhouse gas emissions, building dams and mitigation efforts, such as restricting housing in coastal areas affected.

Rapid-onset hydro-meteorological hazards
Climate change has already contributed to an increase of extreme weather events and may intensify. Better disaster preparedness for this in the form of education, training and infrastructure is needed. Disaster responses need to be improved. Different systems of early warning are needed for storms, floods, forest fires and droughts.

Rapid-onset geophysical hazards
Earthquakes, volcanic eruptions and their possible extreme consequences also need improved early warning systems and better disaster preparedness, improved disaster response and clear

guidelines for post-hazard reconstruction activities.

Man-made disasters
Such events can consist of technical, industrial and traffic accidents or of a combination of these.

A fourth phase of environmental security research

After two decades of research, environmental security can now move to a fourth stage of synthesis and reconceptualisation (Dalby 2002a, 2002b, p.96, Oswald et al. 2009). The first three phases were primarily focused on the nation- (Dalby et al. 2009) , but Oswald et al. (2009) suggest that during the fourth phase a people-centred perspective needs to be included (Brauch 2003a, 2005a, 2005b, 2006a, 2006b). Environmental security should include societal and gender issues, and sectoral approaches such as water, food, health and livelihood security as well as eco-feminist perspectives (Oswald 2001, 2008a, 2009). Furthermore, of the concepts of securitisation should be widened to include global, regional, societal, community, family and human levels. This research phase on HESP should combine the structural factors of global environmental change, based on expertise from the natural and social sciences, with outcomes and conflict constellations (Brauch 2003a, 2003b).

Research agenda for HESP

Research on HESP should combine the structural factors of global environmental change, based on the expertise from the natural and social sciences, with outcomes and conflict constellations. The fourth phase of social science research on HESP could aim at the 10 conceptual and policy goals listed below.

Scientific orientation and approach

- *Orientation.* An equity-oriented Grotian perspective to support multilateral environmental efforts in international organisations and regimes.

- *Spatial approach.* Analysing environmental security issues on a regional level requires a spatial approach which may be called a political geo-ecology.
- *Human security focus.* The reference for research and policy should be human beings, individual victims and communities of distress migration, disasters, crises and conflicts.
- *Sustainable development and sustainable peace.* A human security perspective in analysing environmental security issues to aim at an enduring, sustainable peace.

Scientific focus on causes, impacts and extreme outcomes of global environmental change

- *Causes.* The research should include both environmental degradation and environmental scarcity and their impact on environmental stress and on natural and human-induced hazards. This requires an interdisciplinary approach with close interaction between social and natural sciences.
- *Outcomes.* The research should include hazards, distress migration and environmental refugees as well as the complex interactions among these outcomes.
- *Policy process.* Case studies should include the policy processes, that is, how the state and the society have responded to the challenges and outcomes. They should emphasise the role that knowledge, learning and capacity building has played in developing adaptive and mitigation strategies to reduce vulnerability and to strengthen resilience.
- *Regional orientation.* This requires regional natural science models of climate, soil and water and comparative social science case studies on the policy processes at the regional level.

Policy goals

- *Policy goals on the societal and individual level.* Studies should contribute to strategies for reducing the impact of environmental stress, decreasing vulnerability and strengthening coping capacities and resilience.

■ *Policy goals on the communal, sub-national, national and international level.* Strategies for coping with outcomes of environmental stress should be developed by improving disaster preparedness and response and by integrating disaster reduction into development planning.

The resolution, prevention and avoidance of violence resulting from environmental stress should become a major policy goal. Such a research agenda should be developed within a culture of prevention:

■ to reduce exposure, the impact of, and vulnerability to hazards and to build resilience
■ to address the root causes of environmentally induced distress migration
■ to focus on linkages between disasters and distress migration and examine how they intensify the potential for domestic socio-economic and political crises
■ to analyse the causes and processes that resulted in violent environmental conflict
■ to develop policy-relevant strategies to resolve environmental crises
■ to prevent environmental crises escalating into violence by addressing their root causes.

In conclusion, the policy relevance of HESP is to recognise early-warning indicators and to examine both the environmental consequences of wars and the existing conflicts over scarce resources that may lead to environmental stress. These studies must aim at preventing them from escalating into violence and developing long-term priorities for developed and developing countries. They must help international organisations to avoid the extreme violent and fatal consequences of weather-related hazards and to contribute to regional environmental good governance.

A policy strategy should use international environmental regimes and governance as a tool for conflict prevention. The realisation of these goals requires interdisciplinary cooperation between scientists from both the North and the South, from the natural and the social sciences from environmental specialists, disaster and migration experts with the peace and conflict research community. Finally, policy-relevant initiatives need to be developed in close consultation and cooperation with policy-makers.

An integrated HUGE

Oswald (2001, 2004, 2006) suggested widening the security concept by combining a broad concept of gender, including children and the elderly, with a human-centred focus on environmental security challenges. The HUGE concept analyses violent, patriarchal, exclusive structures of the family, questioning the existing process of gendered social representations and roles. It includes environmental security concerns, where hazard impacts can be reduced by a healthy environment and increasing the resilience of highly vulnerable groups (especially women).

The exchange of experiences reinforces the empowerment of the vulnerable. Immediate and efficient support for isolated regions affected by social and natural disasters can prevent long-term effects such as famine and violent conflicts. HUGE may overcome the consolidated gender discrimination and help to overcome discrimination through specific governmental policies and legal reinforcements. HUGE creates world solidarity to support the poorest countries with financial aid and debt reductions.

The focus now shifts from concepts to action, focusing on threats and challenges posed by climate change, desertification, water stress and natural hazards for human security.

Environmental challenges for human security

After a brief discussion of the environmental security threats of the six pressures contributing to global environmental change, the impacts of three eco-systemic causes of global environmental change will be discussed. These are climate change, soil degradation and desertification, water scarcity, degradation and stress, and weather-related natural hazards.

There are possible linkages between environmental causes, stressors, impacts or outcomes that may pose security threats and challenges for human beings or humankind within their respective natural environment. Natural and human-induced hazards are rapid-onset events that are also influenced by long-term, creeping or structural factors, processes referred to in the survival hexagon as supply-side factors, such as climate change, deforestation, soil erosion, desertification and drought and water scarcity and degradation. Both the hazards themselves and hazard-induced distress may trigger socio-political consequences that have hitherto been outside the traditional analytical scope of the hazard community. The peace and conflict research community has not systematically studied hazards as a cause of conflicts.

Climate change as a challenge to human security

Impacts of climate change on society

Many analysts are focusing on the impacts of climate change. These include the IPCC. The IPCC has three working groups. Working Group I deals with the science of climate change; II with its impacts, adaptation and vulnerability and III with mitigation of climate change. There is also a task force on greenhouse gas inventories.

Approximately every five years the IPCC prepares a comprehensive and up-to-date assessment of the policy-relevant peer-reviewed scientific, technical and socio-economic dimensions of climate change.

The IPCC distinguishes between sensitivity (the degree to which a system is affected by climate-related stimuli), adaptive capacity (the ability of a system to adjust to climate change) and vulnerability (the degree to which a system is susceptible to, or unable to cope with, adverse effects of climate change, including climate variability and extremes). It also refers to possible impacts of a substantial and irreversible damage in the next hundred years, modest impacts to which systems may readily adapt, and impacts that would be beneficial for some systems. The Working Group II's Third assessment report (TAR) admits that progress in mitigation strategies has been made, but less so in assessing vulnerabilities (IPCC 2001b, p.25).

The analysis of climate change impacts during the twenty-first century are based on several scenarios for the years 1990 and 2100 that include a range of socio-economic assumptions. The WG II's TAR analysed in detail a range of projected impacts of the different climate change, such as scenarios on coastal zones and marine ecosystems, human settlements, energy and industry, on insurance and other financial services and on human health. It includes input factors such as population and economic factors and three output factors: the concentration of CO_2 in the atmosphere, global temperature change and the global rise in the sea level.

In 1998 the IPCC released a special report that explores the potential consequences of climate change for 10 continental or macro regions. The report tries to explain "how projected changes in climate could interact with other environmental changes" (IPCC 1998, p.ix).

The report used primarily qualitative methods. It offers an "anticipatory adaptation in the context of current policies and conditions", and so-called "win-win" or "no-regrets" options that would have positive effects, even without climate change impacts.

So far, the conflicts arising from environmental stress have not yet been adequately addressed in the IPCC's first four assessment reports (IPCC 2007a, 2007b, 2007c, 2007d) although these questions have been analysed since the early 1990s in the social sciences (WBGU 2008; Brauch 2009). This body of research is primarily conducted by environmental, peace and security specialists in the North on environmental refugees, security and conflicts. It has not yet been assessed by the IPCC and most social science analysis focuses primarily on demand-driven environmental scarcity. A study for the German Environmental Ministry (Brauch 2002a) urges

■ the scientific community to focus on the socio-economic and political impacts of climate change that may lead to environmental stress
■ the international political community to recognise the long-term potential root causes for human catastrophes and to aim at longer term cooperative strategies to address these challenges

In the scientific community, causal statements on the links between the symptoms of global change and conflictual human outcomes are not yet possible at this early stage. In addition to the global climate modelling approach of the IPCC, a regional and nationally focused approach to climate change impacts is needed.

Several international organisations, programmes and regimes have translated scientific knowledge into political declarations, action plans and political strategies. Their work on climate has mainly focused on science, with little consideration of the link to security or conflict. The IPCC is now the major international epistemic community translating sound scientific knowledge on climate change into political action. It may thus be worthwhile for the IPCC to consider whether social science research findings should be included in its future scientific agenda. Social science research has dealt with the linkages between environmental degradation and scarcity (input factors), the impact of both on environmental stress and the impact of this stress on man-made hazards and crises.

The goal of this dual scientific and political agenda setting is

- to contribute to the early recognition of potential root causes for conflict
- to stimulate scientific research and conceptual thinking on strategies for avoiding environmental conflict
- to motivate national and international cooperation and action to counter the root causes by sustainable energy policies

This approach has differed from social science approaches that focus on political efforts of conflict prevention and rely on short-term early warning indicators.

Studies of climate change and conflicts

Two studies by Brauch (2002a) and by Schwartz and Randall (2003) have a have analysed the possible impacts of climate change on security policy and conflict. As global and local carrying capacities are reduced, tensions could mount around the world, leading to two fundamental strategies: defensive and offensive. Nations with the resources to do so may build virtual fortresses around their countries, preserving resources for themselves. Less fortunate nations, especially those with ancient enemies with their neighbours, may initiate struggles for access to food, clean water or energy. Both studies make

different assumptions, have a different worldview and approach to security (Grotian versus Hobbesian) and use different security concepts. However, they agree that climate change can lead to significant consequences for security policy.

By securitising climate change, the key questions that must be addressed are security for whom, against what and by which means, to achieve what end? Climate change will affect all objects of security: from individuals to humankind, from nation-states to global systems. But it cannot be addressed by a limited Hobbesian security perspective and with military means. It can be solved only by cooperation within multilateral organisations such as the UN.

Security impacts of climate change and extreme weather events for small island states

The interactions between rapid-onset situational events (hazards) and long-term creeping or structural processes (climate change, desertification) are most obvious for many small island states in the Indian and Pacific Oceans and the Caribbean. This group of small island states have contributed less than 1 per cent of global greenhouse gas emissions but they are the most vulnerable to the adverse effects of extreme weather events and the rise in the sea level. Those with high levels of poverty have only limited resources to adapt to and mitigate both rapid-onset hazards and the long-term impact of climate change. If the sea level rises as anticipated there be serious consequences for their social and economic development.

The rising sea levels are expected to be further worsened by increasing storm surges and flood risks. In some areas, beach erosion will increase, coral reefs may be weakened and many mangroves will be put under additional stress. Water supply is very vulnerable in the atoll states of the Pacific and in the low limestone islands of the eastern Caribbean. The population density may increase due to the resulting shrink in territory, especially for the atoll states.

There will be direct and indirect effects on tourism, agriculture from climate change directly and human settlements. Health threats include heat waves, drought and floods, and an increase in malaria and dengue. Insurance costs have already risen as a result of damage due to extreme weather events, as, for example, in the Caribbean.

The vulnerability of the small island states to major hazards has been demonstrated by the Indian Ocean tsunami in the Maldives, whose population density has been projected to grow significantly until 2050. Climate change is only one of the several challenges the Maldivians will confronted in this century, along with poverty alleviation, high unemployment, housing, education and healthcare facilities. The IPCC suggested that adaptation to climate change should be integrated into risk reduction strategies for sectoral policies.

The two IPCC reports (1998, 2001a) did not include in their discussion the population projections that will increase the severe environmental stress. In the Caribbean the population will increase in Haiti and in the Dominican Republic, but only slightly in Cuba. In all small island states in the Indian Ocean, the projected population growth and the high reliance on tourism may increase environmental stress even without climate change impacts. The most likely implication of the threats posed by climate change for small island states may be a survival dilemma.

Climate change, extreme weather events and hazards as security issues

According to the IPCC, extreme weather events will become very likely during the twenty-first century. The socio-political and economic consequences of the projected increase of hydro-meteorological hazards will raise security dangers for the poor. The impact of climate change will differ with regard to climate zones and world regions, as do the capabilities for adaptation and mitigation. For example, regions in Asia (IPCC 2001a, p.48) differ in their vulnerability to climate change. Boreal regions are moderately vulnerable to slightly resilient, arid and semi-arid regions are not very vulnerable, temperate regions are moderately to very vulnerable and tropical sub-regions are very vulnerable.

The impact of rising sea levels poses existential threats to the survival of many other countries. In Bangladesh a 45-cm increase in the sea level would lead to a loss of 10.9 per cent of its territory and expose about 5 per cent of its rapidly growing population to risk. Due to this high population growth and vulnerability to multiple hazards, environmentally triggered urbanisation and distress migration have already become political issues between Bangladesh and India, and Mexico and the USA, for both the national security of India and the USA and the human security of the migrants (Brauch 2002a).

Environmental factors as security threats and challenges

For Bangladesh, Mexico and Egypt environmental factors have increased human insecurity by confronting the highly vulnerable and poor people with a survival dilemma. Hazard-induced or environmentally triggered distress migration has become a major human and societal security challenge for the twenty-first century. Measures taken in both India and the USA have neither stopped nor prevented immigration: instead, the numbers of illegal immigrants have increased (Oswald and Brauch 2005).

Since the events of 11 September 2001 military perceptions have focused exclusively on weapons of mass destruction and terrorism and used these new threats to legitimate new military missions and expenditures and the use of force. In this mindset migration is perceived as a soft security threat that must be contained by police or by the armed forces. This primarily reactive policy to countering terrorism or containing migration does not address the long-term structural root causes.

From a Kantian perspective, legal provisions offer an effective framework for dealing with these challenges, by establishing international development goals, strengthening existing international institutions and environmental regimes by taking measures against free-riders and violators and using instruments for setting agendas and coordinating policies, including strengthening the International Criminal Court.

From a pragmatic Grotian perspective, international cooperation needs to address not only the perceived short-term and hard military security threats, but also the long-term structural factors, as well as rapid-onset hazards that pose threats to others than the nation-state, that is, to both human beings and humankind. To reduce the impact of climate change more effective implementation of the goals of the UN *Framework convention on climate change* (UNFCC 1992) and of the *Kyoto protocol* (1997), as well as of the evolving post-2012 climate regime, is vital.

Desertification as a challenge to human security

To discuss desertification in terms of security, the interactions between desertification and other human, as well as human- and nature-induced, factors of global environmental change must be understood, together with the possible fatal outcomes of global environmental change.

Definitions and concepts of desertification

Monique Mainguet (2003, p.645) distinguished four meanings of desertification that have changed over time. To start with, Lavauden, (1927a, 1927b) claimed: "Desertification ... is purely artificial. *It is only the result of man.* It is relatively recent, and could still be fought and checked". Later, in response to the severe drought in the Sahel, UNEP offered this definition in 1977: "Desertification is the diminution or destruction of the biological potential of land, and can lead ultimately to desert-like conditions. It is an aspect of the widespread deterioration of ecosystems" (UNEP 1996).

In 1990 the UNEP ad hoc group for the "Global evaluation of desertification" used this definition: "Desertification is land degradation in arid, half-arid and dry sub-humid areas resulting from opposite human impact". Two years later in Rio de Janeiro UNCED adopted this definition: "Desertification is land degradation in arid, half-arid and dry sub-humid areas, resulting from various factors, *including climatic variations* and *human activities*". At this conference the Charter of the Earth was proposed, and the negotiation of a Convention to Combat Desertification (UNCCD) was launched.

The text of the UN Convention to Combat Desertification (UNCCD) of 17 June 1994 used the UNCED definition. Combating desertifica-

tion aims at: "land degradation, rehabilitating partly degraded land and reclaiming desertified land". The term "drought" is used for naturally occurring phenomena that exist when "precipitation has been significantly below normal recorded levels". To mitigate the effects of drought improved drought prediction is needed. The objective of the UNCCD (Art. 2) is to combat desertification and to mitigate the effects of drought, especially in Africa. This is to be done by using "long-term integrated strategies" aiming at "improved productivity of land, and the rehabilitation, conservation and sustainable management of land and water resources, leading to improved living conditions, in particular at the community level" (UN 2003, pp.7–8).

Complex causes and impacts of desertification on society and politics

The UNCCD Secretariat noted that today drylands "are being degraded by overcultivation, overgrazing, deforestation, and poor irrigation practices. Such overexploitation is generally caused by economic and social pressures, ignorance, war, and drought". The UNCCD Secretariat listed among the consequences of desertification, a reduction of the land's resilience to natural climate variability, a decline in soil productivity and loss of vegetation. It also causes increased downstream flooding and reduced water quality and a decline in crop yields and food production. In poor countries this often contributes to famine.

The UNCCD has also pointed to the enormous direct and indirect social and economic costs in Africa, including internal displacement and migration, estimating the global annual income forgone from desertification to be about US$42 billion each year. The UNCCD Secretariat also addressed the manifold interactions between desertification, global change and sustainable development, saying that these are often not fully understood, but are clearly important. While climate change could worsen the effects of desertification, desertification itself may temporarily affect climate change: "This is a recipe for political instability, for tensions between neighbouring countries, and even for armed conflict. Evidence is mounting that there is often a strong correlation between civil strife and conflict on the one hand and environmental factors such as desertification on the other".

Two-thirds of the African continent is desert and dryland, and the southern shore of the Mediterranean is severely affected. In northern Mediterranean countries land degradation has been often linked with poor agricultural practices. As a result, soils often become salinised and unproductive in response to a combination of natural and human-controlled activities, notably overtilling and overgrazing. Modern intensive agriculture and the growth of industry and tourism have put coastal areas under stress.

These general statements on linkages and claims of causality are not all supported by research in the social sciences as researchers have not considered either the interactions among causes of global environmental change, or their societal consequences (Brauch 2003a, pp.65–92).

Linkages between desertification and climate change

The IPCC (1996a, pp.95–324) assessed in detail the climate change impacts on land degradation and desertification. It stated with certainty that "most deserts are likely to become even more extreme if climate changes as projected by current scenarios; most desert regions are expected to become hotter" (1996a, p.161) and opportunities to mitigate greenhouse gas emissions in desert regions are few. But the IPCC also stated that human-induced desertification may counteract any ameliorating effect of climate change on most deserts. It argued that it is impossible to separate the impact of unsustainable land-management and climate change, but they do interact to produce a negative cumulative effect on the soil.

These effects are seen in Mediterranean, Middle Eastern and North African countries (Mainguet 1994; Mendizabal and Puigdefabregas 2003; Portnov and Hare 1999; Puigdefabregas and Mendizabal 1995; Williams et al. 1996) (see Figure 2).

Desertification has been a major contributor to environmental degradation, scarcity and stress. Economic production and consumption patterns on both shores of the Mediterranean are influenced by economic globalisation. Together they impact on global environmental change. It is doubtful that these complex and often combined environmental and socio-economic challenges can be solved by military means. However, military services can be used – and in some cases have been successfully used to combat desertification (such as in Tunisia).

Analysing desertification as a security challenge

Soil erosion, degradation and desertification may contribute to environmental scarcity and degradation, as well as to environmental stress that may influence violent societal outcomes. In addition, climate change has already resulted in an increase of extreme weather events. Desertification may contribute to the intensity and length of periods of drought. It is the impact of these two natural – partly human-induced and economically driven – factors on famine and distress migration that causes environmental, human, food, health and livelihood security issues. The relevant policy questions are:

■ How can the processes of soil erosion, degradation and desertification be successfully countered?
■ How can the societal consequences be curbed, and their impact be reduced?
■ How can policy implementation be improved and corruption curbed, so that the humanitarian aid quickly reaches the most affected people?

The dual task is to focus on the causes and the violent outcomes. However, this requires mainstreaming actions for coping with environmental hazards and conflict prevention. There is no simple strategy to counter and combat desertification and its outcomes. Instead, a complex set of strategic components in different action plans by different national and international, societal and economic actors is needed. For this to work, knowledge creation and anticipatory and reactive learning, can become important tools.

Desertification poses no military threats to objective or hard security but, as a regional environmental challenge, it severely undermines people's well-being. From a subjective perspective, desertification, drought and famine contribute to environmental and human as well as food, health, and households' livelihood insecurity. Thus, desertification poses a severe challenge to human security. It poses no national security threat in developed countries where military logic and the armed forces can be a solution.

Desertification can force people into internal displacement, urbanisation and transborder migration. Social and ethnic groups may become the focus where national identity is perceived to be at risk. Immigrants are often perceived as a threat, depending on specific circumstances. National security may be threatened by general strikes and hunger riots, and the value at risk may be regime stability and the survival of governments. For instance, the severe droughts and famine in the Sahel during the 1970s and 1980s resulted in violent clashes between nomadic tribes and resident farmers.

In the early years of this century desertification, drought and famine and migration have been perceived as human security threats by the CHS. Drought and famine have been addressed as challenges to food security by the FAO (1996, 2005), the World Food Programme and the International Fund for Agricultural Development, as well as to health security (WHO 2002).

In North America several hundreds of thousands of Mexicans leave their rural dryland homes each year to migrate to the USA. During the last few decades in China many villages have been lost to expanding deserts, sand drifts, dune movement and sandstorms. In Haiti land degradation reduced the per capita grain production to half its 1960 level, thus contributing to the chronic political unrest that has contributed to the emigration of 1.3 million Haitians since the 1980s. The political agenda-setting has just started.

Desertification-induced drought, migration and famine as security issues

Desertification is a slow-onset environmental challenge to security and survival. In some developing countries, they are part of a vicious circle: poverty contributes to desertification and desertification often intensifies poverty. Thus, there exists a complex mutual causal relationship. Desertification may also contribute to the intensity and length of periods of drought. The impact of these two natural factors that are partly human-induced and economically driven cause environmental, human, food, health and livelihood security issues.

Human needs assessment and index of human insecurity

Two of the diagnostic tools and resources available for analysing these interactions are European Community Humanitarian Office (ECHO)'s Global Humanitarian Needs Assessment and the "Index of human insecurity" by Lonergan et al. (2000).

Among the nine countries on the top of the ECHO's global humanitarian needs assessment, Sudan experiences a high level of natural disasters, refugees, internally displaced persons and conflicts in a complex emergency situation. But the high occurrence of these four events does not necessarily mean they are causally linked. To observe linkages requires structured and focused comparative case studies (George 1979), using the same methods and addressing the same questions to all cases.

Of nine countries most in need on the ECHO list, four are in the Nile basin and seven are in Africa, where processes of soil degradation and desertification, as well as the impacts of drought on famine, have been severe for decades. Eight of the Nile basin countries (except Egypt) and several Sahel states have experienced repeated periods of severe droughts and famine. One long-term early warning indicator, the projected population growth in the Nile basin until 2050, indicates that a major human catastrophe is in the making, with a massive projected population growth.

However, in their "Index of human insecurity", Lonergan et al. (2000) distinguish between countries "based on how vulnerable or insecure they are, and groups together those countries that possess similar levels of insecurity". They saw the highest human insecurity not in countries in the Nile basin but in countries in West Africa. Some of these countries are in the arid and semi-arid zones, but in others it is abundance in precious resources (such as diamonds and others) instead of scarcity that has contributed to state failure and conflicts.

Desertification, migration and conflicts: claims and scientific disputes

In 1988 about 10 million people were considered to be environmental refugees. These were defined by El-Hinnawi (1985) as "persons who have been forced to leave their traditional habitat, temporarily or permanently, because of a marked environmental disruption that has jeopardised their existence and/or seriously affected the quality of their life". For Myers (1995) "neither environmental push nor economic pull need be a wholly sufficient cause of migration", but a number of intervening contributory factors would not negate the link between the environmental cause and the migration effect. Among them are "non-adaptive institutional structures, deficient planning systems, and disempowerment of women".

While processes of environmental degradation due to pollution and soil erosion, leading to desertification, are caused by regional developments, global warming and the resulting climate change is caused by global greenhouse gas emissions (Brauch, 1997a, 1997b, 1997c, 1998, 2000–2001, 2002a, 2002b, 2003d).

On the socio-political dimension, the Almería Statement (1994/1995) referred to the projected high population growth that may result in an exclusion "of vulnerable groups, who are subject to suffering, oppression, and dependency on fragile ecosystems under stress". The Statement referred to conflicts in the early 1990s: "Of the 50 or so armed conflicts currently in progress, some 20 have an environmental dimension or are partly environmentally induced. Half of the latter are associated with arid lands". The Statement called for several policy and action priorities, including research to achieve a better understanding on the "relationship between environmental degradation and migration".

But 12 years later the empirical research on the impact of desertification on migration remains unsatisfactory. General estimates that are not substantiated by detailed statistical accounts seem to prevail (Myers 2002). Systematic social science research on linkages between fatal outcomes and natural hazards their potentially violent consequences so far hardly exists. This is because there is a lack of multidisciplinary, transdisciplinary and interdisciplinary research integration in the global change community, for example, between desertification and climate change specialists, and among specialists on the six factors of the survival hexagon. What assessment of the linkages between environmental change and forced migration there is remains controversial. While Myers (1995) has claimed that the link is close, Black (1998, 2001) has challenged this hypothesis and Castles has argued that "general forecasts and common sense linkages do little to further understanding" (Castles 2002).

Shin-wha Lee (2001), who explored the environment–security nexus, stated "that both Bangladesh and North Korea illustrate Amartya Sen's principle that the roots of famine lie not in lack of aggregate food supply, but in the failure of individuals' entitlements to food. The problem is primarily political and social – not environmental". Castles concluded that the concept of the environmental refugee "is misleading and does little to help us understand the complex processes at work". For him, environmental factors are "part of complex patterns of multiple causality.

Combating desertification and avoiding conflict

The threefold task is to focus on the causes and triggers of global environmental change and on local environmental scarcity, degradation and stress, to focus on its fatal outcomes and potentially violent consequences and to mainstream research efforts and policy activities on environmental hazards with conflict prevention.

Desertification, drought, famine and hunger riots must be analysed as part of a causal chain linking global environmental change and its outcomes. They require long-term cooperation among scientists and practitioners using traditional, local and advanced technological knowledge. They also require broad, long-term, proactive local capacity-building.

Desertification and drought mitigation: some policy conclusions

Combating desertification and drought is not only a major technical environmental task, but it has also become a non-military security task for agricultural and environment policy. Coping with drought and famine are major preoccupations of many international governmental and non-governmental organisations. Beyond scientific dialogue and research, more proactive policies by states and international organisations in the Mediterranean may be needed to address the manifold causes of desertification. Among these are population growth (in the South), market forces (in the North) and climate change impacts (on both sides).

The systematic knowledge that is needed includes analyses on the commonalities of technical forecasts of hazards and political assessments of conflicts. We need to know more about the policy processes of warning and analysis and policy responses by international governmental organisations and governments. The potential of remote-sensing techniques and satellite systems for dual early-warning tasks must be assessed for the Mediterranean region. Comparative case studies on the integration of different technical early-warning systems (e.g. on crops, drought, migration, crises and conflicts in the Nile basin, Sahel, and southern Africa) could become a helpful instrument. These studies could include work on the cooperation of government agencies with international organisations on early warning for disaster reduction and response, as well as conflict prevention and crisis management activities. Finally, they may be helpful in producing success stories (best cases) and accounts of the failure of early warning systems.

Although mainstreaming early-warning activities and focusing on both natural hazards and conflicts, has been discussed as an emerging issue at the second Early Warning Conference in Bonn (2003) the task of bringing together both conceptual and operational communities remains a long-term aim.

Water stress as a challenge to human security

Water as a natural resource is conceived in two ways in science: in research on global environ-

mental change it is linking it with the five other factors of the survival hexagon (Figure 2) that results in water stress and contributes to environmental stress and as a topic of research on conflict and cooperation in social science discourses on water security. Water has become a key concern of many international organisations outside and within the UN system, and in networks, multinational enterprises, and research projects on global environmental change.

Water as an international political and research object

Water has played an important role in the UN Millennium Declaration (UN 2000), the MDGs, the Millennium Development Project (2005) and the Millennium Ecosystem Assessment (2005). The seventh MDG "to ensure environmental sustainability" listed as target 10, halving by 2015 the proportion of people without sustainable access to safe drinking water.

Since 1989 water security has become a topic of international politics (Wouters 2005, pp.166–168) and increasingly also a theme of national and human, as well as food and health, security. Water has also become a major topic of three programmes on global environmental change. These are the International Geosphere-Biosphere Programme the IHDP and the World Climate Research Programme. It is also the concern of the Global Water System Project that deals with water governance and the global water system, and aims at a dialogue with interest groups and political decision-makers.

Water scarcity, degradation, stress as security dangers and concerns

The human impacts of the global water system have resulted in several areas of conflicts where water scarcity and a decline in food self-sufficiency were defused by virtual water (Allan 2003). Since 1995 fresh water stress has existed in Mexico, the Middle East and North Africa, in central, west and south Asia, as well as in southern Africa. It will increase in these regions and spread to other countries until 2025. Alcamo and Endejan (2002) have analysed the linkage between water availability and food crises, based on historic data for 1900–1995, pointing to high risks of food crises due to drought and bad harvests. The crisis potential may increase further until 2050 and significantly affect the global food situation and several countries that export quantities of virtual water (like the USA and Canada) may experience severe food crises.

Thus, problems of water scarcity have become key issues of water policy as well as of water and food security in the affected regions.

Water as a research topic in the natural and social sciences

Water is an indispensable source of life, but too little or too much water may also be a threat to human lives and the economy. For 5,000 years the water cycle has been influenced by human behaviour, by deforestation, agriculture and the construction of dams, canals and irrigation systems (Steffen et al. 2004, pp.111–115). Climate change and global environmental change influences the availablity and quality of vital water resources. In 2000 about one-quarter of the global population (1.7 million) experienced water stress. Due to population growth, water demand will rise and, due to climate change, water supply may decline in some regions, resulting in an increase in water stress during this century. These processes directly impact on politics from the local to the national and global level.

Although water is primarily a preoccupation of the natural sciences, in three core projects of IHDP (GECHS, industrial transformation, institutional dimensions of global environmental change) and in the Global Water System Project, political scientists are involved. WG II of the IPCC (2001b, pp.191–234) devoted a chapter on hydrology and water resources to the state of our knowledge. It discussed linkages between climate change and hydrology and assessed our knowledge on the retreat of the glaciers and the decline in water quality due to higher temperatures.

According to the IPCC the impact of climate change on water resources requires more research in many areas. Effective adaptation to climate change in the water sector requires efforts in five main areas: data for monitoring, understanding patterns of variability, analytical tools, decision tools and management techniques. Many scientific studies have addressed the climate–ocean interaction, the implications of climate and sea-level changes and the impact of climate change on coastal areas. More research is needed at regional and national levels on the likely impact of climate change on water resources, precipitation and evaporation levels.

Researchers at the Potsdam Institute for Climate Impact Research have developed two scientific approaches in this area that are relevant to political scientists: the earth system analyses (Schellnhuber and Wenzel 1998) and the syndrome analysis for systems of global change (WBGU 1994; 1996).

Water as a topic of environmental, water and food security

The term "water security" was used in several Ministerial Declarations and UN documents but it was not defined. According to Gutierrez (1999), water security goes beyond the availability of water and includes the individual right of access to water as well as the national sovereignty over water. Wouters (2005, p.168) defined water security as "the state of having secure access to water; the assured freedom from poverty of, or want for, water for life". The discourse on water security is influenced by Annan's three pillars of human security:

- Water security is based on three core freedoms
- Ensuring water security may lead to a conflict of interests, which must be identified and effectively dealt with
- Water security, like water, is a dynamic concept that needs clear local champions and sustained stewardship (Wouters 2005, p.169)

Wouters (2005, pp.171–180) discussed the specific contribution of international water law to water security. This includes transborder water basins, the vulnerability of water supplies to industrial accidents and attacks by non-state actors (terrorists). Water security may also be threatened in armed conflicts, where the water supply for millions of people may be interrupted (Boutruche 2000; Tignino 2009).

Water has been used as a weapon since the war of Persia against Babylon until today although since ancient times, contaminating wells as a means of warfare has been prohibited (Greenwood 1999, p.13) and, in contemporary international law, water is protected in times of war (Tignino 2009).

The role of water in conflicts does not exhaust its relevance to international relations. Instead, water should be analysed in all its manifold connotations. Water was included in the first three phases of research on environmental security. During the first phase it was conceived primarily as a US national security issue but in none of the three early programmatic articles was water seen as a key security challenge for humankind.

In contrast, in the second research phase authors have addressed, both in their theoretical approaches and in their empirical case studies, water scarcity, degradation and water stress as a central security challenge, albeit one considered primarily as a national and not a human security issue. During this empirical phase, one research group led by Homer-Dixon analysed the relationship between water scarcity and conflicts in several case studies. Another group led by Bächler and Spillmann discussed the effects of water scarcity and degradation on conflicts and cooperation. Both research groups analysed water scarcity as a consequence of human interventions in nature, the growing demand for water, declining precipitation and growing evapo-transpiration due to temperature increases and (improved water management and virtual water). Water degradation is often a consequence of inadequate sanitary systems in rapidly growing slums, industrial pollution, the energy and transportation sector, the intensive use of nitrates and phosphates in agriculture and industrial accidents. Water scarcity and drought have often resulted in the over-use of ground water and fragile soils, which has contributed to progressive desertification. The consequence is growing water stress, due to a growing demand and a declining supply of water, and in some cases an increase in water pollution. This has contributed to water-borne diseases. The growing water stress has also contributed to progressive environmental stress and vulnerability, leading in the past to low-level violence.

In the third research phase (Brauch 2003a, pp.101–120), questions of water policy and security were considered in the framework of IHDP by the Global Water System Project and GECHS, among others. A significant social science literature now exists on issues of water policy, water security, water cooperation, water conflicts and water wars exist, using different theoretical orientations. In the political debate, the complex linkages were discussed as "water wars" or as "water peace".

Political controversy on water conflicts and water cooperation

The water stress resulting from water scarcity and degradation in transboundary river basins may result in manifold domestic and international tensions, conflicts and, in extreme cases, in low-level violence (such as that between nomads and herders). So far it has not led to a major war. Thus, an international, regional or national security perspective for the analysis of water stress may be less pertinent than a people-centred human security focus.

Water and environmental stress, as well as extreme weather events, may expose the people who live in poverty and with high social and environmental vulnerability, to a survival dilemma. Those living under conditions of extreme poverty, i.e. women, children and older people, often have only the first survival strategy available, that is, to endure it at home, while the young and better educated often leave their countries, legally or illegally, to support their families with remittances (Oswald and Brauch 2005).

Several Egyptian politicians have warned that future wars may be fought over water. A relationship between water scarcity and conflict was noted by Westing (1986), Homer-Dixon (1994), Toset et al. (2000), Shiva (2002) and Oswald et al. (2005b). There is a controversy over whether or not there have been water wars, with Gleick (1991, 1993a, 1993b, 1993c, 1994, 1998, 2000, 2004) and Wolf (1998, p.8, 2002) Yoffe et al. (1999, 2000, 2004) taking up contrary positions. More empirical research is needed including on the theories and methods of the political sciences.

Natural hazards as challenges to human security

Meteorological and geophysical natural hazards, such as earthquakes, volcanoes and tsunamis are part of the earth's history. But, besides geophysical processes and natural climate variability, the human impact on climate and weather-related hazards has significantly increased and has been projected to increase even further during this century. In addition, technical hazards (industrial, transport) have increased, and may increase further due to nuclear accidents and the use of nuclear and chemical and biological weapons by terrorist organisations. While natural hazards cannot be prevented, their impact can be reduced by early warning, disaster preparedness and rapid disaster response.

Defining natural and technical hazards and disasters

In UN terminology a hazard has been defined as: "A threatening event, or the probability of occurrence of a potentially damaging phenomenon within a given time period and area" while a disaster has been described as: "A serious disruption of the functioning of society, causing widespread human, material or environmental losses which exceed the ability of affected society to cope using only its own resources. Disasters are often classified according to their cause (natural or man-made)". Risk has been described as the expected losses due to a particular hazard. Based on mathematical calculations, risk is the product of hazard and vulnerability. Finally, vulnerability refers to the degree of loss (from 0 to 100 per cent) resulting from a potentially damaging phenomenon.

Hazards are the result of a natural or human-induced process that can be increased or reduced by human actions. Hazards impact on people, goods and on the environment. Environmental hazards may be natural or man-made, with intensive or diffuse effects. Natural environmental hazards are caused by external forces. The human sensitivity to hazards is a combination of physical exposure and of human vulnerability. In contrast, technological hazards or disasters are created by the spread and failure of high-risk technologies. Hewitt (2002, pp.480–484) distinguished between five groups of natural hazards: atmospheric, hydrological, biotic, compound and complex. Keith Smith (1996) also identified five but different types of environmental hazards:

atmospheric, hydrological, geological, biological and technological. The source of these hazards, according to him, were hydro-meteorological, geophysical and man-made. On their scope and impact, Aptekar (1994) differentiated between local accidents and regional and global disasters. On the temporal level, he distinguished between short-term, medium-term and long-term developments. Environmental disasters are often the result of human factors and physical triggers (environmental events), and natural disasters are the result of "ecologically destructive practices and from putting ourselves in harm's way" (Abramovitz 2001, p.6).

Hewitt (2002b, pp.297–303) has also pointed to the ways in which disasters may be magnified by global environmental change. These are dangerous trends, such as drug-resistant diseases, magnified risks, such as drought, fire, pest, novel threats, such as the escape of genetically engineered organisms, and increasing social vulnerability and adaptive capability. In the twenty-first century, natural hazards and associated risks may increase due to these factors:

- higher magnitudes of given natural forces and events
- higher frequencies or recurrence of given dangerous conditions
- combinations of adverse conditions that become more frequent, prolonged or intense
- changing geographies of one or all the above (Hewitt 2002a, p.491)

Life could become more hazardous but it could also become less hazardous if effective vulnerability mitigation and improvements in emergency preparedness and humanitarian assistance occur.

In research on global environmental change, vulnerability assessment evaluates the sensitivity of a particular ecosystem, resource or activity to a broad range of environmental and socio-economic stresses. According to Kasperson et al. (1995, 2001), a vulnerability assessment could be conducted through critical thresholds of different stresses and risks. For Hewitt (2002a, 2002b), a vulnerability perspective considers how communities are exposed to dangers, the ways in which they are readily harmed and the protection that they lack. Thus, vulnerability is created by the social order.

Kasperson et al. (2001, pp.1–54) distinguish between systemic risks and cumulative environmental change that may cause short-term and long-term consequences. Global environmental risks threaten international security and the peaceful relations among states. The key driving forces are population growth, technological capacity, affluence or poverty, political-economic forces and beliefs and attitudes.

A joint UK Department for International Development, EU, UNDP and World Bank Study (2002) linking poverty reduction with environmental management argued that drought, floods and other disasters can wipe out any development gains that poor people make. Competition for scarce natural resources contributes to conflict and complex humanitarian crises. Ecological fragility and the likelihood of natural disasters contribute to vulnerability to such disasters. With expanded social protection, better access to climate information and related measures to protect infrastructure and improved disaster preparedness, the exposure of the poor to risk can be reduced.

Natural hazards: developments of events and impacts (1900–2005)

Since the 1990s the International Decade on Natural Disasters and the adoption of an UN ISDR, concerns for disaster response, reduction and preparedness have also become a major concern of national and international organisations. While the number of all reported disasters has steadily increased since 1950, the number of deaths, has declined due to medical progress, but the number of people reported to have been affected by such events has increased since 1960, and so has reported economic damage. However, for natural disasters, a different long-term trend has emerged since 1900. The number of all reported natural disasters has significantly increased, as has the number of affected people, especially since 1960.

National efforts and international activities for an improved assessment and mitigation of natural hazards have intensified (International Federation of Red Cross Red Crescent Societies [IFRC] 2001, 2002, 2005). According to the World Disaster Report 2001 of the International

Federation of the Red Cross the total number of reported disasters increased from 454 in 1991, to 752 in 2000, reaching a total of 4,703 events from 1991 to 2000. In 1991 170,093 persons were killed (most in Bangladesh) and, over the decade to 2000, 752,521 people died and 2,108,025 were affected by disasters causing damage amounting to US$809,785.8 million (in 2000 prices). While the numbers of victims of natural hazards can be estimated, no similar data exist on the consequences of global environmental change as well as of environmental and of water stress.

Conclusions

Addressing the environmental dangers to security requires a complex combination of strategic instruments and policies to reduce vulnerability to natural hazards and the related risks for human beings and the societal groups affected. Thus, a dual strategy is needed for dealing with short-term situational impacts of extreme weather events and natural hazards, and the long-term structural impacts of global environmental change. A conceptual and policy-oriented mainstreaming is needed that will address both impacts (Brauch 2005a, 2005b).

The response to the tsunami of 26 December 2004 has shown a preference for short-term reactive policies of disaster management, and there is continued hesitation towards long-term proactive climate change policies by reducing greenhouse gas emissions in domestic energy and transport. Three groups of vulnerability and risk indicators are needed: for climate change and hydro-meteorological hazards, for specific hazards and temperature increases and rising sea levels. Effective climate policies with legally binding obligations may be the most cost-effective solutions to counter the increase in extreme weather events and hazards. To respond to these security threats proactive non-military policies and measures are needed.

UNDP and UNESCO have been the lead agencies in the UN system. In international organisations a dual mainstreaming is needed to incorporate a human security perspective in environmental security initiatives, such as in the ENVSEC Initiative of OSCE, UNEP, UNDP and NATO, which joined the ENVSEC initiative in 2004. In the European Union, the European Council in Thessaloniki (2003) launched the EU s green diplomacy (Kingham 2006; Brauch 2009).

UNESCO, the UNU and UNU-EHS can enhance the mainstreaming efforts in the UN system through their scientific forum function and through human capacity-building activities for freedom from hazard impacts. However, to introduce member states to vulnerability concerns in the human security concept and support them in adopting these concerns requires the active involvement of many other UN agencies and programmes.

The ethical challenges of human security in the age of globalisation

J. Peter Burgess

Human security: needs and ethics

The long debate on the meaning, nature and scope of the concept of human security has come full circle. Its epistemological pretences and methodological abilities have been discussed by analysts seeking to better grasp the world around them and to draw clearer and more meaningful conclusions about the security landscape as it is. Less well explored is the field of the actions the concept of human security calls on us to perform. For, like many concepts, human security is both a epistemological tool for describing empirical reality and a normative concept signalling the way the world should be and marking where change is needed.

The problem, long known to social scientists and in particular to philosophers of the social sciences is that the call to engagement implies a weakening of the concept's objective foundations. According to the doctrine formulated by Weber over 100 years ago, science that is normative is not objective and is thus not science at all. However, this opposition between the normative and the descriptive has since been deconstructed, and the necessity for a normative or quasi-normative power basis to science has been reaffirmed by many (Foucault 1994; Latour and Biezunski 2005; Latour and Guilhot 2006).

J. Peter Burgess is Research Professor at the International Peace Research Institute, Oslo (PRIO). He is the leader of PRIO's Security Programme, and Editor of *Security Dialogue*. He was a trained in mechanical engineering, comparative literature and philosophy in the USA, Germany, France and Norway. He has published 11 books and over 45 articles in the fields of philosophy, political science, gender, history and cultural studies. Email: peter@prio.no

The moral innovation of human security is also its terrible Achilles' heel. In a globalised world, where the values of the global view are imposed upon most people with the force of necessity, the concerns of individuals resist global action. At the very moment when individual concerns are put on the agenda, the possibility for achieving anything local is nearly erased by the weakness of individuals in a world of massive collective interests. What can the particular interests of individuality make claim to in such a strong environment of universality?

The purpose of this chapter is to approach the philosophical challenge posed by just such an engagement. If, as Chomsky once said, it is individuals that are moral, not states, then the imperative of human security to refocus the notion of security on individuals is well guided. At the same time, one cannot simply discard the state as custodian of security. The moral force of the human security is, following Chomsky, from individual to individual, not from state to state, nor even from state to individual. So, even once we have established what is to be done to strengthen the human security of humans where strengthening is needed, a second-order, normative question arises: through what institutional mechanisms can and should such changes be made? Given that we accept the challenge of acting, how do we get from here to there?

Definitional challenges

The aim of this chapter is to underscore the ethical dimensions of the concept of human security in as far as it relates to the principled discussions of ethics and international relations. The rich and engaged debate on international ethics that has taken place over recent years has, by and large, concerned the applicability of human security as a scientific concept (Burgess and Owen 2004; Owen 2004).

The other side of the coin of universal verifiability is universal applicability. If human security is a valid concept, should it not bear the same meaning and have the same scope and reach in any given setting? The challenge in answering such a question arises from the fact that different settings usually means different cultural settings. Different cultural settings relate to a different ethos, different values and ethical principles. Can one concept of human security then apply to the multiplicity of cultures, in particular when cultures differ fundamentally from one another? This approach opens up human security issues to their ethical consequences and presuppositions.

The United Nations Development Programme (UNDP) report formulation of "human security"

Most analytical and conceptual considerations of human security take the 1994 United Nations *Human development report* as more or less the source of human security thinking (UNDP 1994). Although the report is not the first to use the concept in general, the force of its impact on global discussion is undeniable.

In the wake of the Cold War, it has become clear that, for the developing world, "security" holds an entirely different set of priorities than when nationalised super-powers were concerned with "mutually assured destruction". The UNDP report is both provocative, in arguing that the long-standing tradition of using "security" to refer to geopolitical issues is entirely misguided, and reconciliatory, in the sense that it proposes human security as a supplement to existing terms.

The report notes that, in the developing world, the moments of insecurity arose from issues such as disease, hunger, unemployment, social conflicts, crime and political repression. This suggests that security studies have simply got it wrong and analysts need to retool and take aim at a new object. This simple methodological imperative is underpinned by the recognition that development has been neglected and over-shadowed by a certain use of the term "security". The UNDP report defines security as "freedom from fear, freedom from want". Here the notions of "fear" and "want" mark the transition from one understanding of security to another. The "fear" to which the UNDP refers is widely construed as fear from physical violence, from attack by a physical aggressor, be it individual or collective. The notion of security as protection from physical violence is thus designed to include the traditional notion of security. Absence from want tends to cover issues more traditionally the concern of development studies and developmental politics. It refers to poverty and lack of food, water or shelter. The agenda of human development is thus reflected. In this way, both continuity and novelty are embraced by the new concept of human security. The ethical imperatives of development studies are linked with the ethical imperatives of international relations and global geopolitics.

Fear and insecurity are imaginary, based on images of what could happen, what is likely, what is threatening, what is risky. The UNDP report suggests that a different scope of imagination is relevant for the two conceptions of security. For the global level, the threat concerns the collapse of an entire way of ordering facts and ideas, peoples and societies. Insecurity in the larger sense is related to the possibility of a general collapse, the possibility of a shift in the conditions for relating to the world at all. By reason of scale, these are always forcibly on a level that cannot be grasped by any one individual. It is supra-individual. A consensus on the shared experience of insecurity is difficult at best.

The UNDP report shifts from such imaginary constructions towards concrete individual relations in an individually determined world. The global dimension has not gone, but fear and insecurity remain connected to the imagined possibility of what could go wrong, cause damage, pain or other suffering.

The UNDP report, like its successor, the Commission on Human Security's (CHS) *Human security now*, sets out the shape of an ideal world, one in which security on an individual level is generalised across all communities in all parts of the world. However, it also provides a powerful moral voice for the needs of those subject to human insecurity by locating security and insecurity on the personal and small group level. This location (or relocation) of the focus of security and insecurity is the foundation of an ethics of insecurity.

Assumptions of the UNDP and CHS reports

In the debates on the concept of human security that have followed, the UNDP 1994 report has become associated with widening the concept to understand "violence" as physical violence, based on discrete and more or less quantifiable characteristics and capable of measurement. It is based on the changes in the reality of security threats and on the way we actually think about these threats.

First, the UNDP report sketches a picture of the historical evolution from a Cold War-oriented world in which the conditions of life of ordinary people simply fell under the radar of global attention. While there is, according to the UNDP report, little empirically new about the security situation of the societies of the developing world, our perception of the situation has changed. The weakness of this approach is that these perceptions are authored by the *We* of the developed world. There is thus no essential empirical basis for explaining the emergence of the concept of human security. Rather, it is a question of perceptions and of awareness. These perceptions lead to the second assumption of the UNDP report: an evolution in security thinking. There is a change in both the reality of threats in the real world and in the way we think about and experience threats in everyday life as well as in the way that the human and social scientists, as well as technology industries, conceptualise security and security threats. Second, it advances an activist, even ideological position about the appropriate coverage of the concept.

"Security", according to the UNDP report, is traditionally based on a territorial understanding of threat, whereby all that is threatening comes from "outside" the national boundary. Other sub-national spatial determinations of insecurity are either neglected altogether or toned down in importance. From the point of view of security or the ethics of violence, aggression itself takes a spatial, even linear, form. Violence in this model is discrete and identifiable, with a finite and limited origin. Its aim is linked with an intentionality, with a reasoned purpose or goal, namely harm, destruction or suffering of another human being.

In other words, even though its final object is human life, and it is therefore intersubjective in its character, physical violence is instrumental in a way that other kinds of violence are not. It inevitably involves a mediation, such as a tool or a weapon that exists in time and space and is discretely measurable. Even if it originates in human intention and a logic of intentionality, even if its ultimate aim is to obtain advantage through human suffering, it requires an instrumental middle, without which it falls.

The instrumental dimension is therefore also the pragmatic key to ending it. The practical consequence of this way of understanding violence is that it can be stopped by equally instrumental means. No matter how vicious are the intentions of the person or group that would cause violence, it is impossible without the knife, the gun or the rocket-launcher. Without these material means, the violence will not take place. This observation provides a means to differentiate threats to human security from other kinds of threats. It contributes to solving the categorisation problem by shifting the focus from the object to the means. It thus also enters the definitional debate around human security by suggesting that the meaningfulness of the concept is not based on its wideness or narrowness, but rather upon the nature of the means used to pursue it.

The classical concept of security

The analytical reach of the UNDP report places the emergence of human security in the geopolitical lineage reaching back only to the Cold War. For this reason, its emphasis is less on conceptual issues, than on a concern for what happens in the field. The concept of human security, as it is used by the UNDP in 1994, is the sign of a change in politics and political consciousness, and is far more than a revolution in epistemology. It is a reference to the emergence of an authentic need for individuals, agencies and states to address a problem that has emerged in the geopolitical spotlight, but which has lain unnoticed for some time.

The state is traditionally regarded as the primary unit of security. The notion of "security" that is operative in this conception implies two principal dimensions: outwardly, it refers to the notion that the state should function as a unified, finite and clearly delimited body, both the actor of security concerns in relation to other, equivalently constituted states, and the object of the security regard of other states and internally, the state, according to the contractualist, Hobbesian perspective, has an implicit relation and responsibility to its citizens. The citizens of the Hobbesian state pledge their allegiance to it in exchange for security. This security is, however, not uniquely directed toward the external other, but rather also from other individuals. It is, as we have suggested, the basis of individual, domestic security as well.

The rarefied state and its limits

This statist version of security presupposes a rarefied, even idealised, notion of the state. In the conception of the state at the foundation of conventional security, the collective unity that it reflects has no corresponding cultural cohesion. The state has a primary prophylactic function. It provides protection unconditionally, regardless of the cultural composition of the citizens it encompasses. This original form of the state precedes historically the consolidation of the concept of "nation".

The idea of the "nation-state" of the eighteenth and nineteenth centuries was scarcely used at the time when the original theories of state itself were formulated. To the degree the nation is understood as an ethnically charged entity, based on shared language, religion and cultural heritage, it should be expected to protect the cause of common interests, most obviously by preserving, among other things, the language and religion that provide cohesion to the group. The nation-state is self-preserving in a way that is quite different from the rarefied state. To put it inversely, if an identity-based collective group, a nation, is not supported and indeed driven by a force of self-preservation, then by definition it is not a nation. The substance of the rarefied state, however, consists precisely of not having any substance independent of the contract that gathers its members. It is pure contractuality, empty territoriality. Though we overstate the ideal form of the rarefied state, this is how it is conceptualised in the genealogy of modern state security.

Ethical starting points

Background concepts of human security

Globalisation involves a general evolution in the relation between inhabitants of the globe. It implies an interconnectedness, for better or worse, in terms of economics and information, a flattening of cultural differences in some areas and a radicalisation of differences in other ways. We are more universally involved in the value decisions attached to actions that will have knowable consequences for people far away. At the same time, our increased knowledge and awareness of the locally determined challenges and threats of individuals brings a great imperative for understanding and evaluating appropriately the premises and consequences of our actions for the security and insecurity of others.

Liberalisation refers to the consolidated evolution of one axis of globalisation through the ideology or discourse of economics. In order to increase the efficiency of the national and transnational systems, there is a general trend in global economics and politics to bring value decisions to the individual level. Universal protection systems, be they social welfare or economic support, are prioritised less, since they are taken to be at odds with the economic and social advantages of a free flow of capital, services and individuals. This tends to give a common basis for a strengthening of the individual in the moral sense of the term. Both the focus of human security and the emphasis on the question of what and whose responsibility it is, is implicated in it.

The globalised, liberalised world has at the same time become more democratic. More people have more access to representative political institutions. Political representation implies the ability and the responsibility to participate in the process of political representation. Democracy is considered by most to be a participatory active process. Thus, the liberalist dimension of democratic representation engages a responsibility to take one's voice seriously, to take responsibility for self-expression. The individualised notions attached to the doctrine of human security are easily associated with a certain spirit of political liberalism.

Social and cultural differentiation of human security issues

Social and cultural conditions determine security and insecurity in two distinctly different ways. On the one hand, there is an absolute and immediate insecurity caused by poor social and cultural living conditions such as poverty, poor health, environmental dangers and exposure to violence on a personal level. On the other hand, such social conditions and their consequences do not constitute insecurity in the proper sense of the word. Social and cultural ills and their derivatives are direct causes of suffering, but poverty itself is not insecurity. Insecurity, as we have underscored above, is the experience of openness in the future to dangers and suffering. Poverty causes immediate suffering without either ambiguity or speculative moment. At the same time, as with all aspects of insecurity, the fragility of socially, culturally, naturally and economically based suffering raises the threshold for future crises, exposes one to dangers to which other would more easily resist. The threat of human insecurity, it must be remembered, is not based on discomfort whose cause one feels, nor by the threat we know; it is caused by the experience of the unknown, by the calculus of unknown danger, based only on the robustness of the present.

Historical aspects of the concept of security

The long history of the concept of security has seen considerable changes over the course of the centuries, but more radical changes in the twentieth century. Before the twentieth century, the concept of security was only seldom applied in international relations, even as late as the 1940s. The turning point in the contemporary evolution of the concept of security is its mutation into its own sub-category: national security.

Security and the nation

This condensation of security around the concept of the "nation" itself corresponds to a shift in the very concept of nation. Like security, the perceptions and realities of the nation vary widely in time and space and the actual character of the nation-state is far from unitary in both historical and geographical terms. Moreover, they do not share a common or ideological political form.

While in ancient Greece "security" was primarily associated with the spirit and spirituality, in classical Rome concept of *securitas* meant something close to what we today call "safety", that is, firmness and solidity. The Roman notion had a distinctive and objective character. Yet the concept remained, in a narrow sense, subjective in the moral or psychological sense retained by the Greeks. If one is in a situation of security, one is without care, without concern. The thread of moralism thus remains present even today in interpretations of the concept.

At the same time, we can understand security in a different way. For, if we are in a situation of security in the sense of being without care, we are equally care-less or lacking in vigilance, either with respect to ourselves or with respect to others. Security is also a lack of need to be aware of our environment, those close by, and ourselves. In this way another moral dimension is introduced in the historical evolution of the concept. Security is the equivalent of lassitude, an entirely negative spin on a notion that was primarily construed as favourable. To have *securitas*, in this sense, means not having any doubt in the belief in God. Indeed, "belief" is no longer the appropriate notion: something more like "knowledge" characterises the relation between the individual and God. For someone with *securitas*, in this regard, the Christian notions of doubt, despair and uncertainty fall away and are replaced by the un-Christian notions of arrogance, hubris and arrogance.

Finally, the historical divorce between *securitas* and *certidudo* brings the last major dimension to the evolution of the concept of security. *Certitudo* replaces the religious meaning of *securitas* with a sense that differentiates between the notion of arrogance associated with certitude in the existence of God and the security measure in terms of a certain secular relation to the world, its risks and dangers. *Securitas*, freed from this negative connotation, evolves towards a situation where one benefits from protection.

Security and politics

This new mutation precedes the association of security with politics. In the twelfth and thirteenth centuries security took on a political form, referring to the protection of material objects against enemies, understood simply as those who would steal them. The introduction of a notion of political power corresponds to the return of the objective side of security: safe-making and safe-keeping of material things.

The objective turn gradually adopts a certain phenomenological aspect about the position of the object with respect to the threats it encounters or confronts. Thus, in English we differentiates between safety and security, in Italian between *sicurità* and *sicurezza* and in French between *sûreté* and *sécurité*. In each case, the former refers to an objectively identifiable threat, foreseeable, and for which a defence can easily be planned. The latter refers to more vaguely definable, less foreseeable danger.

Institutionally speaking, the early form of political security probably arose in the form of feudal princely states, in which security concerns were articulated and services provided according to politicised economic models. Security, understood as service provided by the prince, and later by the state in its more institutionalised forms, first arose in this way. Historically, a certain notion of security service became increasingly

implicit in the early understanding of the state. Service is associated with efficiency and the state is, for purely technical reasons, because of the economies of scale, by far the most efficient provider of security. This efficacy becomes thoroughly engrained, as we know, in the course of the evolution of the modern state. The notion of the obligation to provide security as a service is further nuanced through its association with the notion of the "people". The people – the collective identity whose basis is its affiliation with the state – becomes, in one sense or another, associated with the notion of protection from dangers, both profound and incidental. The people are also the identification point for the individual as a member of the state. This constellation of actors in the security field is first outlined in the work of the early political philosophers, most notably Hobbes.

Hobbes as the first theoretician of human security

In the Feudal era of European political history the city-states were managed by local princes (Chélini and Riché 1991; Duby and Dalarun, 1996). As part of the management of economic and natural resources, the princes made security a natural task of the state. Through the intermediary of the prince, security was thus provided to the people. The need for the prince became associated with a need for the collectivity that was both the labour force for and of economic interest to the state. The logic of security of the feudal period culminated in an early form of the relationship between people and security, a popular group identity as the basis for a notion of collective values that in turn might form the basis of a need for collective security. The Thirty Years' War – which, for most conventional purposes, marks the conclusion of the feudal period – shattered the religious anchoring of the European political order. Emerging from this context was an unlikely theoretician of the basic principles of human security: Thomas Hobbes.

If we are to understand human security as the result of a particular relationship between the individual and the state, between threats, dangers and concerns on the personal level and those on the collective level, then Hobbes' theory of security is instructive. It is he who first theorises the relationship between the individual and the state in European modernity. The point of departure of Hobbes' theory is the notion that the preservation of the self lies at the very foundation of individuality and the basic aim of all individuals. Moreover, and even more radically, individuality does not exist a priori for Hobbes. Instead, it emerges at the moment where the state announces itself as being preoccupied with the well-being of the collective. To the degree that the state seeks to preserve itself, it conceptualises the units that then make up the basis of that self-preservation. From the point of view of the newly formed individual, on the other hand, the pursuit of the preservation of the self constituted the very kernel of individuality.

At the same time, and somewhat paradoxically, the individuality is built upon a renouncement of individuality. The founding act of individuality in the philosophy of Hobbes is when individuals transfers the personal control of their life to the sovereign, the Leviathan. Individuality in Hobbes' perspective is a modality of choice. It is the moral ability of individuals to transfer their personal sovereignty to a sovereign authority. In other words, individuality is defined by the freedom to renounce individuality. The motivation for such a renouncement is, in the perspective of Hobbes, security. The direct purpose of sovereignty, and the motivation for any given individual member of society to turn over personal or individual sovereignty, is to enjoy the advantage of collective protection from the dangers posted to all members of society.

Thus, in a double movement of legitimating collective action, Hobbes theorises a system of collective security based on the particular fears of individuals. The particular security issues of individuals in their diversities are in this way condensed into a collective concern for general security. It is not the particular content of the security concerns of the individual that counts, but the fact that there are security concerns. All varieties of individual threat are transformed into a collective guarantee of security.

Security in international relations theory

The major changes in the structure of global security have effects on the scholarship which seeks to study them. Just as the late modern notion of security was born in the heat of the Cold War, security studies too arose in that same climate and with the aim of studying and understanding security as it was then practised. It is largely for this reason that the field of security studies has traditionally been dominated by a realist perspective. In the academic field of international relations these changes came through a number of significant methodological developments that took place during the Second World War and immediate post-war years. They took place in studies conducted from the standpoint of Anglo-Saxon political and intellectual perspectives, the techniques of objective measurement and the premises of rationality in international relations theory.

The ethical subject in realist theory

By necessity, the nationalisation of security studies through the Cold War structures of the East – West opposition oriented perspectives toward national interests, and primarily toward the interests of the major powers of the East – West axis. "National interest" was understood as primarily existential, in the medium-term or long-term. The national interest was all that contributed to maintain the integrity of the nation-state as it was (Morgenthau 1951). It is thus radically conservative in its basic premises. If one can speak of value at all, it can be a question of only one value, and that is the value of the nation-state.

Given the fact that "national values" belong to and apply to the nation-state alone in opposition to other national values, they can hardly be universalised in the same way as universal rights, "human" or otherwise. Moreover according to its core principles, the nation-state must by necessity oppose itself to ethical principles that might permit it to recognise rights, obligations and other values that support human security in its most universalistic form. The founding moment of modern security studies reflects the founding challenge of human security studies: not only do the political institutions and bureaucratic make-up of the nation-state tend to resist the novelty of a new geopolitical distribution of institutional task in the form of a human security agenda, but the value agenda of human security is also structurally opposed by the nation-based nature of human values in late modernity.

Thus, the study of international relations bracketed the entire question of values and ethics, arguing that it is simply foreign to the decision-making processes that characterise international relations. This is true only under a relatively special set of methodological conditions. The actions of actors in the sphere of international relations are value-free, only on condition that the actor is perfectly rational, instrumental and strategic. In realist theory, the actor of international relations is reduced to an atom, a subject without interiority. None of the interior political, social or cultural processes are presumed to be present in the actual political processes of the subject.

Secondly, the premise of the value-free "real" political subject of international relations requires the notion of "interest" to be abstracted from ethics. The interest of states must be regarded as entirely instrumental, dissociated from values that might be reducible to any kind of ethical reasoning. National interest, the normative guideline for actions in international relations in the realist perspective, is at the heart of the matter.

Ethics and international affairs

The realist theory of international relations revolves around its premises about human subjectivity and the notion of agency it implies and supports. The logic of diplomacy has thus been profoundly motivated by realist thought. Its possibilities and limitations revolved around those of the relations between nation-states, as represented by the tasks and activities of the diplomat.

Among the many variants on security theory since the end of the Cold War realist thinking dominates a certain understanding of ethics in the theory of international relations. A large variety of English language works have appeared in the last six years (for a critical review, see Walker 1994) but the traditional absence of ethical reflection in the field is, by and large, consistent with its predominantly realist orientation. A basic tenet of political realism is

that politics supplants ethics and that the political dynamics of security national interests on the international playing field contain no moral dimensions. Based upon a Weberian-inspired understanding of interest in international politics, the realist and neo-realist branches of international relations theory have built upon the more or less coherent conclusion that the resolution of differences between opposed international entities must be based upon questions of power, understood as a strategic, military and technological dimension and connected to the security of a given nation-state. Indeed, international politics is considered an device for translating the perilous metaphysics of all values into the universal language of military power. In other words, the essential differences between states may derive from metaphysical value differences, but they are negotiated on the secular field of international politics.

Security and international values

Since the high point of realist notions of security in international relations, the concept of security has undergone other changes that have consequences for the development of the notion of human security. The question of the meaning of the concept of security has thus become more and more associated with the question of what is under threat, what is in a situation of insecurity, and what is in need of security. This preoccupation has led to a kind of "neighbouring" effect. The conviction that the nation-state should stand as the sole beneficiary of security coverage or, inversely, that insecurity stops at the frontiers of the nation-state, gradually ceased to have universal currency.

This shift corresponds in a number of ways to the shift in subjectivity of the nation-state itself. Who speaks when the nation-state speaks, and who responds? The logic of state-to-state communication in the form of diplomat-to-diplomat contact has changed significantly. The changes brought about by globalisation in general, transnational economic arrangements and, more recently, transnational terrorism have brought a kind of porosity to the nation-state that has immediate consequences for the question of its security. Once the nation-state itself is divided, fragmented, and re-arranged into overlapping unities that have, in some cases, only partial correspondence with the security and insecurity of the nation-state what is the object of security?

In this condition the "interior" dimensions of the nation-state became the concern of security. Institutions, infrastructures, subgroups and individuals became implicated in the insecurities of what was once considered only state-oriented. These new objects of security also became associated on an international level and the subsequent networks of sub-national groups and interests required a retooling of security thinking altogether. This is the deeper theoretical background for the emergence of a literature of human security. It complements the developmental issues that lead to the pragmatic emergence of the concept and explains in some sense the richness of ethical issues involved. The result of this evolution in the general theory of the security subject is that security became accepted across a variety of discourses, from psychology to biology, from economics to physics.

From security to securitisation

Buzan's 1983 *People, states and fear* is a milestone in the evolution of the concept of security, opening the concept of security to a more penetrating analysis. It was also the first in a long line of increasingly sophisticated work on the nature of security, generally taking its point of departure in a critique over the narrow interpretation of security as "military" security. Through the development of the Copenhagen School, the theoretical problematisation of the concept of security has become a field unto itself. The fundamental originality of the Copenhagen School is twofold. First, and in general, it has developed and systematised the notion of security as a system of reference, based in part on the semiotic theory of Greimas. According to this approach, the meaning of security lies in the use of its concept, in the act of securitisation, whereby, the exact definitional criteria of securitisation "is constituted by the intersubjective establishment of an existential threat with a saliency sufficient to have substantial political effects" (Buzan *et al.* 1998, p.25). This methodology of analysing the security discourse as extended strategies of securitisation redefines the concept "security" as a pragmatic function, as the transitive act, of "securitisation". Indeed, in latter years, it has become more strongly construed as a "speech act" carried out by a "security actor" (Buzan *et al.* 1998, p.40), inspired by Austin's speech act theory.

The semiotic structure of securitisation differentiates between "referent objects", "securitising actors" and "functional actors". A "referent object" of securitisation is something that is considered to be existentially threatened. In most cases the security referent is the state, though Wæver *et al.* (1993) recognise that this is not necessarily the case, as the semiotic system of analysis covers a much broader set of referent objects than is covered by conventional security analysis. A "securitising actor" is the actor who actually performs the speech act of securitisation by declaring the referent object "existentially threatened" (Buzan *et al.* 1998, p.36). A "functional actor" is a participant in carrying out the pragmatic consequences of securitisation.

The most important theoretical innovation of the securitisation approach of the Copenhagen School is its differentiation between the subject and the object of security. The subject of securitisation carries out an act ascribing security valence to the referent object. Security is never objectively given. According to the suppositions of constructivism, there is no implicit, objective or given relation between the subject – the security actor – and the object of securitisation. Rather, this relation is constructed intersubjectively through social relations and processes (Buzan *et al.* 1998, pp.30–31).

From security to human security: the path of political ethics

The human paradox of security

The continuity between conventional security and human security grows out of a tension at the heart of the historical concept of security. In its present use, security has both a subjective and an objective form, an indeterminate and determinate usage: on the one hand it can be used to designate "a security", a guarantee, a symbol of value, something not to be lost, not to be wasted and, moreover, presentable as the replacement for something wasted or lost. On the other hand, it is used in international relations theory as a determinate object, as the security of a thing, individual or collective. In the broader end of the spectrum emanating from this determinate sense, security is understood as a negative thing. It is the mark of the absence of some kind of danger or another, be it threat or fear, known, imagined, or unknown. This absence is often conceptualised as liberty.

This double face of security finds its fullest expression in the study of its historical evolution. In order to make sense of human security, its relation to more conventional or tradition-bound notions of security must be clarified. What is the essence of "security" in human security? Is there one at all? And, inversely, what of the human can be derived from the notion of security? Security in its deepest roots is a human-oriented concept, a notion bound up in an individual, subjectively determined experience of the world. And yet the concept of security has undergone a transformation from the expression of subjective, even moral, well-being into a measure of objective threat or lack of threat. What does this transformation of the notion of security tell us about the human values and the ethics that is their expression?

In order to fully understand the implicit ethics of human security, the concept must be developed along a number of lines of inquiry. What are the variables involved in conceiving, understanding and practising security? From what intellectual and political traditions do they arise? What lines of authority serve to legitimate them? What actors use them, and to what ends? First, like any concept, the notion of security is historically determined, lying along a linear path of progress and development, past and future, between continuity and discontinuity. The parameters of security are thus determined by dimensions outside the security field. The very notion of security and its origins and aims grows out of a certain set of values and interests. Second, the relation between security and human security builds upon a complex relation between the security of the individual and the security of a collective unit. Collective security and individual security are different but tightly interrelated. Third, the relation between the individual or community and what philosophers call its ethos, its "ethical substance", rests on the cultural, spiritual, religious or social values that determine its perception of the secure and the insecure. Fourth, since security itself rests upon stable notions of the subject and the object of security, a theory of the security subject is a decisive element for the security picture.

Continuity and discontinuity

The new notion of human security is a part of the development of the concept of security. This continuity between these concepts assures the salience of human security in general, and gives ethical meaning to the general notion of security. In human security the object of security is the individual. Can the individual express or embody the kind of human values that could form the basis for ethics? As discussed above, this is not the right question. The shift from the nation-state or collectivity to the individual as the object of threat does not entirely, correspond to a shift from an objectively experienced, verifiable, consensual threat to an individual, personal and purely subjective experience of danger or threat.

The ethos of security

A threat is not simply an unknown danger lying in wait, to be launched upon us in some unknown way at some unspecified time. Threats are not entirely incidental or accidental, nor is the effect of a threat independent it targets. Threats are co-determined by those who are under threat and those who threaten. Certain infrastructures creates threat by virtue of creating value as threats are implicitly linked to what has value for us and to the possibility that what we hold valuable could disappear, be removed or destroyed. The key to understanding threats therefore lies in understanding the value systems that link human interests and values and things, such as infrastructures.

How are values, threats and fear linked? The ideal threat against security seeks to a perfect fit between what we value, the fear of its loss implicit in that value, and the political interests sought by those who carry out the act, though this link is, however, never perfect or ideal. While infrastructure experts know and understand technical weaknesses in critical infrastructures, the threat analysis must also take into account the potential destruction of both material things and the social, cultural, spiritual and even moral values they are associated with. It is less our physical security that needs assurance; rather, it is our *moral* insecurity.

The evolution of subjectivity

Human security does not only constitute a change in the object or the subject of security. While it is both these things it also constitutes a shift in the very notion of subjectivity and the point when threats enter subjectivity, contributing to the constitution of the subject. Subjectivity is henceforth defined as the experience of threat, in which the political subject becomes the subject of threat.

Which values for human security?

If it is the case that human security expresses a new set of values, what are these values? Human security not only focuses on the individual but it also opens the very notion of the individual, problematising the sovereignty of the individual. For, in order to focus on the individual as the primary unit of security, one must first ask what it is that makes the individual insecurity, what are the coordinates of its fragility?

Human security and responsibility

Ensuring human security does not mean taking away from people the responsibility and opportunity for mastering their lives. On the contrary, the concept of human security stresses that people should be able to take care of themselves: all people should have the opportunity to meet their most essential needs and to earn their own living. This will set them free. Human security is a critical ingredient of participatory development (UNDP 1994, p.24).

The report of the UN CHS, *Human security now*, underscores the need for a new conception of security by re-affirming the "vital core of human lives" (CHS 2003). It emphasises "empowerment" as a fundamental component of human security. This concept brings a variety of practical issues to the individual level. Whereas rights provide the moral foundation for action, empowerment implies the ability to act upon rights. Empowerment is the practical capacity to deploy principles and to give them form and reality. Yet the ability to take action toward the realisation of a principle implies the oblique obligation to do so. Thus, when the CHS invokes the empowerment of the individual as the key to human security, it implies a shift of responsibility from the higher levels of social protection to the individual level. Human security is not only an ethics of the international organisations, NGOs and third-party states, it is an individual ethics. The basic premise that the nation-state no longer assumes its traditional responsibility to protect the individual shifts that responsibility to the individual.

Human security: from human rights to a new contractualism

Like identity-based security communities, human security appeals to a logic opposing the rarefied state. It not only resists territory, it also confronts the fundamental contractual presuppositions of the state by proposing a different contract: that of human rights, or natural law.

Types of human security

One axis of human security, namely the various kinds of violence that can be considered as causing insecurity and that must be averted to establish security, has been analysed and debated at length. Yet a series of interrelated questions is left undetermined. These are the questions of "who", "when" and "where". If social, cultural, ethnic and religious specificity is to be respected we need to examine whether the concept of human security covers these dimensions equally.

Recognition

The concept of human security has a special character, based on the fact that it emerged from the media-shaped and geopolitical shadow of the Cold War. Human security is thus only a new phenomenon in the sense that it was not hitherto perceived. While there is little new about the individual needs that is revealed by the discourse of human security, what is new is the need to focus on the individual in general. This is the new-found status of the individual, with all that might characterise or be associated with the individual.

The needs relative to human security of the individual that is the subject of human security, from a farmer in rural China to a factory worker in urban India, are distinct from each other. Human security is a concept that reflects needs that are never the same, that vary from person to person. Paradoxically, if human security was a reflection of the same needs for all, it would simply not be human security. If needs were the same for all, they would be a collective matter, a sub-state collective concern.

Tolerance

The issues of tolerance surrounding human security are many. Toleration is the action of allowing something, which in essence is not allowed, which is discredited, devalued, or frowned upon. Toleration is a response to difference; to something that is not me, not us, not this, something that is implicitly in opposition to, or possibly in open conflict with, my identity. This opposition can range from a simple perception of difference to an existential conflict. Tolerance is not just the experience of the something that we might find difficult to accept. It is the experience of the difference between my religion and the other, my music and the other. The ethical burden of tolerance is the need for recognition of the validity of the cultural particularities of another. In this way, toleration always lies in a paradoxical place, between full recognition of the other and full rejection. Toleration is both an expression of the right of something else to exist, and the assertion of the right to oppose it.

Toleration takes place on many levels, from the individual to the global. The precondition and guarantee of toleration is simple: the existence of another subject. In any given community, certain political interests and desires must coexist with others. In religious settings – the historical origin of the very concept of toleration – certain sub-groups must tolerate others. Ethnic groups coexist in different settings.

Human security and political ethics

Realism and idealism

Prior to the general academic evolution of the mid-twentieth century on, international relations were the domain of diplomats and international politicians and competing interests and political compromise were seen more as modes of action, or the tools of a certain professional activity. Idealism as a practice was launched in the USA in the 1940s. In international relations theory, "idealism" is a blanket term for a number of approaches to the link between ideas and empirical reality, emphasising the norms and values of political action in the international arena. Idealism refers to normative international thinking, generally referred to as "moralism", "utopianism", "revolutionism" and, in some cases, "liberalism". In general, idealism builds on claims that ideals do exist about how international politics should be carried out, and a public policy driven by principles is a realistic alternative to one that is not (Hutchings 1999, p.13).

The term can be related to a more philosophical kind of political idealism with its roots in Enlightenment political and ethical philosophy. The obligatory station in this immense literature is Kant's 1795 essay "On perpetual peace" (Kant 1991). Kant provides a model for conceptualising the opposition at the root of idealism between politics and morality. Politics, according to Kant, is a response to the laws and necessity of nature and to the facts of the world. Morality, on the other hand, concerns to the capacity of human reason to understand right and wrong. Schematically put, morality is a question of doing what one should, based on reason and force of will, politics is a question of what one is constrained to do by force of necessity (Hutchings1999, p.13; Kant 1991).

The concept of realism springs from the historical debate which opposes it to idealism. It, was first and best formulated by Carr in 1939, though repeated and nuanced subsequently Morgenthau, 1948). Political realism focuses on the nation-state as the central actor and subject of politics, the aim of politics is the survival of the state, and this imperative supersedes any other normative imperative. Power is both the means and the end of politics. States are seen as autonomous, as are the foundations of their principles.

The concept of human security intersects both of these debates

The human security concept represents an idealist approach to international relations although qualifications need to be made. The ethical imperative behind human security is far from clear. There is little consensus concerning what the protection implied by human security means, nor is there consensus concerning who the objects of ethical consideration should be. Concrete criteria have not been produced to determine when human security crises exist and who should determine at what level the object of human security should be placed (an exception is Owen 2004).

On the side of realism, human security admits the primacy of the nation-state as the primary security provider. As internationalist as it may be, human security understands the nation-state as the fundamental reality, as the challenge for which operational solutions must be found. As the state is the reality that drives the need for human security, human security adopts the principles of realism.

In terms of power, the other essential pillar of realist thought, human security possesses still another focus. In the human security focus, power determines the formation of the concept of the individual and is the axis around which human security revolves. But individuals and their rights and obligations are situated at a level below state authorities who organise and control their status in political and social systems. Indeed, the contentiousness of the concept of human security lies in its struggle for control of that status, for the right and political position to define rights and obligations of individuals in society. Power is thus, from one point of view, the crux of the human security debate, not, in terms of the power to act, but instead to conceptualise and categorise human security.

In the tradition of Hobbes, a general scepticism towards any universal principles of international relations expresses itself in two

ways. First, for the classical realists, international relations precede principles of right, which are thus inapplicable to international relations. Second, realists claim that assertions of normative principles are not necessarily universal, but rather contingent and particular (Hutchings 1999, pp.19–20). The latter distinction has clear consequences for the condition of cultural, social, economic or ethnic particularity at the heart of the problem of human security. The object of security is clearly a sub-state entity, thus a sub-state ethics or even sub-international humanitarian law, in as much as it is construed as a trans-state phenomenon. The novelty and force of the doctrine of human security depends largely on this dimension of particularity in the eyes of traditionally universal principles of humanitarian international law.

It is for this reason that the particularity of human security as an ethical concept must be displaced into a different domain. It is meaningful only when the universality of international humanitarian law, a common support mechanism for humanitarian efforts, if not human security efforts, is compromised by the particularity of locally determined needs, wants and fears.

The notion of realism was revised in neo-realism through Waltz's *Man, the state and war* (Waltz 1959), among other works. Waltz nuances the idealism – realism opposition by underscoring the need for a theoretical opposition between domestic and international politics. The opposition between morality and politics at the heart of the realist view, is somewhat variable, according to levels, in the system of Waltz. For the question of ethical foundations of human security, this nuance opens for the calibration of moral guidelines specific to individual levels and thus groups that do not fall along the discrete lines of nation-state politics (cf. Telhami 2002).

Cosmopolitanism

Cosmopolitanism is not a moral theory in and of itself, but a class of theories. It grows out of the stoicist tradition (the same tradition as theories of national law). In its broadest articulation, it implies that the standards for human conduct are innate, inscribed in nature and available to human rationality. Ethical substance, according to this point of view, is both universal (it covers the cosmos) and independent of any human institutions, including state forms. The ethical properties of individuals cannot depend upon the laws or regulations of states or other international organisations. Though the consequences of embracing moral cosmopolitanism are openly political, its origins are not. By the same token, moral cosmopolitanism can be used to argue for (or against) particular political orders that might more or less embody its doctrines (Pogge 1992). Cosmopolitanism instead embodies a form of global ethics whose political determinations are unspecified (Dower 1998).

The status of cosmopolitanism, implicitly disconnected from political institutions, is essential to clarifying its relation to the notion of human security. Indeed, the fact that cosmopolitanism encompasses an entire class of notions about the commonality of human values makes particular state-based arrangements difficult to justify. In this sense, one might also say that cosmopolitanism is not forcibly at odds with the notion of realism. For cosmopolitanism the state need not be a moral entity, nor must it be concerned with deploying any given arrangements designed to realise any given principles. If one may talk about the purpose of cosmopolitanism, it would be to articulate standards that are not necessarily related to human institutions, to establish "truths about humanity that transcend political debates, while at the same time providing guidelines for them" (Amin 2004; Anderson-Gold 2005; Beck 2002; Brennan 2001; Brown 2005; Dallmayr 2003; Dobson 2006; Fine 2003, 2006; Foster 2003; Hutchings 1999: 40–41; Hutchings and Dannreuther 1999; Nagel 2006; Robbins 2003; Sivaramakrishnan 2005; West 2002.)

The difficulty posed by cosmopolitanism for human security is its transcendentalism, the very source of its power. Its most important contribution to the debate is the fact that it nourishes a kind of idealism in its most general form. Unfortunately, this also constitutes its primary weakness. By principally lifting itself above the fray of both domestic and international politics, it must sacrifice its capacity to grasp and engage the baseline issues involved in the differentiation within the human community. It is precisely this differentiation that lies at the heart of the notion of human security. The problem is that differentiation occurs along lines that are not state-based and layers that coincide with state-based political and non-political issues. Cosmopolitanism exemplifies the paradox of cultural particularity by both justifying its existence and denying its particularity.

Communitarianism

According to communitarianism, moral values exist only in one type or another of public or shared space. It thus opposes most forms of liberalism, which see the individual as the cradle of values; it opposes realism, which regards morality as something utterly foreign to political community; it opposes idealism, which considers the sphere of values to be autonomous from contingent empirical references and it opposes cosmopolitanism, which regards all individuals as part of one, unified community.

In the communitarian philosophical perspective, the principles upon which social, economic and political arrangements are legitimised are based on actual community-based practices, traditions and historically determined facts (Hutchings 1999, pp.42–43). While communitarians differ on a wide variety of perspectives, they essentially share the view that one form of community or another is the basis for morality and, in political terms, legitimacy. Where they tend to differ is on what constitutes a community, how legitimacy is derived from community and the limits and scope of the moral community beyond the borders of the "actual" community (Archibugi 2004; Bellamy and Castiglione 1997; Bellamy and Warleigh 1998; Brown 2002; Cochran 1996; Hayden 2005; Irwin 2001; Kaufmann 2000; Lacroix 2002; Makinda 2005; Melchior 1999; Parker and Brassett 2005; Stychin 2000, Thaa 2001, Woodhouse and Ramsbotham 2005).

Communitarianism opposes not only the idealist position that moral laws and guidelines are universally available, but also, regardless of the actual situation, it does not accept such a universal position, moral or otherwise. Just as with people in all regards, so it is also impossible that moral standards can be universally established, provided on a universal basis, and accessible to all people and peoples.

Communitarian ethical theory permits Waltz, for example, to argue that the nation-state has a primacy in terms of the ethical foundation. The robustness of the community, its internal cohesion and its external solidity give it a privileged status as an author of its own moral virtues through processes of internal consensus. The people possess an extraordinary moral substance, which makes it, in the analysis of Waltz, the source of what is right.

The implication of this ethical position for the project of human security is somewhat ambivalent. Something like individual security cannot be supported by a communitarian approach, since the ethical foundation, the cohesion between individuals, would be absent. The human security of certain minority groups would, in some sense, be protected by a communitarian approach. The moral robustness of the collective would be determined in part by its size, and by the breadth of its collective foundation. This would provide considerable moral impetus for larger minority groups, but would leave smaller groups exposed, perhaps more exposed than without the approach.

Building the agenda of human security: policy and practice within the Human Security Network

Keith Krause

Introduction

In May 1999 ministers and representatives of 11 governments met in Lysøen to found the Human Security Network (HSN). This innovative and flexible grouping of like-minded states committed themselves to combating poverty and contributing to sustainable development and sustained broad income growth, promoting respect for human rights and international humanitarian law (IHL) and strengthening the rule of law and good govern- ance. It also sought to foster cultures of peace and peace- ful conflict resolution, con- trol instruments of violence and end international impu- nity for gross violations of international law.

A wide range of practi- cal initiatives to achieve these goals was presented and dis- cussed at this first meeting, including the campaign to eliminate anti-personnel land- mines (APLMs), the excessive and destabilising accumula- tion and spread of small arms, the needs of children in armed conflict and the ratification and implementation of the International Criminal Court, as well as strengthening adherence to international humanitarian and human rights law.

This novel multilateral initiative was the fruit of a series of bilateral discussions, first between the Norwegian and Canadian Foreign Ministers, and later with other key states such as Switzerland and Austria. It was also in part a personal initiative born out of the experience of working together on the international negotiations to ban APLMs, which closely involved all four of these states. This initiative seized the mood of the times that seemed to capture and crystallise an emerging vision of security and cooperation that fitted well with the needs and opportunities presented in the post-Cold War world.

In order to assess the achievements and shortcomings of the HSN, this chapter first traces the origins and animating ideas of the HSN, situating it against the broader emerging discourse and practice of human security. It then discusses in detail the de- velopment and pursuit of several specific policy in- itiatives in the HSN and by HSN members, to demon- strate its vision of human security and the achieve- ment of its policy goals.

The third section ex- amines the way in which the HSN states (either individually or collec- tively) have helped set the agenda of contemporary multilateral security initiatives beyond the nar- row focus on the specific policy initiatives of the HSN. Issues that are examined include the idea of a "responsibility to protect" and the "protec- tion of civilians" agenda in contemporary conflicts. This section demonstrates that a full appreciation of the ongoing impact of the HSN requires an understanding both of its formal diplomatic and political efforts and its contribu- tion to the setting of the human security agenda worldwide.

Keith Krause is Professor at the Graduate Institute of International and Development Studies in Geneva, Switzerland and Pro- gramme Director of the Small Arms Survey, a research non-govenmental orga- nisation (NGO) he founded in 2001. His research interests include the changing nature of armed violence, concepts of security and multilateralism and the United Nations (UN) system. He has published *Arms and the state* (Cambridge), co-edited *Critical Security Studies* (Minnesota) and *Culture and Security* and authored many journal articles and book chapters. Email: keith.krause@graduateinstitute.ch

Finally, the last section considers the future prospects and options for the HSN, including recommendations for expansion, refocusing, deepening or reorienting its work. It concludes with some reflections on the place of the concept of human security in broader discussions promoting international peace and security, and argues that the discourse and practice of human security is now a durable feature of the international landscape, in part due to the efforts of the HSN.

The concept of human security and the origins of the HSN

While it is presented as a joint Norwegian–Canadian initiative, there is little doubt that the HSN was a Canadian initiative. As early as February 1996 Foreign Minister Axworthy was using the phrase "human security" as a cornerstone for the new foreign policy that he intended to pursue. He cannot, however, take sole credit for launching the concept of human security as his initial reference leaned explicitly on the articulation of human security in the 1994 United Nations Development Programme (UNDP) *Human development report* and referred to his participation in the Copenhagen World Summit on Social Development in 1995.

The idea of human security articulated in the 1994 UNDP report and subsequent developments and UN initiatives are discussed by Brauch and Owen in this volume. Although the reference to human security in this document was dropped from both the subsequent Copenhagen Declaration on Social Development and the Programme of Action of the World Summit for Social Development, for reasons that are unclear, the nascent HSN picked up the baton. After a series of informal meetings the Canadians and Norwegians released the Lysøen Declaration (11 May 1998), agreeing, among other things, to establish a framework for consultation and concerted action to enhance human security. This framework was the seed of the HSN, since it emphasised the need for flexible diplomacy, engaging civil society and NGOs, involving other countries and meeting annually at a ministerial level. Neither human

security itself, however, nor even the umbrella concept was at the forefront of this agenda; it was merely one item among five.

By September 1998 the outline of the HSN was in place when Canada and Norway convened a Ministerial meeting on the margins of the General Assembly. By this point, human security had crystallised as the umbrella for the initiative, and ministers expressed interest in establishing an informal partnership to promote human security. The emergent definition of human security adopted by the HSN – a focus on freedom from fear – was also reflected in the statement that the initiative would "concentrate political efforts on those security issues that have a direct impact – positively or negatively – on the safety and well-being of individuals and their communities" (Ministerial meeting, 1998).

In February 1999 Norway and Canada convened a "Retreat on Human Security" to flesh out the conceptualisation of human security that they wished to promote in light of the upcoming meeting of what would become the HSN in May that year. At this meeting, the main elements of what would become the "narrow" conception of human security, focusing on conflict, violence and "freedom from fear", were discussed. As the subsequent Canadian policy document explained, "in essence, human security means safety for people from both violent and non-violent threats".

By the time of the first Ministerial meeting of the HSN in 1999, membership had been broadened to include both The Netherlands and Greece. Although discussions over the concept of human security were "unfocused", the participants managed to agree on elements of a common agenda. The Chairman's summary invoked both freedom from fear and freedom from want (the two terms that have become associated with the narrow and broad understandings of human security). But the list of objectives and the overall language of the declaration reflected an orientation towards the narrow vision of freedom from fear, with the language of human development reserved for the broad idea of freedom from want.

The next section traces the development of the policy agenda in two phases, and is followed by a longer discussion of specific areas in which HSN states have been active.

Institutionalising the HSN

Policy development in the HSN 1999–2002

In the next three years HSN Ministerial meetings were held in Lucerne in 2000, in Petra in 2001 and in Santiago in 2002. It is convenient to treat the period from the first meeting in Norway to the Santiago Ministerial as the first phase of the HSN. This period was marked by a desire to put on the table the issues that had been proposed for attention at the first Ministerial, rather than to pursue concrete initiatives.

The agenda of action for the HSN was open-ended, in the sense that states could propose a set of activities without excluding or dropping other commitments. The Chair, which rotated among the hosts of the Ministerial summits, could set the priorities for the year that culminated in their Ministerial, with the expectation that they would sponsor or promote specific activities in these areas. This did not, however, give rise to disorder in the proceedings, since most topics proposed followed the original logic of the freedom from fear agenda. Some states paid little heed to the violence-centred implications of the HSN definition and followed a much broader path, as will be seen below.

The second Ministerial held in Switzerland, drew attention to two issues: small arms and light weapons, and the role of non-state actors in conflicts. The discussion on small arms was especially important, given that the Ministerial took place in the period leading up to the 2001 UN conference on the "Illicit Trade in Small Arms and Light Weapons in All its Aspects". The HSN served to create a coalition of like-minded states committed to achieving a strong programme of action at the New York conference, and its cross-regional membership facilitated agreement among the different regional groupings that still dominated negotiations in New York. The HSN itself made a statement to that conference.

The issue of non-state actors and human security has proven to be a particularly thorny one, and it is discussed in detail here to illustrate the complexities involved with attempting to trace the impact of the HSN. HSN members recognised that the term "non-state actors" encompassed three distinct entities: organisa-tions engaged in humanitarian assistance, non-state armed groups in conflict and private (corporate) actors. Although the focus of its attention was on non-state armed groups, the HSN undertook to pursue work along all three axes, to

- create a database on armed groups world-wide
- promote dialogue between humanitarian organisations, the private sector and inter-ested governments to improve understand-ing and practical options ways in which the private sectors can contribute to conflict prevention
- work with humanitarian organisations and to develop practical and effective strategies of engagement with armed groups

The background for this was increasing concern over ensuring respect for international humani-tarian law (IHL) and humanitarian workers, as well as the potentially negative role of private (corporate) actors in conflict zones.

A wide range of subsequent initiatives, most of which were spearheaded by non-governmental organisations (NGOs), resulted from this com-mitment to pursue work on non-state armed groups. Initiatives include the network/website launched by the University of British Colombia for disseminating research on non-state armed groups and the support by Switzerland and other HSN members of the work of Geneva Call, an NGO launched in 2000 devoted to encouraging non-state armed groups to respect the ban on using and producing APLMs. Another initiative was the launch by two Geneva-based NGOs, the CHD and the Small Arms Survey, of field-based and practical analyses of humanitarian engage-ments with armed groups, or with their impact on humanitarian operations, focusing in parti-cular on Central Asia, Colombia and West Africa. All these initiatives were the direct result of the HSN and illustrate the interaction between governments and civil society in the HSN. Given the sensitivity of states dealing directly with non-state armed groups, the HSN format provided a particularly useful means to explore and advance the issue.

The Jordanian and Chilean Ministerials broadly followed this core agenda, focusing mainly on issues on freedom from fear. At the

2001 meeting in Petra the ministers focused more directly on the issue of small arms and added the question of children in armed conflict. In Santiago in 2002 the concept of human security was framed within the notion of "public security", on the security of people and communities in great urban centres. Public security, which includes issues such as crime and corruption, terrorism and penal institutions is of special importance for Latin America, given the high levels of public social violence in such places as Brazil, Colombia and much of Central America.

At the 2001 UN conference, the HSN called upon the UN conference to adopt a multi-dimensional approach to small arms, to recognise that "cooperation and coordination between and among states, international organisations, regional bodies and civil society is essential" and to "acknowledge that both suppliers and recipient countries bear responsibility for finding common solutions to counter these problems". These three elements went well beyond the positions of many states at the UN conference, who argued instead for a narrow focus on the security dimension (arms control and disarmament), inter-state (traditional) diplomacy, and a supply-side approach to the problem. The final UN Programme of Action was closer, in many respects, to the position of the HSN than of these more traditional states.

The policy of the HSN on children and human security built on a report commissioned by the Canadian Department of Foreign Affairs and International Trade followed the preoccupation with the issue of children in conflict that was present even at the first Ministerial meeting (Stichick and Bruderlein, 2001). This initiative fed directly into the UN General Assembly Special Session on children (2001), for which the HSN prepared a wide-ranging policy agenda for dealing with the special needs of children in armed conflict and post-conflict situations.

Thus, during this first phase of its activity the HSN had managed to promote an impressive array of initiatives focusing on the core topics that had been identified at the outset and new but closely related freedom from fear issues. Already, however, the tendency to broaden the agenda beyond the freedom from fear concept had begun to manifest itself. In addition to the three issues of small arms, non-state actors, and children in armed conflict, the two Ministerials

discussed the impact of the HIV/AIDS pandemic on human security, human rights education and the link between security and development.

Expansion of the agenda, 2003–2006

The Santiago report represented a compilation of old and new issues for the HSN, permitting an evaluation of its evolution and impact after four years. Fourteen overlapping issue areas were mentioned. In at least four of these – the protection of civilians (treated below), armed non-state actors, landmines and small arms – the HSN could claim a leading role in promoting international policy initiatives. In others, such as conflict prevention, children, corporate citizenship, respect for IHL and transnational organised crime, it could only with difficulty claim to have played a leading role and in still other areas the HSN had expanded its agenda beyond its original vision.

The period from 2003 to 2006 thus presents a mixed picture for the HSN. On the one hand, it expanded its membership (in 2005) to include Costa Rica, and it continues its now-regular meetings at the Ministerial level, and on the margins of various international forums. But the degree of high-level participation in the Ministerials themselves seems to have diminished. It is also somewhat more difficult to find high levels of policy coordination at the international level, although this may be due also to the generally changed climate for multilateralism and the breadth of the agenda that has been taken on.

Four Ministerial meetings have been held in this period (in Graz in 2003, Bamako in 2004, Ottawa in 2005 and Bangkok in 2006). The meeting in Austria focused on human rights education and children in armed conflict. The Austrian government launched the "Graz declaration on principles of human rights education and human security". A secondary focus was the issue of children in armed conflict. The result of the work of the HSN was a support strategy that included a commitment to rapid ratification of relevant international instruments on child rights.

During this period the HSN addressed several statements directly to high-level institutional bodies, including the Security Council on the issues of civilian protection (2002), children and armed conflict (2003), women, peace and security (2004), the UN Commission on Human Rights (2003) and the Permanent Council of the Organisation for Security and Cooperation in Europe (2003). These statements raised and consolidated its institutional profile in the UN system and had a potential impact on agenda-setting in these organisations, especially in the UN system.

The most significant aspect of the sixth Ministerial meeting, held in Bamako in 2004 was the adoption of a Declaration on Food Security. This declaration illustrates well the tensions inherent in keeping a diverse set of interests and states focused on an intellectually and program-matically coherent agenda. It was adopted with strong encouragement from the Malian govern-ment, but without overwhelming support by other states. It contained no practical proposals, except to intensify a dialogue with relevant international organisations and it has not been followed up with subsequent work.

The Ottawa Ministerial in 2005 broke no new ground for the HSN. It was almost entirely preoccupied with debating UN reform and the process leading up to the World Summit of that year (see below). Concerning the "freedom from fear" agenda, it witnessed the pre-launching of the first *Human security report* (formally launched in late 2005) and laid the ground-work for the "Second HSN medium-term work plan", launched in collaboration with the Thai chair, in late 2005. This work plan redefined the priority areas for the network, under seven headings.

From this overview of the activities of the HSN itself, it is clear that it operates with a shifting and open-ended, agenda that revolves around a core set of concerns that have been ranked in different orders and added to in an ad hoc fashion. One can perhaps best picture the agenda as a series of concentric circles, in which the original issues are supplemented by a second sphere including human rights, IHL and conflict prevention, with the outer sphere including HIV/AIDS, food security and reform of multilateral institutions. The test of the influence and effectiveness of the HSN depends on a closer examination of some of these issue areas, which is undertaken in the next section.

From policy to practice: the HSN in action

This section looks more closely at three sets of issues that have been repeatedly identified as forming the core of the "freedom from fear" agenda for the HSN: APLMs, small arms and light weapons and the civilian protection agenda and IHL. In each section a brief summary of the pre-HSN and post-HSN position is given, recognising, of course, that the achievements listed cannot be entirely (or, in some cases, even mainly) attributed to the activities of the HSN. But, where possible, the section goes on to highlight the contributions that the HSN has made, either by individual members or collec-tively, to advancing the specific issue in the multilateral arena.

The campaign to ban APLMs

Although the international campaign to ban APLMs, took place before HSN took up the campaign starting here shows that the develop-ment of the entire human security and freedom from fear agenda was ad hoc and based on the experience of middle-power states working together.

The movement to ban APLMs began in the early 1990s with the launch of the International Campaign to Ban Landmines (ICBL) in 1992 by a coalition of NGOs including Human Rights Watch, the Vietnam Veterans of America and Handicap International. This coalition quickly grew to include more than 1,000 NGOs from around the world. In 1997 an international treaty banning the production, procurement, sale, transfer and use of APLMs was negotiated in Oslo and signed in Ottawa. Today more than 150 states have ratified the treaty, making it one of the more successful instruments in the field of international security and arms control. While many important states – including Russia, China, India, Pakistan and the USA – remain outside the treaty, the USA, substantially adheres to it and provides extensive resources for its goals and Russia has signalled their eventual support for the treaty.

From a human security perspective, the aspects of the Ottawa Treaty process worth highlighting are the close cooperation among like-minded states, the nature of the relationship between states and NGOs and the efforts towards practical implementation that followed the ratification of the Ottawa Convention. The process that led up to the signing of the Ottawa Treaty was marked by relatively close coopera-tion between four states that subsequently played a major role in the HSN: Canada, Norway, Switzerland and Austria. Each of them, by 1995 (or 1996, in the case of Austria), had committed to an outright ban on landmines by their own states and armed forces and although other states joined the ban they coordinated the steps that led to a treaty.

The meeting that launched the call for negotiation of a treaty banning APLMs was held in Ottawa in October 1996. Fifty governments participated and the Oslo conference that finalised the treaty was attended by 121 states. The most important feature of this cooperation, however, was that these states, in particular Canada, took the lead in supporting a multi-lateral process that was outside the traditional diplomatic framework, although other states that supported international action continued to argue that the landmines issue should be negotiated in traditional forums.

This process included an equally close collaborative relationship between states and NGOs. Traditional arms control and disarma-ment NGOs had previously had a relatively adversarial relationship towards states, conceiv-ing of their role as lobbyists and remaining outside the process. In the case of the landmines treaty, however, the ICBL was given the status and rights of an observer at the Oslo conference, and in negotiations and other informal forums, states and NGOs participated on a more or less equal footing. Not only did states and NGOs work together closely, but when they differed, it was not automatically the views of the NGOs that lost out.

This collaborative relationship carried into the treaty itself, when attention shifted towards universalisation of the treaty, practical humani-tarian demining and assistance to victims and survivors of landmines. Partnerships with civil society organisations and NGOs, often at the local level (such as villages and districts) has been important to successful demining opera-tions. The work of the ICBL has been supported by contributions from five of the HSN member states, although it has also received substantial support from a larger number of non-HSN states.

Throughout the process HSN states played a central role in the lead up to the Ottawa Treaty and beyond. They were crucial to crystallising the treaty negotiations and worked together on a flexible multilateral process, developing new and innovative ways of working with non-govern-mental actors. They have also consistently worked in HSN Ministerials to expand adher-ence to the treaty, and to practical implementa-tion of these efforts. In short, they set the international agenda on the landmine issue.

Despite the fact that it originates before the HSN was created, the Ottawa process, treaty and implementation could thus be considered as the hallmark of the human security approach, since it is difficult to conceive of this initiative emerging as long as one remains locked into a state-centric concept of security.

Small arms and light weapons

Before the mid-1990s the issue of small arms and light weapons proliferation and control was almost completely absent from the international security agenda. Until the early 1990s many policy-makers argued that conventional weap-ons "are not a proliferation issue". Behind this was the belief that the right of states to defend themselves legitimised their possession of most types of conventional weapons. Similarly, var-ious types of small arms were deemed to have legitimate civilian uses to be regulated within nations through gun control policies, for exam-ple. By the World Summit in 2005, however, the situation had changed to the point where the one arms control and disarmament issue on which world leaders could agree was that of small arms and light weapons. How did the situation shift so much in one decade?

In the late 1990s there were three shifts in the international context in this regard. The first was rise of illicit (but sometimes also legal) trafficking of weapons from the newly indepen-dent states in central and Eastern Europe. The second was the reports of shipments of weapons to the Rwanda before the genocide in 1994, as well as to other armed groups (Musah and Castle, 1998; Goose and Smyth, 1994, pp.86–96; Human Rights Watch 1995) and the third was the increasing insecurity facing UN peace-keepers in places such as Somalia. This was coupled with the growing recognition that practical disarmament initiatives were essential in order to consolidate post-conflict peace-building efforts in places such as Mozambique.

Most of the early initiatives to deal with this issue were not, however, led by like-minded states committed to human security, but emerged within the UN system, starting with Secretary-General Boutros-Boutros Ghali's invocation of the problem of "micro-disarma-ment" (1995, p.14). These early efforts were followed by the establishment of two successive UN Groups of Governmental Experts, in 1995 and 1997. The reports of these two groups in 1997 and 1999, respectively, played a central role in defining the nature of the problem and some of its parameters. Alongside this, the UN decided to convene an international conference on this issue in 2001.

Although HSN states cannot be said to have been central to the genesis of the small arms agenda, after the success of the Ottawa process, three key HSN states – Canada, Norway and Switzerland – very quickly sought to capitalise on their recent success to catalyse further action. Canada played a role in the creation in 1998 of the International Action Network on Small Arms, the worldwide NGO network on small arms. Norway helped to sponsor the creation in December 1997 of the Norwegian Initiative on Small Arms Transfers, which brought together the resources of three major groups to promote international action on small arms. In 1998 Switzerland commissioned what later became their major initiative in this arena, the Small Arms Survey project. These initiatives all represented an engagement with civil society, rather than a diplomatic process. A partnership between NGOs and governments was increas-ingly seen as a way for a state to play a significant role on an issue. Second, in a situation where there was no reliable information and analysis on which to base practical policies, it made sense for leading-edge states (not just HSN members) to support civil society experts and research organisations, sometimes with millions of dol-lars per year, to widen their knowledge base for policy-making.

This does not mean that diplomatic initia-tives were absent, and in fact some HSN states have also been prominent in the development of specific proposals and initiatives. The 2001 UN conference generated a Programme of Action that set the international framework for broad action in the small arms area and most of the early work at this time focused on the more traditional arms control and disarmament or supply-side initiatives than on the wider rela-tionship with development, human rights and public health. Following the successful negotia-tion of the UN Programme of Action, individual states took the lead in policy development on specific issues. HSN members have been dis-proportionately over-represented in this role. The first initiative that led to international negotiations concerned the marking, tracing and record-keeping of weapons. A second issue has been the fight to combat illicit arms brokering. Eight of the 18 participating states in this meeting were members of the HSN, illustrating the way in which the HSN formed a convenient core group around which to develop broader initiatives. A group of governmental experts (GGE) that examined this issue in 2001 was chaired by a Canadian. A second GGE was launched in late 2006, chaired by the Dutch.

The issue of small arms also figured highly on the agenda of most of the HSN Ministerial meetings themselves, but discussions in this forum concentrated rather more on the "huma-nitarian" or human security aspect of the problem. HSN states also assembled in a loose coalition on the margins of relevant small arms meetings in New York (in 2003 and 2005) and in Geneva, to brainstorm particular initiatives, although no concrete steps resulted from this.

In light of this, it is appropriate to ask what, if any, has been the distinctive contribution of HSN states to the development and implemen-tation of the small arms agenda. At least three achievements warrant highlighting. The first is the strong support they have given to NGO and civil society activity. There is no doubt that the major contributors to this have been Canada, The Netherlands, Norway and Switzerland – all HSN states, who probably contribute approxi-mately half of the funding that NGOs receive for small arms and light weapons activities inter-nationally. The second achievement is the HSN states' leadership role on the key issues of marking and tracing arms and arms brokering.

These issues were singled out early on as being ripe for international action, and Norway, Switzerland and The Netherlands continue to play a key role in policy development and negotiation in both areas.

The third contribution has been to expand the agenda of small arms and light weapons to include second-generation issues that go beyond single issues to embrace the full logic of human security. For example, work to develop practical policy measures to curtail demand has been supported by Canada, and also encouraged by Japan – a human security promoter (see Atwood et al., 2006; Jackman and O'Brien, 2006). The broader link between small arms, armed violence and development has been actively promoted by The Netherlands, Norway and Switzerland at the UN in activities that have pushed the small arms issue towards a human security perspective. The only high-profile non-HSN state involved in these issues has been the UK. Thus, it is fair to conclude that the main drivers of the HSN agenda have acted as agenda-setters in the small arms issue, even if their voice overall is one among the many states and international organisations active in this area. The emphasis on demand reduction, armed violence and development would not be prominent without their support.

The civilian protection agenda and IHL

The longstanding and close links between the concept of human security and the protection of civilians has been highlighted by many commentators. One could argue that the concept of human security itself originated with the work of the International Committee of the Red Cross and the humanitarian community. While there are differences between the two concepts and contemporary notions of human security are inspired by many sources, the challenges to the doctrine and practice of IHL posed by the transformation of contemporary conflicts increase the importance of the more inclusive concept of "civilian protection" that is part of the human security agenda.

Most of the activity concerned with the protection of civilians in armed conflict has focused on the UN, and on Security Council resolutions concerning contemporary peace-keeping operations. These resolutions respond to the perception that the fundamental rights of civilians, vulnerable groups in particular, are increasingly violated in contemporary violent conflicts, and that the existing legal and institutional mechanisms for dealing with this are inadequate. Many HSN states have participated actively in these debates and the protection of civilians agenda also figures prominently in the second medium-term work plan for 2005–2008 of the HSN. This specifically pledged to focus on the implementation of Security Council Resolutions on children affected by armed conflict and the protection of civilians in armed conflict at the UN and in regional forums, increasing HSN advocacy on the protection of civilians agenda and strengthening the international humanitarian system.

Promoting human security beyond the network

The activities of the HSN were part of a broader tapestry of initiatives that have been pursued multilaterally over the past decade to promote human security beyond the network. These initiatives included the Canadian-sponsored International Commission on Intervention and State Sovereignty (ICISS), support for the publication of the first *Human security report*, promoting the human security agenda in the UN and a wide array of non-governmental initiatives. Some of these initiatives were either influenced by the HSN, or driven by the same agenda-setting (and sometimes by the same actors) that animated the HSN. Overall, it concludes that the HSN has served as a reference point for many of these initiatives and, through the regular interaction of officials from HSN member states, facilitated the diffusion and "uptake" of the language and practice of human security within the broader international community.

The responsibility to protect

Against the backdrop of the war in Kosovo (1999), the genocide in Rwanda (1994) and the collapse of state authority in places such as Somalia, many advocates and analysts began to argue that the international community could no longer tolerate abuses of human rights on a massive scale, standing by as thousands of lives were placed at risk in the name of the abstract principle of sovereignty or non-intervention. Within the UN system, this was partly met by the expanded definition of threats to international peace and security, which emerged in the mid-1990s (for interesting recent overviews, see Holzgrefe and Keohane, 2003; Wheeler, 2003; Welsh, 2004). The policy community recognised the need to rethink the circumstances in which the international community ought to intervene in matters that had hitherto been considered as essentially falling within the domestic jurisdiction of states.

Naturally, this debate also implicated discussions around the concept of human security. Many critics of human security, particularly from the global South, voiced their concern that the idea of human security promoted an expanded agenda that could give rise to an unfettered right of intervention in the internal affairs of states. Whether or not this "logic of intervention" might involve the use of armed force to overthrow a government, or was expressed through more subtle pressure was largely irrelevant. The perception was that a "people-centred" vision of world politics might pit individuals against their states.

The efforts to promote human security and rethink the scope and justification for international intervention were linked in one practical way. One of the last major initiatives of Canadian Foreign Minister Axworthy was to launch the ICISS in 2000. This was a High-level Panel with a geographically diverse set of representatives, co-chaired by a former Australian Foreign Minister and Special Advisor to the UN Secretary-General, Mohamed Sahnoun. Its mandate was to examine ways of "reconciling the international community's responsibility to act in the face of massive violations of humanitarian norms while respecting the sovereign rights of states".

While this was not formally an HSN initiative, it included members from three HSN states, its concluding report was presented to the Santiago Ministerial in 2002 and has including the 2006 HSN Ministerial in Thailand.

The conclusions of the report, *The responsibility to protect*, illustrate how proponents of human security attempted to answer the concerns raised by the critics. It adopted a definition of human security close to that of the HSN, noting that "human security means the security of people – their physical safety, their economic and social well-being, respect for their dignity and worth as human beings, and the protection of their human rights and fundamental freedoms" (ICISS, 2001: 15). Second, it acknowledged that a commitment to human security meant taking a cautious approach to the circumstances under which force could be considered an appropriate means of promoting human security.

As a result, the ICISS report leaned heavily on the language and tradition of "just war" thinking to develop the conditions that must be met for any forceful intervention to protect human lives to be justified. The most important ones were "just cause" and "right authority". Under the rubric of "just cause", intervention for human protection can only be considered, according to the ICISS, when there is: "serious and irreparable harm occurring to human beings, or imminently likely to occur, of large-scale loss of life, actual or apprehended ... which is the product either of deliberate state action, or state neglect, or large-scale "ethnic cleansing", actual or apprehended, whether carried out by killing, forced expulsion, acts of terror or rape" (ICISS, pp.xii, 32–25).

With respect to the debate concerning "right authority", the debate on intervention has focused almost exclusively on the role of the UN Security Council in authorising intervention. The ICISS report stated that "Security Council authorisation must in all cases be sought prior to any military intervention action being carried out" (ICISS, p. 50). But it also went beyond an exclusive focus on the Security Council to note that, when the Security Council is unable or unwilling to act, alternative means of fulfilling the responsibility to protect have to be considered, including action under the authority of the General Assembly or regional organisations. Consistent with its focus on human security, the ICISS stated that "If collective organisations will not authorise collective intervention against regimes that flout the most elementary norms of legitimate governmental behaviour, then the pressures for intervention by ad hoc coalitions or individual states will surely intensify" (ICISS, p.55).

In circumstances under which a coalition of concerned states, act, and seek to justify their action in the name of protecting people and communities from harm, the justification for their action will have to be accepted by a strong consensus of states. It will need to demonstrate "right intention": that "the primary purpose of the intervention . . . [is] to halt or avert human suffering. (ICISS, pp.xii, 35–36).

According to this reasoning, intervention in Rwanda, Kosovo, or Somalia-type situations might be justified, but not in very many other cases. It is also noteworthy that the American-led invasion of Iraq was not couched in human security terms, and would not have been accepted had anyone tried to do so.

Although the HSN contributed to the overall climate in which the ICISS conducted its work. Several individuals involved in founding the HSN were part of the ICISS secretariat provided by the Canadian Department of Foreign Affairs. In that sense, one can conclude that the HSN has influenced a broad rethinking of the relationship between human security and state sovereignty.

The Human security report

A second initiative that is worthy of note was the publication of the first *Human security report*, by a team led by Professor Andrew Mack at the Human Security Centre at the University of British Colombia, Canada. When seeking financial support and an institutional home for the project, Mack naturally turned to the HSN, and the idea was endorsed by several governments, with financial support from within the HSN coming from Canada, Norway and Switzerland Together with additional funding was provided elsewhere. The report itself is not a product of the HSN but it owes its existence to the support provided by HSN members and it adopts the narrow definition of human security promoted by the HSN.

The idea of such a report was first mentioned at the 2002 HSN Ministerial in Santiago. As it argues, "in absence of official statistics on political violence or human rights abuses around the world, there is a clear need for a comprehensive annual report that tracks trends in these and other human security issues". The reception that the first report received

confirmed this level of interest, as its release garnered wide press coverage in news outlets in more than a dozen languages.

The main message of the report was that the number of wars, and victims of wars, has been declining and is perhaps at or near an all-time low; and that one explanation for this decline is the concerted action of the international community. The evidence in the report seems to indicate a consistent decline in the number of lives lost directly in war, to around 20,000 in 2002 and 2003, and to all forms of political violence as less than 30,000 in both those years (UN 2005, pp.30, 73). While other sources include much higher figures, all tend to agree that the number of direct conflict deaths has declined. The number of indirect victims is many times higher, and a consequence of the transformation of contemporary conflicts seem to be an increase in the proportion of civilians who are directly affected by violent conflicts, especially internal or communal violence.

Other issues that fall within the core of the human security agenda, such as child soldiers and the indirect costs of war were all addressed in the report. Despite its strengths one criticism of the report is that it actually focuses too narrowly on war and places too much emphasis on the conflict-related aspects of key human security issues, such as child soldiers (as opposed to children affected by armed conflict). In its defence, the authors of the *Human security report* intend intends to cover indirect costs and victims of conflict in subsequent editions, but its first edition highlights the difficult choices between narrow and broad understandings of the concept of human security.

The *Human security report 2005* notes that many factors have contributed to the decline in violent conflict. It does, however, emphasise the role of the UN in complex peace operations, and related mechanisms such as international tribunals or wider post-conflict reconciliation efforts. It notes that "two-thirds of UN nation-building missions examined were successful" and that, over time, this success rate will lead to a sustained and durable decline in violent conflicts (UN 2005, p.154). Whether or not this optimism is misplaced, the *Human security report 2005* represented a key contribution of the HSN to the debate on human security that would not have seen the light of day without its support.

Human security in the UN system

Although the HSN itself represents a new and flexible multilateral arrangement, members of the HSN have also been committed to promoting the agenda of human security within the UN system. Eight of the network members have been members of the Security Council since 1999, testifying both to their degree of engagement in the UN and to the practical results of working together.

With respect to specific issues, there is evidence that the agenda of issues promoted by the HSN has assumed a prominent place in UN debates and activities. This is well illustrated in the outcome document of the 2005 World Summit and the various reports that preceded it. Human security itself received a subheading and was treated in paragraph 143:

Human security 143. We stress the right of people to live in freedom and dignity, free from poverty and despair. We recognize that all individuals, in particular vulnerable people, are entitled to freedom from fear and freedom from want, with an equal opportunity to enjoy all their rights and fully develop their human potential. To this end, we commit ourselves to discussing and defining the notion of human security in the General Assembly.

This wording addresses both the narrow and broad concept of human security, but the term, "freedom from fear" is directly derived from the HSN. Similarly, issues such as civilian protection, small arms and light weapons, APLMs, children in armed conflict and HIV/AIDS receive prominent attention in the report (General Assembly 2005).

Another way to demonstrate that the HSN influenced the inclusion of these issues is to examine not only the *Outcome document*, but also its two forerunners, the Secretary-General's report *In larger freedom*, and the report of the High-level Panel, *A more secure world: our shared responsibility* (Annan 2004). The former should be viewed as an internal UN product, reflecting its agenda, concepts and priorities, and the latter as an external product more susceptible to influence from the views of states such as the HSN.

The Secretary-General's report only mentions human security once, without definition or elaboration. Its Annex, however, develops the triumvirate of freedom from fear, freedom from want and freedom to live in dignity, although here, too, the freedom from fear section cannot be said to follow closely the logic of the HSN. Although the report does discuss themes that also emerge from the HSN, it cannot be said to align closely with the HSN's agenda, and it thus reflects the way in which the views and priorities that were generated within the UN system are broader and more diffuse than the action agenda of the HSN.

By contrast, the report of the High-level Panel is closer to HSN concerns. The panel was chaired by the former Prime Minister of Thailand, and included another member from an HSN state (Norway). Its consultations included meetings in Switzerland and Norway, and a dedicated workshop on small arms and light weapons was held in New York, among the 40 workshops and regional consultations that it held.

The report attempts to give equal weight to state and human security. Human security is mentioned numerous times alongside state security concerns, and although the authors remain vague about which concept they adhere to, their usage is closer to the broader or inclusive vision than that of the HSN. Specific issues, however, such as APLMs and small arms do receive particular attention, as does the protection of civilians agenda. In general, the concept of human security is more central to this document than to *In larger freedom*, and it can be concluded that the Panel's members were somewhat more open to the influence of the new ideas and agenda promoted by the HSN member states.

Human security, civil society and the new diplomacy

From the outset the HSN tried to build on the flexible arrangements with NGOs that had been the hallmark of the Ottawa process on APLMs. Non-governmental representatives have been associated with a formal part of the agenda at almost all Ministerial meetings since Lucerne in 2000. To start with participation was skewed towards the narrow understanding of human security, and the first set of participating NGOs included the International Federation of Red Cross and Red Crescent Societies, the International Committee of the Red Cross, the

ICBL and Save the Children Alliance, among others.

In general terms, this engagement was based on the growing recognition that a working relationship with civil society actors could increase the leverage of states themselves. This permitted privileged access to expertise, so that states were better able to formulate creative policy initiatives, and augment the scarce resources (mainly human) that were available to them on any given issue. From the civil society perspective, engaging with the HSN and the human security agenda overall made sense for similar reasons, giving them greater access and opportunities to influence policy development and a privileged position vis-à-vis decision-makers.

The HSN also attempted to catalyse related NGO work within network member states. Although it is difficult to argue that a full-scale network exists (with NGOs linked to each other, working together on a common agenda and meeting regularly), there is a long list of engagements by HSN member states with nationally based NGOs, academic institutions or other bodies. A preliminary, list would include:

Austria. The European Training Centre for Human Rights and Democracy has organised an International Summer Academy on Human Security and published a manual on human rights education.

Jordan established, with Canadian support, the Regional Human Security Centre which sponsored regionally oriented work on small arms and light weapons, multiculturalism, the International Criminal Court and human security in the Arab World (with UNESCO).

Greece announced in 2003 the creation of a regional centre for human security in Athens.

Thailand associated researchers from Chulalongkorn University with its HSN presidency in 2006.

Norway worked closely with (and through) the International Peace Research Institute, Oslo to promote policy-relevant research on a variety of human security themes, including child soldiers, gender and human security and post-conflict transitions.

Canada established a Human Security Fund that supported the creation of the Canadian Consortium on Human Security and the web-based information resource gateway as well as supporting the creation and work of the Human Security Centre at the University of British Colombia.

Chile has worked with the Facultad Latinoamericana de Ciencias Sociales, UNESCO and the Canadian government to pursue the themes of democratic security, public security and security sector reform in Chile and South America.

Switzerland has actively and financially (through core funding) supported the work of four centres in Geneva pursuing the human security agenda: the CHD; the Small Arms Survey; the Geneva International Centre for Humanitarian Demining; and the Centre for the Democratic Control of Armed Forces.

In addition to these nationally specific initiatives, Switzerland, Norway, Canada and, to a slightly different extent, The Netherlands, have provided large amounts of financial support to other centres or projects worldwide, on key issues such as APLMs, child soldiers, small arms, the *Human security report* and the International Criminal Court.

Not all of these initiatives are of equal importance, or are equally active. The Greek initiative, for example, which was announced in 2003, does not yet appear to have taken off. The Jordanian Regional Human Security Centre is less active than before 2005, when its founding director moved to a government post, and the Thai level of engagement with civil society is limited. In other cases, such as Norway or Canada, the work of the Peace Research Institute, Oslo, already had a significant human security cast before the HSN, and nothing fundamental has changed in the nature of their engagement. But in the most active cases (Switzerland, Canada, Norway and Austria) there has been a significant opening-up of the policy process and a wide range of informal links and cooperation between civil society organisations exists. That more work remains to be done was recognised in the second medium-term work plan of the HSN.

Beyond the HSN, a number of other programmes, centres or initiatives have emerged that have only been loosely connected (if at all) to the work of the HSN. The list is long, but core institutions or programmes would include the Programme on Humanitarian Policy and Conflict Research at Harvard University, the Institute for Human Security at the Fletcher School of Law and Diplomacy (Tufts University), the Centre for Peace and Human Security at the Institut d'Etudes Politiques de Paris (Sciences Po), the Centre for Research on Inequality, Human Security and Ethnicity (Queen Elizabeth House, Oxford University), the Ford Institute for Human Security (University of Pittsburgh) and the Institute for Environment and Human Security (Bonn, United Nations University).

Most of these are research institutes. Advocacy organisations are far too numerous to be listed, but many of them receive financial support for their work from HSN donor governments, including Canada, Switzerland, The Netherlands and Norway.

Observations and conclusions

The HSN, in both its direct policy-focused and indirect agenda-setting activities, has had a sustained and important impact on the recent development of the international peace and security agenda. Direct impacts include

- sustaining international attention and commitment to dealing with the problem of APLMs
- developing consensus around the importance of dealing with the proliferation and misuse of small arms and light weapons
- working towards international action concerning children and armed conflict, including child soldiers
- advancing respect for human rights, especially through the International Criminal Court or the Human Rights Council

Indirect impacts include

- opening and expanding the debate around humanitarian intervention towards the ethic of a responsibility to protect

- contributing towards an expanded network of civil society organisations and NGOs working on human security issues
- reframing the debate around international peace and security to include protection of civilians and the human security agenda (especially in the UN context)
- developing and spreading new means of flexible multilateralism working through ad hoc coalitions and purpose-build cooperation among like-minded governments

Although the HSN cannot take exclusive credit for all of these developments without this initiative, many of these issues would have had difficulty gaining momentum in the international arena. Counterfactually, this is especially true if we imagine a world dominated exclusively by the discourse and practice of the "war on terror" as the primary foundation for thinking about international peace and security.

Two questions loom large, however, when thinking about the future: to what extent is the concept of human security a durable feature of contemporary world politics and what should be the scope and orientation of future activities of the HSN? In order to answer these questions we need to be clear about how the issues emerged and were placed advanced by the HSN.

First, the states that came to the human security agenda did so, in many cases, with their own set of policies or initiatives that they wished to promote. For example, Switzerland encouraged its traditional emphasis on IHL as part of the activities of the HSN and Japan folded many of its established development assistance policies under the banner of human security. Policy entrepreneurship and niche diplomacy on the part of states, NGOs and international organisations was a crucial feature of the rapid development of the concept and practice of human security. Hence, the need for the umbrella of human security to embrace practical and politically "winnable" initiatives should be taken into account.

It would be a mistake, however, to consider that the use of the concept of human security was an afterthought, or just a label applied to policies that states were already pursuing. Although the concept of human security emerged after (and out of) its practice (notably in the APLM campaign), the recognition by different actors that disparate threads of policy and practice could be powerfully linked together under a common umbrella does represent an innovation. The issues that come under the heading of human security today were almost completely absent from the international scene 20 years ago.

Second, there is sometimes a perceived gap between the principles and practice of human security. Although it promotes a people-centred agenda, the focus is still mainly on states and their interactions, and there are limitations to civil society participation. Including the voices and views of a few handpicked international NGOs does not necessarily mean that the human security concerns of civil society have been effectively taken on board. While opening up the process to all interested parties is not practicable, it is important to ensure that civil society participation represents the real human security concerns of a particular groups. This can be done through effective on-the-ground research and analysis, such as is reflected in the World Bank's *Voices of the poor* studies, and should be a key element of any freedom from fear agenda (See Narayan et al., 2000a; Narayan et al., 2000b; Narayan and Petesch, 2002).

Third, the agenda of human security and the HSN remains somewhat a donor-driven process. With only a few exceptions the issues that are central to the HSN are not taken up in the domestic political agenda of HSN partici-pating states. In fact, most of the activities that attempt to develop and highlight the human security concerns of states in the global South have been undertaken outside the HSN frame-work, through the work of UNESCO. Confer-ences held in Latin America, East Asia, the Middle East and Southern Africa have brought together a wide range of scholars to debate and discuss the meaning and relevance of human security for their regions, and their perceptions did not always accord easily with the freedom from fear versus freedom from want debate. The project also resulted in individual monographs exploring the meaning of human security in different regions, which again could usefully inform debates within the HSN (see Chourou, 2005; Lee, 2004; Fuentes and Rojas Aravena, 2005).

Finally, there remains a critical tension between the narrow (freedom from fear) and

broad (freedom from want) agenda. There is no need, except for the sake of conceptual neatness or intellectual rigour, to choose a definition; most major political concepts such as democracy or justice do fine without clear or universally accepted definitions. On the other hand, there is a risk that too broad a concept will cease to have practical utility for policy-makers. Overall, if the concept of human security remains focused on freedom from fear – from the threat or use of violence – it can be linked to a coherent practical agenda that is rooted in a particular under-standing of the liberal state, including those of Hobbes and Weber. In light of this, one can conclude that the concept of human security has become an enduring feature of the international peace and security landscape. Human security is thus here to stay.

This leads logically to six major recommen-dations for the future development of the HSN:

- to deepen collaboration beyond Ministerial and policy staff to working-level officials in HSN member states, to ensure that they can build coalitions and maximise their influence in international forums,
- to expand partnerships with other like-minded donor states in a position to support human security work (the UK, Sweden and Finland) on issues of common interest,
- to strengthen cooperation between Northern and Southern members of the HSN, and expand the Southern reach of the HSN through direct partnerships on key issues,
- to initiate a process of reflection in existing Northern HSN states that catalyses and enhances their commitment to human secur-ity issues,
- to develop a work plan for the period beyond 2008 that reflects an agenda focusing on the acknowledged strengths and value-added of the freedom from fear agenda
- to maintain flexible and open-ended working arrangements, especially with civil society actors responsible for the practical realisa-tion of the human security agenda

These recommendations are based on the ob-servations and analysis of the strengths and weaknesses of the HSN in this chapter, and on the success of recent initiatives such as the Geneva Summit on Armed Violence and Development, which mobilised both HSN and non-HSN member states around a core human security agenda. They also take note of the fact that engagement with the HSN agenda is often weak at the working level, thus hampering the ability to mobilise the HSN behind initiatives such as the Dutch-sponsored resolution on small arms and development in the UN General Assembly First Committee. Finally, they are based on a belief that the ultimate success of the HSN is not measured by its Ministerial declarations, or by the promotion of resolutions and initiatives in multilateral institutions, but by mainstreaming human security concerns into specific and concrete programmes launched by foreign ministries or development cooperation agencies. Only when freedom from fear for communities around the world becomes a practical reality can we really conclude that this unique initiative has been successful.

Gender aspects of human security

Ghada Moussa

Introduction

This chapter examines the evolution of the concept of gender in international and national agendas, and the opportunities it offers for changing existing power relations, in addition to global human security. Gender equality has to be understood as a core component of human rights. Thus, gender-based abuses are human rights abuses and they affect security. About 3 billion persons are subjected systematically and casually to various forms of violations because they are female. Gender inequalities are caused by states, non-state actors, and individuals. Institutions such as the family, community and the state have failed to protect women from social, economic oppressions and exploitations and political violence and men still dominate power in public and private spheres worldwide and thus continue to determine the patterns of women's lives and the extent of rights granted to women (Ashworth 1995, pp.5–7).

Primary assumptions

Gender and human security were officially born from world policies and then acquired their social dimensions. By relating gender to human security we can capture the socio-cultural

Ghada Ali Moussa is an Director of the Governance Centre in Egypt and Coordinator of the National Committee for Transparency and Integrity. She has a PhD in political development from the faculty of economics and political sciences, political sciences department. She is currently teaching human rights and civil society courses at the Future University, a private university in Egypt. She has written several research chapters on children's rights, child labour, the role of civil society in advocating for human rights, capacity building for non-governmental organisations (NGOs), the concepts of social security and social development, combating corruption, and economic transformation and its influences on society in Iran, Turkey and Lebanon. She is also a volunteer in several rehabilitation activities in armed conflict areas such as Lebanon and Palestine. She currently works as an advisor to the Minister of State for Administrative Development in Egypt. Email: llaghada@hotmail.com

dimension of the concept of human security, and identify the correlation between gender and human security and their mutual influence on each other. Thus, although gender inequalities may not cause wars they can cause societal conflicts and instabilities and tensions that may pave the way to cultural conflicts and to trade-offs between political and social justice.

Gender inequalities are universal, but they are not uniform, either across space or over time. There is now a body of work testifying to the existence of a "geography of gender" – regional differences in the forms and magnitude of gender inequality. While family and kinship ideologies and relations play an important role in the construction of these inequalities, they are also reinforced, modified or transformed by the interaction between family, kinship and wider social processes, including state legislation, public action and macro-economic change. Furthermore, achieving gender equality does not have the same impact on human security in different parts of the world, although there is a link between achieving gender equality and overcoming the dichotomy of human security and national security.

While women strive to achieve individual security through circles of resistance, especially in the family, these strategies impede gender equality. Using the broader concept of gender allows us to move away from the idea that the security of a state or regime is identical with the economic, political and social well-being of its citizens and to address basic needs, and the concept of empowerment of individuals, especially women, to improve their social, economic and political status. With it we can explore the strengths and weaknesses of the concept of human security relating to women's needs and examine how different states see human security as matters that belong within their own competence, rather than international issues. This could be because, in some states, gender equality is a security issue that clashes with the state's own interests.

Gender equality is a prerequisite for achieving security. It should be tackled using a new discourse that deals with the threats embedded in cultural and social structures when applying to developed and third world countries. Up to now, the introduction of a wide range of international policies and initiatives concerning gender mainstreaming have failed to achieve gender equality and to ensure social peace. Gender mainstreaming can achieve freedom from want and freedom from fear through NGOs and international aid without necessarily resorting to state apparatuses. In addressing gender issues and concerns, women have used the non-governmental arena as a launching point.

Human security and gender equality as manifestations of globalisation

The end of the Cold War was seen as the beginning of an era of peace and prosperity, a turning point that would make it possible for the world to focus attention on problems such as under-development, poverty and the environment. Today we live in a world of vastly increasing complexity and of shrinking alternatives. The corollary of dramatic increases in wealth for the rich is a dramatic increase in the number of those suffering from absolute poverty. There is despair among those who do not benefit from the new world order, leading them to retreat to traditional security communities such as family, clan, ethnic group and religious identity. These often compete with each

other for the shrinking resources necessary for their survival. The result is increasingly violent conflicts within states that may lead to radicalisation (Korean National Commission for UNESCO 2003). By the end of the millennium local conflicts have increased in number, and they have political and cultural dimensions.

One of the features of globalisation is the proliferation of women's organisations, especially non-governmental organisations (NGOs), which have created worldwide networks, among them security networks and are indispensable partners and political allies in the protection and promotion of human security. Another important feature of globalisation is the use of telecommunication and the dissemination of internet services to empower people, despite their high costs in developing countries. Overcoming the digital divide became one of the main challenges to achieving gender equality and human security and the internet is now used for education, work and communication in poor areas in Africa.

Another manifestation of globalisation is the emergence of grassroots movements and feminist groups examining structural causes to women's insecurities in different cultures. Last but not least, it could be said that the end of the Cold War gave countries space to revise their security needs and threats facing them. Unlike western countries third world countries are concerned with security issues emanating from their environmental, political or economic circumstances.

International declarations and conventions addressing gender

The most important of these are the "Universal declaration of human rights (All human rights for all)" (UN 1948) and "The convention on the elimination of all forms of discrimination against women" (CEDAW) in 1979. When CEDAW was adopted, after decades of work by women's movements, it was by no means welcomed by all UN member states. The greatest tension was between religious and secular concepts of the role of women in society, the former conceiving women's rights as embedded in women's roles in family and society, while the

latter emphasised women's autonomy and
individuality.

CEDAW calls for the equality of men and
women in public and political life, before the law
and with respect to nationality rights, in education, employment, the provision of health care
(including access to family planning services),
and in marriage and family matters. It explicitly
urges states to suppress the exploitation of
prostitution as well as trafficking in women
and to improve the situation of rural women as a
particularly disadvantaged group.

The evolution of gender

Richard Ullman introduced, in his article titled
"Redefining security" published in International
Security, a new agenda to international security
by incorporating non-military considerations
described in Brauch and Owen in this volume.
The emergence of gender as a key concept on the
international agenda emerged in the 1994 United
Nations Development Programme (UNDP)
report.

Much human behaviour is not the result of
individual preferences but is governed by
institutional rules, norms that have powerful
effects on people's lives that may be written or
unwritten, explicit or implicit, codified in law,
mandated by policy, sanctified by religion,
upheld by convention, or embodied in the
standards of family, community and society.
Their influence is obvious in the division of
labour between production and reproduction in
different parts of the world.

The sex/gender system is primarily a
cultural construct that is constituted by social
structure. These gender systems appear in
different forms in all societies and are influenced
by different types of political regime and state
ideology, the division of labour in the household
and the gendered division of labour at the macro
level. This dynamic is an important source of
women's disadvantaged position and of the
stability of the gender system, together with
juridical and ideological sources are also
important. Men and women have unequal access
to political power and economic resources, and
cultural images and representations of women
are fundamentally distinct from those of men –
even in societies formally committed to gender
equality. Inequalities are learned and taught,

and the non-perception of disadvantages of a
deprived group helps to perpetuate gender
inequality (Papanek 1989, p.15).

Where the state's policies, rhetoric and
official and popular discourses stress sexual
differences rather than legal equality, an apparatus exists to create stratification based on
gender.

Gender, according to Sophia Phoca, is a
conceptual system that replaced the notion that
masculinity and femininity are essential attributes with the notion that all gender configura-
tions are performed and constructed by
socialisation processes (1997, p.60).

On the other side, gender equality is one of
many dimensions for feminists. Feminism is the
belief that women are treated inequitably in
patriarchal societies. In this way women are
denied equal access to the world of public, as
well as cultural, representation. Feminism challenges these cultural forms. (Gamble 2003,
pp.14–15).

"Gender" refers to the rules, norms, customs and practices by which biological differences between males and females are translated
into socially constructed differences between
men and women and boys and girls, so that the
two genders being valued differently and are
given unequal opportunities and life chances.
The argument for addressing gender inequality,
therefore, is not simply that it exists in all
societies but that it exists at all levels of society.
It makes the effects of poverty worse for women
and biases the form taken by economic growth.
To overcome gender inequalities the gender
equality approach was urged. The most recent
of these was the Gender gap report, which
quantifies the size of the gender gap in 58
countries, and measures the extent to which
women have achieved full equality with men in
five critical areas.

"Gender equality" means both equality of
treatment under the law and equality of opportunity. In addition, since these do not take
structural inequality into account, it also
includes substantive equality and equality of
agency. Substantive equality means that the
different circumstances and characteristics of
men and women have to be considered to avoid
unfair gender-related outcomes. For example, in
a case where a man and a woman both have the
qualifications for a particular occupation, the

latter may be unable to take it up if there is no childcare available. Equality of agency means ensuring that both women and men can make strategic life choices for themselves and help determine the conditions under which these choices are made.

The gender equality approach

The struggle for gender equality was still in its early stages at the establishment of the United Nations (UN) in 1945. Of the original 51 member states, only 30 allowed women equal voting rights with men or permitted them to hold public office. Nevertheless, the drafters of the UN Charter had the foresight to deliberately refer to the "equal rights of men and women" as they declared the Organisation's "faith in fundamental human rights" and the "dignity and worth of the human person". No previous international legal document had so forcefully affirmed the equality of all human beings, or specifically targeted sex as a basis for discrimination.

During the first three decades, the work of the UN on behalf of women focused primarily on codifying women's legal and civil rights, and gathering data on their status around the world. With time, however, it became increasingly apparent that laws, in and of themselves, were not enough to ensure the equal rights of women.

The struggle for equality entered a second stage with the convening of four world conferences by the UN to develop strategies and plans of action for the advancement of women. The efforts undertaken have gone through several phases and transformations, from regarding women almost exclusively in terms of their development needs, to recognising their essential contributions to the entire development process, to seeking their empowerment and the promotion of their right to full participation at all levels of human activity.

The first world conference on the status of women was convened in Mexico City to coincide with the 1975 International Women's Year. It was called on by the UN General Assembly to focus international attention on the need to develop future-oriented goals for the advancement

of women. Three key objectives on the Conference were full gender equality and the elimination of gender discrimination, the integration and full participation of women in development and an increased contribution by women in strengthening world peace.

The Conference responded by adopting a World Plan of Action, a document that offered guidelines for governments and the international community to follow for the next 10 years. The Plan of Action set minimum targets, to be met by 1980, focusing on securing equal access for women to resources such as education, employment opportunities, political participation and health services. Whereas previously women had been seen as passive recipients of support and assistance, they were now viewed as full and equal partners with men, with equal rights to resources and opportunities. A similar transformation was taking place in the approach to development, with a shift from an earlier belief that development served to advance women, to a new consensus that development was not possible without the full participation of women.

The second world conference on women held in Copenhagen in 1980, reviewed and appraised the 1975 World Plan of Action. It found that governments and the international community had made strides toward achieving the targets set out in Mexico City especially in the adoption of CEDAW. The Convention now legally binds 165 states, which are required regularly on the steps they have taken to remove obstacles to implementing the Convention. An Optional Protocol to the Convention in 1999, enabled women victims of sex discrimination to complain to an international treaty body. This put the Convention on an equal footing with other international human rights instruments with procedures for individual complaints.

Despite the progress made, the Copenhagen Conference recognised that there was a disparity between the rights that had been secured and women's ability to exercise these rights. To address this concern, the Conference pinpointed three areas for specific, highly focused action. These were equal access to education, employment opportunities and adequate healthcare services.

The third world conference on women held in Nairobi in 1985 reviewed the UN Decade for women. Participants referred to the Conference as the "birth of global feminism". The women's movement had now become an international force unified under the banner of equality, development and peace. Behind this milestone lies a decade of work. At the same time, delegates were confronted with shocking reports. Data gathered by the UN revealed that improvements in the status of women and efforts to reduce discrimination had benefited only a small minority of women. Improvements in the situation of women in the developing world had been marginal at best. In short, the objectives of the second half of the UN Decade for Women had not been met.

This realisation demanded a new approach. The Nairobi Conference was given a mandate to seek new ways to overcome the obstacles to achieving the Decade's goals. This resulted in the Nairobi Forward-Looking Strategies to the year 2000, an updated blueprint for the future of women to the end of the century. It declared all issues to be women's issues and recognised that women's participation in decision-making and the handling of all human affairs was their legitimate right as well as a social and political necessity. At the heart of the document was a series of measures for achieving equality at the national level. Governments were to set their own priorities, based on their development policies and resource capabilities. These were constitutional and legal steps, equality in social participation, and equality in political participation and decision-making. In keeping with the view that all issues were women's issues, the measures recommended by the Nairobi Forward-Looking Strategies covered a wide range of subjects.

The fourth world conference on women held in Beijing in 1995, witnessed a new chapter in the struggle for gender equality. The Beijing Conference recognised the need to shift the focus from women to gender and that the entire structure of society and all relations between men and women would consequently have to be re-evaluated. Only a fundamental restructuring of society and its institutions could fully empower women to take their rightful place as equal partners with men in all aspects of life. This change represented a strong reaffirmation that women's rights were human rights and that gender equality was an issue of universal concern, benefiting all.

The Beijing Platform for Action sparked a renewed global commitment to the empowerment of women everywhere and drew unprecedented international attention. The Conference unanimously adopted the Beijing Declaration and Platform for Action that stands as a milestone for the advancement of women. By adopting the Beijing Platform for Action, governments committed themselves to the effective inclusion of a gender dimension throughout all their institutions, policies, planning and decision-making. What this meant was that, before decisions were to made or plans implemented, their effects on the needs of both women and men would have to be analysed. For example, instead of striving to make an existing educational system gradually more accessible to women, gender mainstreaming would advocate reconstructing the whole system so that it would suit the needs of women and men equally.

After the Beijing Conference, the General Assembly called for a special session to review progress after five years. The special session was convened in New York in 2000, under the theme "Women 2000: Gender Equality, Development and Peace for the 21st Century". The special session provided the opportunity for governments and civil society to share good practices and examine current challenges and obstacles in implementing the Beijing Platform for Action.

Gender equality, when studied in its relation to human security issues, raises issues of transformation and social change. Students of social change tend to regard certain societal institutions and structures as central: the family, the market, the state, religious hierarchies, among many key institutions. As cultural institutions and practices, economic processes and political structures are interactive, it is important to concentrate on this interactive relationship among key institutions.

Gender and human security

Despite their known negative impact on gender equality, institutions provide a structure, and hence a degree of stability, to everyday life. They reduce uncertainty, make certain forms of behaviour more predictable and allow individuals to cooperate with others to produce results that they would not be able to achieve on their own. However, institutions rarely operate in egalitarian ways but instead tend to support hierarchical relationships organised around unequal ownership, achieved or acquired attributes (education, skills, contacts) and various socially ascribed attributes (such as gender and age).

A variety of explanations and justifications are given for these hierarchies, including merit, capacity, aptitude, biology, nature or divine will. Institutional rules of access and exclusion intersect and overlap. However, culture is the most powerful framework for explaining how individuals and social groups not only start from different places, but also have different opportunities to improve their situation in the course of their lives.

Culture consists of the norms, values and traditions, including religions, that govern human beliefs and attitudes. Thus, culture powerfully determines individual's relationships and gives actions their significance. As there is a fundamental relationship between religion and culture we need to understand the complementarities and interconnections between the heritage of faith and ways of conceiving of reality and oneself, one's heritage of faith and social ties, and one's ways of thinking of oneself as a member of a community. The gender configuration draws heavily on the religious and cultural norms that govern women's work, and political practices. In the Middle East, among other regions, religion and culture have a major effect on gender equality, though the position of women in the Middle East region cannot be attributed to presumed intrinsic properties of Islam. According to Moghadam (1993) Islam is neither more nor less patriarchal than other religions, including Judaism, Christianity and the teachings of Hinduism: all share the view of women as primarily mothers and wives.

Despite guaranteeing women rights and placing women and men on an equal footing (Shalabi 1997, pp.51–62) personal status laws in Muslim countries still discriminate between men and women, due to various interpretations of the Qur'anic verses addressed to women and discussing their issues. According to Nawal Al Fa'oury, "this explains the failure of Muslim societies to preserve the straight path of Islam" (Al Fa'oury 2004, p.47).

The dimension of religion permeates all social life and transcends the dimensions of beliefs. Thus, religions, which represent the hard core of any culture, affect security in social and political levels which impact directly upon the dynamics of security and creating an ideological framework for action. They can also destabilise political regimes and conservative movements in many parts of the world, depending on the social and cultural context.

Institutions causing gender equality

Four key social and political institutions are causing gender inequalities: the state, the markets, civil society and community and kinship and family.

The state

This section deals with the responsibilities of states, their performance in gender issues and ways of measuring that performance. The state is responsible for the overall governance of society. It enforces the rules and procedures that regulate how different institutions interact. Access to state resources, including employment, is through its legislation, policies and regulations. Gender inequalities cannot be attributed to poverty or patriarchy alone. They result from a specific combination of poverty, patriarchy and the state's public policy. For instance, the 10 best performers measured by the relative status of women include two high-income Scandinavian countries, one upper middle-income, previously socialist, country and seven lower middle-income countries, of which six were previously socialist. The 10 worst performers include one upper middle-income country, one lower middle-income country and a number of low-income countries. In the latter group eight countries are Muslim but they are also mainly deeply patriarchal countries and include three from West Africa. These two regions also account for the 10 next worst performing countries.

This shows the importance of public policies in addressing gender equality in ways above and beyond their income levels. Among the best performers, both the Scandinavian and socialist countries are associated with strongly egalitarian welfare regimes. The presence among the worst performers of middle-income countries like Algeria and Saudi Arabia and the absence of low-income Muslim countries like Bangladesh or the Gambia, shows that gender inequalities cannot be attributed to religion, poverty or patriarchy alone.

An analysis of life expectancy, education and labour force participation, can also contribute to a comprehensive picture of the distribution of gender inequality in both developed and developing countries. At the same time, improvements in human capabilities due to overall improvements must be separated from those that reflect a reduction in gender inequalities. While the absolute level of well-being matters and gender inequality is an ethical problem, there are also policy reasons for investigating women's absolute levels of deprivation, as well as their deprivation relative to men, as these are relevant for different human development outcomes.

Public sector social spending is another indication for gender inequalities, particularly spending that goes on poverty alleviation. Gender issues must be addressed in all parts and at all stages of the planning process in any nation and plans and strategies should be backed by appropriate financial resources and data. Budget analysis can play a number of different roles. It can promote greater transparency of policy processes, helping to demystify the secrecy surrounding official decision-making. It can match policy intent with resource allocation to see whether policy commitments to gender issues by the government are rhetorical or substantive. It can strengthen accountability by making it easier to find out what is actually done with public money.

Gender-responsive budget (GRB) analyses have been conducted at a variety of different levels: national, local, sectoral and even programmatic. They are sometimes, but not always, led by governments. The political climate has an impact on the design of policy. In Australia, South Africa and the UK, for example, GRB analysis gained a place when progressive political parties came into power, suggesting that as the reform was associated with particular political platforms rather than being an essential aspect of development strategy.

Most GRBs focus on expenditure, partly because their direct impacts were easier to assess. Some are expenditures specifically targeted at women, some are intended to promote gender equality in the public sector and some emege from the gendered effects of mainstream budget expenditure (e.g. the educational budget in promoting gender equality in society).

GRBs facilitate public comment on proposed budgets. This was shown in the study carried out by the Women's International League for Peace and Freedom. It initiated a women's budget project in the USA in 1996 at a time when there much public discussion about the national debt crisis and the need to cut government expenditure in order to reduce the public deficit. Noting that very few women benefited from military spending, the project estimated the costs of various defence-related programmes and compared them with the costs of welfare-related programmes, asking women to choose how they would like to see public money spent.

A study in Ghana using benefit incidence analysis noted that government spending on education and health was partly offset by cost recovery that lowered the subsidy element in these services. It found that girls received 45 per cent of subsidies in primary education although their gross enrolment ratio was 67 per cent. This gender bias was more marked among poor households. Because the poor were less likely to go for treatment when they were ill, richer households were found to use both public and private health services to a greater extent. However, women were found to gain more of the public subsidy than men in health, partly because of the existence of gender-specific services targeted to their needs.

The World's Women 2005: progress in statistics showed that designing gender-sensitive budgets relies very much on available data and statistics. It is a follow-up to UN resolutions urging nations to provide complete census data, especially on gender. Only 81 countries representing 28 per cent of the world population completed all five surveys. But for governments to plan budgets and evaluate programmes, they need information on the economic activity of the population, which includes data on employment, unemployment, occupation and wages by sex as well as age.

The market

Markets are organised around a commercial logic – the maximisation of profit – and resources are exchanged on the basis of contracts. Women's economic activity in the public domain varies. In South America, in populations with a strong African or Asian presence their participation rates are higher than in countries where the Spanish influence is stronger. The region as a whole, however, is characterised by low levels of female economic activity in rural areas and higher levels in urban areas. (Boserup 1970).

    Comparing women's labour force participation around the globe is problematic and the difficulty of capturing often irregular, casual forms of work in the informal economy is compounded by the different definitions used in measurement. The discussion here uses the conventional definition of work (i.e., activities done for pay or profit). While this does not fully capture women's contribution to the economy, nor show what is happening in the unpaid economy, it reveals the restrictions to their work in the formal sector.

    The estimated economic activity rate of women and the female percentage of the labour force reached about 45 per cent in East Asia and the Pacific, 46 per cent in Europe and Central Asia, 35 per cent Latin America and the Caribbean, 27.3 per cent in the Middle East and North Africa, 33.3 per cent in South Asia and 42.2 per cent in sub-Saharan Africa.

    The most striking features of labour force participation patterns in the last few decades are that the percentage of women in the labour force has risen and their share of overall employment has increased. In almost every region, there are now many more women involved in the visible sectors of the economy. In addition, women's participation has increased faster than men's in almost every region except Africa, where it was already high. At the same time, the market and its agents actively reproduce and reinforce custom-based gender discrimination. Employers refuse to recruit women, banks refuse to lend to women entrepreneurs, judges think that women get raped through their own fault and states define women as minors (Feldman 1992). These forms of gender disadvantage show how cultural norms and beliefs are also found in the supposedly impersonal domains such as the market.

Civil society and community

Civil society refers to a range of associations whose members pursue a variety of interests. The membership and goals are usually chosen and members determine how resources and responsibilities will be distributed on the basis of some agreed set of principles. Such organisations include trade unions, NGOs and professional associations. "Community" is used here to refer to associations and groups based on what sociologists call "primordial" ties. Membership of these groups is ascribed rather than chosen. Individuals' access to their resources depends on how they are positioned in the group by these ascribed identities. Examples of community include caste, tribe and patron-client relationships.

Kinship and the family

Although gender inequality is found throughout society, institutional analyses generally start by looking at its presence in the household. This is because these are the primary forms of organisation that are inherently gendered. Women's and men's roles and responsibilities in the domestic domain also reveal how the wider society views their nature and capabilities and hence constructs gender difference and inequality. In addition, a great deal of productive, as well as reproductive, activity is organised through kinship and family, particularly among the poor. Consequently, even when women and men participate in the wider economy, their participation is partly structured by relations in the household.

    The most marked forms of gender inequality in the region are associated with regimes of extreme forms of patriarchy. These include the belt stretching from North Africa and western Asia across the northern plains of South Asia and in East Asia. These countries clearly have widely different economies, histories, cultures and religions. However, they share certain historical similarities in the way that family, kinship and gender relations are organised and in patterns of female economic activity. Their kinship structures are predominantly patrilineal, marriage tends to be exogamous and patrilocal and households are organised along highly corporate lines, with strong conjugal bonds and cultural rules that emphasize male responsibility for protecting and provisioning women and children. Household resources and income are pooled under the management and control of the male patriarch.

Female chastity is emphasised (with severe penalties for any transgression). Female sexuality is controlled through a strong public – private divide that keeps women secluded in the private domain. Female seclusion based on norms of honour and shame is practised by Muslims and Hindus, particularly the upper castes. Restrictions on female mobility, patrilineal inheritance and patrilocal marital practices have meant the economic devaluation of women and their overall dependence on men in much of this region. "Son preference" is also marked.

In West and central Africa over 40 per cent of currently married women are in polygamous marriages. In East Africa and southern Africa the figures are 20–30 per cent and 20 per cent or less, respectively. Polygamy contributes to a pattern of separate (rather than pooled) spousal budgets, assets and income flows, which may include separate living arrangements. In such cases women exercise considerable economic agency in the family structure and are not dependent on their husbands in the way that they are in much of South Asia.

Gender equality in the four dimensions of human security

Violence

This section deals with violence as a threat to women and the forms of violence women face. The physical integrity dimension of human security in its relation to gender equality focuses on forms of violence exerted over women, such as human trafficking, bonded labour and girls' child domestic labour. The use, or threat, of violence is an important way in which power relations are maintained in the household. Reasons for domestic violence range from a husband not getting his meals on time to a

mother-in-law asserting her authority over her son's new wife. Violence is also reported in situations where women seek some degree of independence, as when they get access to paid work. Sociological perspectives on violence show that power is based on resources and that violence is the ultimate resource for securing compliance. The exchange/social control model of family violence theorises that violence is used when the rewards are higher than the costs. The private nature of abuse, the reluctance of outsiders to intervene and the low risk of any other intervention reduce the costs of abuse. Cultural approval of violence (for instance, to "discipline" wives) increased the potential of violence (Agnes 1988, pp.28–31. There is also a poverty dimension to domestic violence. The persistence of high levels of poverty in underdeveloped countries, combined with the weakness of democratic institutions, seriously affects the social integration of vulnerable and traditionally excluded groups like women.

The rise in social violence is a human security problem. The increasing rate of violence directed towards women is associated with a combination of factors such as lack of opportunities for women, high levels of poverty and a police system that is concerned with maintaining social order rather than preventing crime (Fuentes and Aravena 2005).

Fighting gender-based violence is one of the United Nations Development Fund for Women (UNIFEM's) major concerns. One in three women suffer some form of violence in her lifetime. Violence became part of an epidemic that devastates lives, fractures communities and stalls development. Despite some progress on this issue over the past decade, its scale remains mostly unacknowledged. New dimensions include the global trafficking of women and girls. UNIFEM's strategy targets several fronts to interrupt the cycle of violence against women, with an overall objective of linking violence to the source that feeds it: gender inequality. Their strategy includes

- establishing legal frameworks to combat violence, followed by plans for specific national actions
- measuring the problem by supporting the collection of data and research on violence against women

- preventing violence before it starts, from the local to the international level
- supporting women's organisations by drawing attention and resources to these efforts;

Forms of violence exercised over women

Human trafficking is one form of violence against women. According to the United Nations Population Fund 2000, four million women are sold each year for the purposes of prostitution, slavery or marriage and two million children are brought into the sex trade. Trafficked women are installed close to military bases for sexual use by soldiers and to supply cheap labour. They are lured by contracts for the purposes of sexual exploitation and for the purpose of organ trading and for transporting drugs.

Another form of violence is bonded and girl's child domestic labour. National and international mechanisms exist to combat discrimination against the girls at home and in the public sphere, especially in the labour market condemned in the Convention of the Rights of the Child and in the African Charter on the Rights and Welfare of the Child, (M'Barek 1996, pp.20–21). Nevertheless, the International Labour Organisation has estimated that 250 million children between the ages of five and 14 work in developing countries, at least 120 million of them on a full-time basis. Of these 61 per cent are in Asia, 32 per cent in Africa and 7 per cent in Latin America. Most working children in rural areas are found in agriculture and many children work as domestics. Urban children work mainly in trade and services.

In some cases, children's work can be helpful to them and their families and working and earning money can be a positive experience. This depends largely on the age of the child, the conditions in which the child works and whether work prevents the child from going to school. The Children's Rights Division at Human Rights Watch has focused its efforts on the worst forms of child labour, including domestic and bonded labour. Bonded labour is outlawed by the 1956 UN Supplementary Convention on the Abolition of Slavery. Yet millions of children are bonded in India alone. Most of these are young girls, as documented in the Human Rights Watch 2003 report.

Needs, poverty alleviation and vulnerability

The needs dimension of human security in its relation to gender equality includes the need to alleviate poverty and the need for combating HIV/AIDS as a cause and as a result of poverty.

Poverty tends to be associated with dependence and the extremely poor include the elderly, the disabled and, in some cases, female-headed households. The World Bank's World Development Report in 2000 included insecurity as one of the three key dimensions of poverty. A certain percentage of the population above the poverty line is vulnerable because they face a high likelihood of falling below it. Vulnerability has now become an integral aspect of poverty analysis. Objective vulnerability refers to exposure to risks, shocks and stress and the inability to deal with them. Subjective vulnerability refers to the sense of powerlessness in the face of threats.

There are at fluctuations in the well-being of the poor as household move into and out of poverty over time. For example, among vulnerable groups in the UNICEF critique of structural adjustment were the "newly poor" – those who had been retrenched from the public sector. A review of 22 national poverty assessments in sub-Saharan Africa in the mid-1990s identified dimensions of poverty that included food insecurity, exclusion from social services, lack of ownership of productive assets, poor quality housing and irregular income flows. In the early post-war years up to the 1960s development was equated with economic growth, economic growth with industrialisation and industrialisation with investment in physical capital formation. The role of labour and human capital was seen almost entirely in terms of "manpower" needs. However, by the end of the 1960s it was obvious that such strategies had failed to bring about the expected reductions in poverty and gender inequality (Kabeer 2003, pp.37–43).

In the 1970s, when greater attention began to be paid to basic needs, rural productivity and informal sector activity, there was growing advocacy on the issue of women in development. This consisted of an argument for economic equity and identifying women as the poorest of the poor. Both started from the premise that women were important economic actors but they emphasised different aspects of women's performance and used different analytical approaches. The economic equity argument focused on the effects of development planning on women's economic status. National governments and international development agencies had not understood that women had productive, as well as reproductive, roles. Conventional measures of economic activity, based on western market-style economies, significantly underestimated the levels of women's economic contributions and failed to acknowledge the magnitude and value of women's unpaid work. This led planners to focus mainstream development interventions on men. At the same time, they directed various welfare programmes, such as maternal and child health, family planning and nutrition, to women. The result was the emergence and widening of a gender-based productivity gap and negative impacts on women's status in the economy.

The argument that women are the poorest of the poor drew attention to the disproportionate number of female-headed households among the poor and the fact that women in poor households were largely responsible for meeting families' basic needs. This led to the spread of income-generating projects for women intended to help them meet these needs, but these had little effect on their marginalised status in the development process. Anti-poverty strategies justified assistance to poor women on the grounds of poverty reduction rather than family welfare. As these would have cost a great deal more they ran into the same problems as "equity-based" programmes. Early initiatives on women in development thus did little to change gender biases in poverty alleviation efforts. The first Human Development Report in 1990 barely touched on gender issues, although it noted that the increasing number of female-headed households has led to a "feminisation of poverty" and that problems of gender inequality were relevant in both the North and South.

Opportunity, empowerment and security

The 2000 World Development Report (World Bank 2000–2001) offered a more complex view of gender than the 1990 Report in its key themes of opportunity, empowerment and security, but particularly in empowerment. The Report recognised the institutional nature of gender inequality and provided a deeper understanding of the relationship between poverty and growth than the 1990 Report and was organised around the three themes of "opportunity", "security" and "voice":

Opportunity was still seen in the context of market-led, labour-intensive growth. However, the notion of the resources of the poor was expanded to include their natural, financial, social and physical resources. The Report noted that lack of resources was both a cause and an effect of poverty and suggested that simultaneous action was needed on several fronts. Security was also much more prominent than in the 1990 Report. This was because of the growing globalisation of production and trade and the financial crisis caused by short-term fluctuations in international capital flow (e.g. in the "miracle" economies of East Asia).

Voice was related in particular to the inability of the poor to influence policies that directly affected their lives. The question of "voice" had recently been given increasing attention in policy discussions about national strategies. Participatory methodologies intended to include the voices of the poor were part of country poverty assessments carried out by the Bank and other donors throughout the 1990s. Worldwide consultations with the poor contributed to the analysis in this report.

The UN millennium development goals

In the course of the 1990s poverty reduction was adopted as an overarching goal by almost every major international and bilateral development agency and as the basis of development cooperation. In 1996 the Organisation for Economic Cooperation and Development countries laid out their strategy for the twenty-first century in terms of a number of international development targets. The first target was halving world poverty by 2015. The targets were subsequently revised to become the basis of the millennium development goals, agreed to at the UN Millennium Summit in 2000 and subscribed to by both developed and developing countries. The main goals concern income poverty, human development, gender equality, environmental sustainability and global partnership. Targets and indicators were set to assess progress in achieving them.

The World Bank's 2001 report

The World Bank's most comprehensive treatment of gender is the 2001 policy research report, *Engendering development: through gender equality in rights, resources and voice* (Mason and King 2001). This documented different aspects of gender inequality using evidence from both the developed and developing world. It noted how important kinship systems are in constructing gender inequality. It drew on the new thinking on "household economics" to explore the structure of power, incentives and resources in the household. It also looked at the ways in which the beliefs and values of households and communities interact with wider legal frameworks to reproduce gender bias in key institutions, including the state and the market.

The report noted that in labour markets around the world women tend to be under-represented in better-paid formal sector jobs and over-represented in the unpaid and informal sectors. As a result, they earn around 70–80 per cent of male earnings in both developed and developing countries. Only 20 per cent of this difference can be explained by conventional economic variables, such as educational attainment, work experience and job characteristics. These inequalities are mainly perpetuated by taboos and prejudices in the labour market.

The report also documented how globalisation is opening and expanding national markets and pointed to the potential gains and costs associated with this. The gains include some signs that the gender gap in wages is decreasing in industries in both North and South. The costs include the failure of legislation to prevent continued discrimination against women workers, as well as the exposure of women in the traded industries to fluctuations in the global economy. As a result, the report concluded that competitive markets may not be the best way to eliminate gender discrimination, so government has a role to play in regulating markets and in providing critical economic infrastructure. The report proposed a three-level strategy to promote gender equality in the development process:

- reforming institutions to establish equal rights and opportunities for women and men
- fostering a rights-based approach to development and growth as the most effective way to reduce gender disparity
- taking active measures to redress persistent inequalities in political voice

Another effort was made by the UNDP, which concentrated on comparing working hours of men and women in nine developing and 13 industrialised countries. The comparison showed that women and men generally worked longer hours a day in the former than in the latter. The average working days were 419 minutes in industrialised countries, 471 minutes in urban developing countries and 566 in rural developing countries. The study also noted that women accounted for 51 per cent of the total work burden in industrialised countries and 53 per cent in developing countries.

These comparisons concentrated on formal economic activities. Activities outside the formal economy are often overlooked in official data-gathering exercises because they tend to be irregular, part-time, subsistence-oriented or else carried out as unpaid family labour. Data on women's labour force participation are most likely to be incomplete and underestimates. This is because more economically active women are likely to be found in the informal economy and in subsistence production and they are more likely to be classified as unpaid family labour than paid workers.

In order to overcome this problem, the International Labour Organisation has adopted two definitions of economic activity. The conventional one includes only activities done for pay or profit and an extended also includes productive work done for own consumption. Estimates of female labour force participation based on the first definition provide information on women's contributions in the "visible" economy. Estimates based on the second definition give a more accurate idea of the extent of their productive contribution across the whole economy. However, neither provides information on women's contribution to the care and maintenance of the family and hence of their own labour efforts in underpinning survival, subsistence and accumulation.

Gender inequalities had a significant negative impact on economic growth. This was particularly so in South Asia and sub-Saharan Africa, the two poorest regions in the world. The 1998 *Status of poverty in Africa* report – which focused on gender, growth and poverty reduction – concluded that sub-Saharan Africa could have added several percentage points to its annual per capita growth rates if it had increased female education relative to male (0.5 per cent) and increased their employment in the formal sector (0.3 per cent) to the levels prevailing in East Asia.

As discussed above, the changing policy discourse of the international organisations' reports and processes has led to the greater visibility of the relationship between poverty reduction and gender equality.

Combating HIV/AIDS

According to Gabriel Siakeu (2000) by 2010 the 23 countries hardest hit by AIDS will lose 66 million individuals. It is not only war and conflict that helped in spreading the disease, but also the effect of peace. The aftermath of complex humanitarian crises presents particular opportunities that accentuate the HIV/AIDS risk Including a lack of income, leading to the sale of sex by women and children and increased child labour. Life after peace in war-affected countries is characterised by a desperation that fosters increases in sexual and domestic violence and abuse, rape and gender inequality. The spread of disease is due to the deterioration of most state services. Poverty eradication assessments say that nearly one billion cannot meet their nutritional needs, the vast majority of them living in Africa (Siakeu 2000, p.47).

The highest rates of HIV/AIDS are currently found in sub-Saharan Africa, which accounts for 79 per cent of people living with the disease and 81 per cent of deaths associated with the epidemic, massively outweighing its share of the global population (10 per cent). However, AIDS is spreading rapidly in other parts of the world, particularly in Asia. AIDS clearly poses risks for all sections of the population, but it also has certain gender-specific aspects. Women are at greater physiological risk than men of contracting the HIV virus from each sexual intercourse and forced sex increases this risk because micro-lesions make it easier for the virus to enter the bloodstream. Women under 25 years of age represent the fastest growing group with AIDS in the region, accounting for nearly 30 per cent of all female victims.

Empowerment

Capabilities

The human security dimensions of capability are made up of the material and human resources available to people to achieve development and security. Capabilities can be available through the empowerment process and empowerment as a vital component in the development discourse related to women. The 1990s saw increasing recognition of the centrality of women's empowerment to the success of development programmes and the notion empowerment was the core of the declarations and platforms for action of the 1990 World Conference on Education for All, the 1992 UN Conference on Environment and Development, the 1993 Human Rights Conference, the 1994 International Conference on Population and Development, the 1995 World Summit for Social Development and the Regional Preparatory Conferences for the 1995 Fourth World Conference on Women. The increased appreciation of women's pivotal role in the development process has also been reflected in the UN system.

Women's empowerment has five components: their sense of self-worth; their right to have and to determine choices, to have access to opportunities and resources, to have the power to control their own lives, both within and outside the home and to influence the direction of social change to create a more just social and economic order, nationally and internationally.

"Empowerment" can mean the ability to make choices. Using the concept of "human poverty" to describe the human development index (HDI), UNDP noted that this "does not focus on what people do or do not have, but on what they can or cannot do". The HDI is thus not a measure of well-being or happiness. Instead, it is a measure of empowerment. Empowerment takes place through agency, resources and achievements. Agency is how choice is put into effect. Resources are the medium through which agency is exercised and achievements refer to the outcomes of agency.

Since gender inequality is inextricably bound up with power relations, empowering women is the goal of efforts to reduce such inequality by such strategies as challenging existing power relations, improving household decision-making and gaining access and control over resources like credit, income and land, as well as subjective variables such as the sense of self-efficacy. Conceptualising power and gender adequately entails understanding its multidimensional nature and realising the multidimensional nature of power suggests that empowerment must take place at different levels and in various spheres.

Dimensions of power

The first dimension of power, "power to", is closely associated with decision-making where there is observable conflict. Here, power is seen as the capacity to affect outcomes. This is the kind of power that is used in making household decisions or in the effects on such decision-making for women who earn an income. The second dimension shifts from the inter-personal to the institutionalised basis of power. This concerns "power over", whereby one group manages to suppress certain conflicts by denying their validity so that are not even put on the decision-making agenda such as the assignment of household and childcare responsibilities.

The third dimension of power recognises that conflicts of interest may be suppressed both from the decision-making agenda and also from the consciousness of the parties involved. Here,

both the dominant and the subordinate parties subscribe to accounts of social reality that deny that any inequality exists. This formulation of power is concerned with ideology and with socio-cultural constructions and patterns of behaviour to which dominant and subordinate groups subscribe.

Women's experience of gender subordination is therefore complex. They may not necessarily be aware of, or desire to realize, their strategic gender interests. This may arise out of women's socialisation into patriarchy or through the restrictions on their mobility and experience that prevent them from knowing other ways of being.

Understanding power and gender also has implications on certain forms of security. It means having to recognise the trade-offs that women make in order to cope with their dependent, subordinate status so that they may subordinate their personal well-being to that of male authority in order to ensure long-term security. Women have a stake in the system and may prefer to make patriarchal bargains. The obedient wife can usually expect her husband to provide lifelong economic support and the compliant daughter-in-law can expect her situation to change with her seniority. They saw women evidence agency in various guises, including in ways that upheld the *status quo* rather than challenged it. Acts of resistance are indirect, for instance in songs (Mukhopadhyay et al. 2003, pp.27–30).

Education: a tool for empowerment

Illiteracy is a form of insecurity in itself. The relationship between education and human security has been recognised ever since the concept of human security originated and evolved towards greater inclusion and leadership for individuals. The world conference on Education for All (Jomtien, Thailand, 1990) treated education as an instrument for empowering people by meeting their basic learning needs, with or without institutional support. It also affirmed directly or indirectly the relationship between gender and human security, as empowering women through education is the cornerstone in achieving gender equality.

Education brings new individuals and social actors, women among them, into the construction of a human security culture. Learning enables people to acquire learning capabilities and both theoretical and practical knowledge, although education cannot on its own guarantee human security (Fuentes and Aravena 2005, pp.170–171).

Education brings about change in a number of different ways. It affects individual cognition and behaviour by promoting agency as the "power to". It improves access to knowledge, information and new ideas as well as the ability to use these effectively for young men as well as to young women, but the former are more likely also to be exposed to new ideas and possibilities through their wider contacts with the world. This may underlie the positive association between women's education and family welfare.

Education increases the likelihood that women will look after their own well-being, as well as that of their family. A study in rural Zimbabwe found that education and paid work are among the factors that increase the likelihood of women using contraception and decrease maternal mortality. It may also lead to a greater role for women in decision-making and a greater willingness on their part to question male dominance in the home and community. A study in India found that better educated women scored higher than less educated women on access to and control over resources, as well as their role in economic decision-making. Educated women also appear less likely to suffer from domestic violence.

The effect of education on women's empowerment could be hampered because of the content of the curricula, particularly in the formal educational system. The content of the curricula can often mirror and legitimate wider social inequalities, denigrating physical labour and domestic activities. The gender stereotyping in the curriculum helps to reinforce traditional gender roles in society and is a barrier to the kind of futures that girls are able to imagine for themselves. In addition, policymakers have tended to see the benefits of educating girls and women as connected to improving family health and welfare, rather than with either their economic opportunities or social transformation. The hidden curriculum of school practice reinforces messages about girls' inferior status on a daily basis and provides them with a negative learning experience, thus creating a culture of low self-esteem and low aspirations.

Social inequalities are also reproduced through interactions within the school system. In India, for example, not only do the children of the poor and scheduled caste households go to different, and differently resourced, schools, but also different groups of children are treated differently even in the same school. There is also evidence of widespread gender bias.

Participation

Participation as a human security dimension refers to the outcome and result of the empowerment process. Political participation affects women's empowerment and their role in peace-building through participation can help to reform the traditional security sector.

Women generally participate in the political process as subjects and not, like men, as citizens. Political literature discussing traditional security issues and political culture and the process of political transformation was written from the men's point of view, based on the common interest shared by all men in the world, including men in the South. As a result, women worldwide and men in the South, are excluded from policy formation.

State policies affect gender equality. They can address women's concerns directly as in legislation and laws related to reproduction, abortion, child care and maternity leave, they can focus on gender relations, especially those associated with power relations among men and women, such as family relations and property rights and they can be neutral with regard to gender relations, in areas such as wars, state foreign relations and foreign trade. Human security issues are embedded in these three categories in different proportions. In addition, all the categories have become subjects of dispute because of many attempts made by feminists to modify and change them.

In achieving gender equality, feminists aim at structural changes that will occur when women are considered as agents. Some feminists are with a bureaucratic background aim at making changes from within the state; others, including NGOs, who oppose patriarchal state institutions, aim at making changes in women's status from the grassroots level (Abdo 1999, pp.38–40; Basut 1995, pp.11–13; Cook 1993, p.22). Feminist movements tend to relate the prevailing gender inequalities to the failure of a state to recognise the distinction between women's practical and strategic interests. This leads to tensions in policies that attempt to meet women's practical needs by improving the concrete material conditions of their lives and those that seek to transform women's position in an unequal society. While the former could serve as a starting point for challenging inequalities in some instances, in many cases they act to preserve and reinforce existing inequalities.

Chun Chaesung sees that gender inequalities are also produced by the existing structure of the political system. This affects how many women are fielded as candidates and how many win. Chaesung stresses the need for gender balance not only in participating in elections, but also in influencing the electoral system, the legislation, the quotas and other measures affecting the political gender balance (Chaesung 2003, pp.244–248).

According to the UN statistics 8 per cent of women on average participated in public life in 2000 in Morocco, 37.6 per cent of women did so in the countries of the North, and 21.9 per cent in Latin American countries, 17 per cent in Africa and 19 per cent in Asia.

The low level of representation of Arab women in political bodies could be explained by two structures for rights: the national liberation right and the personal liberation right. Middle Eastern and third-world countries prioritise the goal of national liberation. Having achieving independence, third-world governments remain reluctant to grant women full citizenship. This argument is still evident in the Gulf states (Jad et al. 2000, p.140). One can conclude that the impediments to women in the Middle East and North Africa from participating in public life are rooted in the liberation and reform discourse itself.

According to Carolyn Hannan (2004), women's opportunities to exercise power are greater on local than the national levels. In India and France policies to increase women's political participation in local elections led to an increase in their presence in national office. Since 1993, one third of seats in local councils are reserved for women. Studies on women's participation in local councils in India have shown

there are positive effects of this empowerment on the women themselves, and that it has the positive impact of making councils more responsive to women's community demands for housing, schools and health. It also helped in improving the implementation of government programmes.

Latin America and the Caribbean have made the most noticeable progress in the area of women's political participation in one decade. Here the number of countries with a very poor representation of women went down from 20 to seven (Hannan 2004, p.5).

In order to secure the legal frameworks guaranteeing women's political participation, the gulf between laws and practices must be bridged. Most women's rights practitioners would agree that getting progressive laws passed to protect women's rights is difficult, but the real battle is in getting them implemented.

Most of the countries where there is a gap between the law and practice were colonised by Northern powers. The new laws did not take adequate account of the power wielded by culture and traditional modes of governance, a power that exists to date and continues to be overlooked. In these and in many other communities, traditional male councils of elders perform a vital quasi-legislative and judicial role, but at the same time perpetuate discrimination against women and violate women's human rights. Customary law in most traditional societies is unwritten, obtained from the usually unreliable memory of the elders and often applied on an ad hoc basis. The advantage of a new legal system existing alongside the ancient system did not necessarily automatically win people over to the western way of thought. They also stress their human right to practise their culture. Cultural relativism has also encouraged the continuation of cultural practices that violate human rights.

In Europe it is recognised that some practices that are said to be based on religious beliefs have a negative effect on women, both women native to Europe and immigrants. Often the line between culture and religion is blurred. The Committee on Equal Opportunities for Men and Women of the Council of Europe recently passed a resolution calling for European states to protect their resident women in Europe against rights violations carried out in the name of religion. It proposes specific policy and legislative measures, such as refusing to accept cultural and religious relativism and enforcing policies against honour killings and female genital mutilation. This raises the question whether human rights are an end in themselves, a means to the end of social justice, or both (Council of Europe 2005).

Peace-building through security sector reform

The International Development Research Centre defined peace-building as "the pursuit of policies, programmes and initiatives that seek to create the conditions for war-torn countries to transform or manage their conflicts without violence in order to address longer term developmental goals".

Women and gender issues connect the suffering of war-affected women and civilians, failed discipline among security forces and a weak justice system across national borders and require cooperative coalitions among societal groups and state apparatuses.

Most contemporary violent conflicts occur in the least developed countries of the world. These conflicts are virtually all internal, generally protracted and brutal towards civilians. They destroy the very physical, human and social capital that developing countries need to pull themselves out of poverty. During the anti-apartheid struggle, a popular slogan was "no peace without justice". In the post-apartheid era, peace also requires long-term stability. To achieve peace, one needs to focus not just on the sources of violence (such as social and political development issues) but also on the material vehicles of violence (such as weapons and ammunition). Until recent years, the international community has not effectively connected those two aspects. It has placed a higher value on short-term peace than on long-term development and stability, while those who do focus on long-term stability place a higher value on the societal and economic elements of development than on the primary tools of violence, such as weapons (Cock 1998).

The role of women's movements in conflict prevention is to improve international capacity and develop local institutions to prevent conflict and build peace. Women's movements are entering a new field of influence by encouraging good governance, especially in traditional security sectors, because failures of governance entail political and social exclusion, inequity, discontent and civil strife. Thus, one of the most vital steps to ensure the day-to-day security of all is to transform the institutions, policies and people who are responsible for the security of communities and individuals: collectively known as the security sector.

Security sector reform seeks to transform the security system using both single-issue reforms, such as disarmament and comprehensive processes based on broad principles, such as good governance. The working definition for the concept of "security" used by the United Nations International Research and Training Institute for the Advancement of Women has moved away from traditional militaristic and state-centric definitions of security towards a concept of human security. It defines security as encompassing the personal and communal state of being secure from a wide range of critical and pervasive threats, including but not limited to all forms of violence, injustice and violations of human rights. The struggle to ensure the human security of women, men, girls and boys is a potentially emancipatory process that includes, at its heart, the elimination of unequal and oppressive gender relations.

Security sector reform is carried out by different actors. There are three kinds of official security sector. The first includes institutions with an official mandate to use violence in order to enforce security, such as international and regional forces (including peacekeeping missions), military, official paramilitaries, police and border guards. The second is responsible for official oversight through the management and monitoring of the security sector and includes a variety of government bodies from national security advisory bodies to parliament or congress. Finally, the third consists of institutions responsible for guaranteeing the rule of law such as the judiciary, prisons, human rights commissions and ombudsmen and customary and traditional justice systems.

In addition to these official institutions, are actors who play an influential role in providing security and holding the security sector accountable for the security of individuals and communities. The first group consists of actors that play a pivotal role in security sector reform. They include donors that support security sector reforms financially. National and international civil society also plays a key role in monitoring the security sector, ensuring their accountability and advocating for security sector reform, including NGOs, women's and professional organisations and the media.

The second group, often defined as non-statutory security forces, takes on the role of security provider without an official state mandate, including armed opposition groups, paramilitaries, private bodyguard units, private security companies and political party militia.

Actors affected by the security sector such as peace activists ethnic minorities, poor people and women's organisations have consistently and actively challenged the structure, purpose and priorities of the security sector, calling for peace, justice, representation and the reduction or elimination of oppressive and inflated militaries (Farr, 2004, pp.2–3).

Donors, states and researchers have recently begun to apply a more formalised, comprehensive approach to security sector reform. Despite the ongoing debates on definitions and efficacy, there is often agreement that the security sector reform agenda must tackle political, institutional, economic and societal security as an interconnected whole. No longer is the focus on single-issue reforms. The security sector must be seen as an interdependent system that can be reformed along broad principles, such as good governance, accountability and transparency.

Recommendations

The steps taken by scholars and international and regional organisations, to mainstream gender equality, despite their progress, are still not enough and further steps should be taken. These are listed under the headings of participation and gender mainstreaming, institutional reforms and empowerment. The tools supporting these are research and economic resources and support.

Participation and gender mainstreaming

- calling upon governments to commit themselves to implementing the binding international agreements that call for full and equal participation of women and gender mainstreaming in all efforts to maintain and promote peace and security
- encouraging women to enter local and legislative elections through institutional support helping women to manage their election campaigns, training women to carry out their roles in an effective manner
- holding intensive consciousness-raising many workshops to minimise legal illiteracy and to increasing society's awareness of women's legal rights
- encouraging women to enter and join political parties and decision-making institutions
- improving and modifying school curricula to enhance gender equality at earlier stages/ younger ages

Empowerment

- empowering women to overcome pressures in the private sphere that prevent them from participating in public life
- introducing affirmative actions in regions where culture marginalises women and where traditional legal mechanisms are strong
- encouraging local media to contribute in a positive way to forming a new image of capable women and of images of women leaders
- introducing fundamental changes into local laws to ban legal discrimination against women

Institutional change

- establishing partnerships between formal and informal institutions, especially between formal security sectors and NGOs working on human security issues in third world countries, to prevent and respond to human

insecurities, create a participatory and democratic security sector, transform cultures of violence and militarisation, respond to gendered insecurities, especially violence against women, redress the under-representation of women in decision-making positions within the security sector, and to condemn discrimination and violence against women perpetrated by members of the security sector
- enhancing the research capacity of developing countries to analyse the impact of macro-economic policies, especially on marginalised women
- providing new instruments for policy and programme design and analysis by developing rigorous analytical tools and poverty-monitoring systems
- assisting the development of community-based monitoring and local development mechanisms
- strengthening the ability of policy-makers to negotiate with international players, such as international financial institutions and other multilateral and bilateral organisations

Research

- bringing together researchers, politicians, government officials and NGOs in policy dialogue concerning gender mainstreaming at the national and regional levels
- promoting the exchange of research knowledge, tools, results and policy measures among developed and third world countries
- building a research portfolio on pressing and specific gender and development issues
- improving the use of funds to promote gender equality and to develop strategies to encourage gender mainstreaming in all policies that have an impact on the place of women in the economy

Economic support

- expanding economic opportunities in areas where women are traditionally under-represented

- empowering and increasing the capacity building of women to respond to economic opportunities and challenges
- eliminating barriers to women's full participation in the economy
- recognising the economic contributions of women's unpaid work
- increasing the availability and quality of sex-disaggregated data research and analytical information
- ensuring the integration of women in the planning, design and implementation of responses to the current economic and financial crisis

Conclusion

Gender is a key organising principle in the distribution of labour, property and other valued resources in society. Unequal gender relationships are sustained and legitimised through ideas of difference and inequality that express widely held beliefs and values about masculinity and femininity. Such forms of power do not have to be actively exercised to be effective, because they also operate silently and implicitly through compliance with male authority, both in the home and outside it.

Women, particularly poorer women, face extremely unfavourable access to land and other valued resources. The terms on which they participate in paid work, including the return on their efforts, do little to improve their subordinate status in the family. They may be actively discriminated against in access to important resources such as credit, agricultural inputs, extension services, marketing outlets and so on. Dismantling these gender disadvantages could play an important role in addressing gender inequalities in the household as well as the economy. Formal legislation on gender equality is one way to address deeply entrenched forms of discrimination in marriage and work. At the same time, it is important to note that legislation alone will not ensure women's rights if customary rules and community beliefs prevent national laws from being implemented. Education and information on these rights are needed, together with effective enforcement machinery and an active civil society prepared to undertake public action to ensure their enforcement.

This analysis has shown that economic and political participation indicators alone cannot explain gender inequalities: institutionalised norms, beliefs, customs and patriarchal practices help to explain the uneven distribution of gender resources and responsibilities in different social groups across the regions of the world. While patriarchal oppression is still very much in evidence, on the last three decades of research, advocacy and activism in the field of development suggests that there has been important progress on a number of fronts. Gender gaps in survival chances, in health and in education and closing. Women now play a far more visible role in the economies of their countries and both educated middle-class women, who enjoy some degree of access to decision-makers, and those in poorer communities, are more aware of their rights.

Basic elements of a policy framework for human security

Paul Oquist

Ontology of human security

The risk that humans will become extinct is total. The risk that you and I will die is total. Existence and extinction, life and death are our absolute reality. Existence and life is our transient opportunity, extinction and death is our eternal destiny.[1] This state of being is beyond our past, present and future control. It is objective. Time is everything. What we can do is seek to increase the time span of species survival and individual existence, as well as to enhance the meaning and the quality of species and individual life. We have a window of opportunity to exist and live to the fullest while we stay alive. Extending the time that we can survive will allow us to realise and expand the human potential for safety, well-being, dignity and freedom. Our security and self-realisation depend on our cultural-historical situation, the goals we desire and the justice we seek for our own and future generations.

Human security aims to reduce the risk to our existence as individuals and as a species and to increase our choices in realising and expanding human potential for present and future generations. Species survival, the quality of individual life and the realisation and expansion of human potential are the content of human security. This concept of human security is historical, ethical and policy-oriented. Each of

Paul Oquist (PhD, Political Science, University of California at Berkeley) is Minister of the Nicaraguan Government and Private Secretary for National Policy of the President. He was Chief of Presidential Advisors in the Nicaraguan government of the 1980s. He has advised the Ecuadorian, Mongolian and Pakistani governments for the United Nations Development Programme (UNDP). He has been Director and Regional Adviser of the UNDP Regional Governance Programme for Asia. He has undertaken numerous governance and peace building consultancies in Asia and Latin America. Email: p30quist@yahoo.com

these basic elements of a human security policy framework is examined below.

Evolution and history of human security

To continually strive for security is part of the human condition. We consciously and unconsciously struggle for survival and to realise ourselves as a species and as individuals. Our physiological, emotional and cognitive processes and our most basic social relations are geared to survival and self-realisation. Our ancestors developed social organisation and language, tools and technologies and cultures and institutions so as to expand their own possibilities for survival and self-realisation. We are a product of their sacrifices, struggles and accomplishments and we likewise, have a moral responsibility to our progeny for their present and future survival, as well as their self-realisation and the expansion of human potential.

Human security and self-realisation are a major driving force in our species history. To understand this fully we need to know about the conditions that have made our existence possible. We also need to know about the history of evolving human security needs and how we have dealt with them across time. Without knowing about our past, we will not be able to fully comprehend our present or our probable futures. A highly summarised approximation of our evolution and history focused on human security follows, organised around the concepts of human and security.

The history of the human species

Humans belong to the genus *Homo*. The superfamily *Hominoidea* contains hominoids, including the lesser and great apes, and humans, who are members of the genus *Homo*, all of which are extinct except for *Homo sapiens sapiens*. *Homo* is a very recent and fast-evolving genus in the evolution of life on Earth that first appeared 2.5 million years ago. The genus *Homo* evolved to *Homo sapiens sapiens* 195 thousand years ago.

Conditions for human existence

The hominoids, *homini* and *Homo* evolved in the Palaeogene and current Neogene periods. Their emergence coincides with the relatively more moderate, cool and dry climate of the current ice age, while the appearance of *hominins* coincides with the intensification of the present ice age through the glaciation of large areas of the planet. The current geological epoch, the Holocene, begins with the end of recent glaciation, only 11,000 years ago. The current loss of ice in the Arctic and Antarctica, as well as receding glaciers elsewhere, indicates that the decline in glaciation is accelerating.

The climatic conditions that accompanied our appearance are reversing. This has been accelerated in the last 200 years and very dramatically in the last 50 by the constant increase in greenhouse gases as a result of burning fossil fuels. Global warming is therefore seen as a threat to conditions that accompanied the emergence and survival of *hominoids, hominins* and *Homo sapiens sapiens*. Some critics point out that global warning has occurred at several points in the history of the Earth. The difference in the global warning of the current Holocene period is that for the first time the consequences of human activities are contributing to climate change. This human security threat will subsequently be described in greater detail.

Human evolution, history and security

Adaptations that accompanied human evolution and enhanced human security include their increased transformative, communicative, cognitive and social capacities. Human history is not linear: civilisations have risen and fallen and there have been periods in which knowledge and capacity have been lost. One such period in Europe was during the 1,000 years after the fall of the Roman Empire, known as the Dark Ages. However, in China, India, South East Asia, Africa, Meso-America and South America, as well as in the Middle East, great civilisations existed at the time, with advanced cultures and knowledge.

The current stage of European history began some 500 years ago with the revival of art and science, known as the Renaissance and the recovery of lost ancient knowledge thanks to the custodianship and contributions of Middle Eastern, North African and Iberian Peninsula Muslim scholars. Advances in European navigation and military technology began the conquest of the world by European mercantile companies and nation-states. The resulting accumulation of wealth financed not only further conquests but also the Industrial Revolution which replaced the simple machines and natural energy of prior civilisations with ever more complex and productive machine tools, as well as an exponentially expanding consumption of fossil fuels that continues to date. In the last 100 years and especially in the last 50, science and technology have geometrically expanded human knowledge and capacity. They have also driven revolutions in information, communications, transportation and military tools.

At the beginning of our evolution our cultural norms, including the emergence of religion, were the principal guides of our behaviour and relations. With the emergence of civilisation and empires, political institutions became predominant, as power, authority and the law organised our societies and social processes, backed by both custom and coercive force. In the last 500 years economic and financial institutions have become hegemonic and political and cultural institutions have become increasingly subservient, acting as support structures for processes driven by economic and financial interests.

The last 500 years have also been the most violent period in human history. The problem is not so much that our behaviour has changed, but that it has not: we have the same propensity to violence that has characterised our evolution and history, but we now have far greater destructive capacity. This has reached its zenith with the creation of nuclear weapons. There are around 20,000 operational nuclear warheads in the world today, of which more than 95 per cent are held by the USA and Russia, with relative parity between the two. There are additionally 19,000 warheads awaiting dismantlement in Russia, giving a grand total of 39,000. Finally, there are 1,500 tons of weapons-grade nuclear waste in Russia, that is, enough fuel for 100,000 warheads. The mutually assured destruction of the Cold War is no longer a strategic doctrine, but the means to undertake it remains in place.

Our historical answers to violence and chaos have been our social organisation and institutions, including law. We have painstakingly developed them across the millennia, yet socially corrosive, highly destructive, violent behaviour and processes continue to be our greatest man-made threat. It is thus ironic that our physical and social adaptations for survival and realisation have reached the point where we are capable of destroying ourselves and most other forms of life as well.

The first stage of human adaptation was driven by physiological processes that increased our manipulative, communicative and cognitive capacity. The second stage was based on our capacity for species and individual learning and knowledge. This stage was driven by organisation and language, tools and technology, and cultures and institutions. This was primarily a social stage of human evolution. In the twentieth and twenty-first centuries human transformations of the environment have created a double evolutionary inflection point that makes our moral dilemma and the underlying value crisis critical. Our early social adaptations that contributed to our survival are now contributing to tendencies that tend toward extinction and the human impact on the evolution of the environment has reached the point where basic eco-systems that sustain life on earth are in decline.

Extinctions and the threat of extinctions

Extinction

Extinction is the end of existence of a species or taxonomic family when the last individuals disappear. This is the ultimate threat to human security. It is also inevitable. It has been estimated that all but 0.1 per cent of all species that have ever existed are extinct. A typical species survives for about 10 million years before it becomes extinct. The difference between species lies in the length of time during which they exist. Extinctions occur when a species cannot adapt to changing conditions, including the appearance of competitors. Ever since life began on earth, there has existed a background extinction rate as some species appear through speciation and others disappear through extinction. An extinction event occurs when a large number of species cease to exist in a relatively short period of time. It would appear that most extinctions of the species *Homo*, with the exception of *Homo neanderthalensis*, were pseudo-extinctions. Parent species gave way to daughter species with a greater adaptive capacity, among other reasons.

Human impact

Most scientists subscribe to the theory that we are now living another extinction-level event, the Holocene event or the sixth extinction. This period of mass extinctions is directly linked to the human impact on the environment. It is from the Industrial Revolution onward that our population and transformative capacity geometrically expanded, with an increasingly negative cumulative impact on the environment. The following factors are involved in these processes: population impacts; climatic and atmospheric impacts; and direct, indirect and habitat impacts.

Population impacts

In 1420 before the European expansion and the Industrial Revolution, the world population stood at 375 million, doubling to one billion by 1802. In 1927 it stood at two billion, in 1961 at three billion, in 1999 at six billion. The world population will crest after 2050 at under 10 million due to declining birth rates. *Homo sapiens sapiens* is literally crowding out other species due to our sheer numbers, our expanding need for space and an increasingly high level of cumulative impact on the environment.

Climatic and atmospheric impacts

Consumption of fossil fuels is one of the best indicators of industrialisation and its impact on the environment, as well as being one of the direct causes of that impact through air pollution, carbon dioxide emissions, an augmented greenhouse effect and global warming. Increases include the global temperature on both land and sea, the volume of atmospheric carbon dioxide and other greenhouse gases. The International Panel on Climate (IPCC) climate models estimate that increasing temperatures will occasion glacial retreats, i eventually reducing summer stream flows critical for irrigation in South Asia and South America. Polar ice caps will also be reduced and sea levels will rise, affecting low-lying islands and coastal areas such as those in Bangladesh. There will be an increase in the frequency of extreme weather events such as floods, droughts, heat waves and hurricanes. All of the above will alter habitats and contribute to biological extinctions.

The phenomenon of global warming is indisputable. The data is conclusive. What has been a matter of controversy since the 1990s is whether or not the rise in temperatures is due to human activity, anthropogenic climate change. The IPCC Third Assessment Report (Watson 2001), explicitly endorsed by the national scientific academies of the G8 countries, concluded that "most of the warming observed over the last 50 years is attributable to human activities".

A second atmospheric effect of industrialisation has been the depletion of the ozone layer in the stratosphere. The assessment of UN agencies has concluded that the global average total column ozone amount for the period 1997–2001 was approximately 3 per cent below the pre-1980 average values, while larger losses occurred over the poles (around 50 per cent on

average). Ozone depletion varies geographically and seasonally. Global concern over the finding by researchers of the relation between CFCs and ozone depletion in 1973 and the dramatic discovery of the Antarctic ozone hole in 1985 led to the *Montreal protocol on substances that deplete the ozone layer* (signed in 1987). What distinguishes this Protocol from other international Conventions is that it has actually had an effect in practice. The ozone layer is expected to begin to recover in coming decades, assuming full compliance with the Montreal Protocol (IPCC/TEAP 2005). By 2015 the Antarctic ozone hole should reduce, while complete recovery will take until 2050 or beyond, other factors being equal. However, indications in 2007 are that the situation is once again worsening. The case of the ozone depletions illustrates the length of time that it takes to undo human-induced environmental damage, even when human security actions are concerted with consensus and implemented with relative effectiveness. It also illustrates that negative synergies between different forms of human-induced environmental damage could also impede recovery.

Direct exploitation, invasive species and habitat change impacts

Some consider that the Holocene event began with the extinction of large mammals at the beginning of the period, including mammoths, sabre tooth tigers and others (10,000 million years ago). Theories on these extinctions include human over-hunting, climate change, disease, or some combination of the above.

Deforestation is the second earliest human impact on the environment, hunting being the first and the two are associated. Fire was used by Palaeolithic hunters to move animals out of woods and later by Mesolithic and Neolithic agriculture and animal husbandry to clear the land. Civilisation led to a greater rate of clearing the land for agriculture and animal husbandry, as well as for cities, roads and other public works. Wood as a source of fuel, construction material and material for making artefacts, added further pressure. Rapid human population growth led to further demand for cleared land and forest products. Reforestation initiated a positive counter-tendency in some places. Pressure on remaining forests has decreased in most developed countries in recent years, but pressure is now on the tropical rain forests and tropical dry forests in underdeveloped countries where there is a loss of two per cent of the forested area per year.

In the last 500 years the pressure from hunting, fishing and invasion and alteration of habitats, including deforestation, has accelerated with the growth of human populations and the complexity of human society. In 2004 IUCN identified 8,321 endangered full species, of which 1,101 were mammals. Large land and sea animals are particularly vulnerable to human activity. A 2002 Report of the United Nations Environmental Programme (UNEP), on environmental damage in the last 30 years, estimates that over 1,000 species of mammals face extinction in the next 30 years, one quarter of the total number.

A 10-year study led by Ransom Myers at Dalhousie University in Halifax, Nova Scotia, determined that, since 1950 when industrialised fishing began, the fish stocks of large species have declined by 90 per cent. The conclusion was that the ocean that is over-fished worldwide. Pollution and global warming are also taking its toll in the degradation of marine habitats in many areas.

The current Holocene extinction event will eventually classify as one of the historic mass extinction events of natural history, according to biologist E.O. Wilson of Harvard University, who estimated in 2002 that, if current rates of human destruction of the biosphere continue, one-half of all species of life on earth will be extinct in 100 years. Once extinctions occur, there is a loss of irreplaceable genetic material and associated biochemicals that form part of life support systems. Global warming and ozone depletion which are causing climate change in the atmosphere, resource depletion and pollution in the lithosphere, pollution and global warming in the hydrosphere and loss of biodiversity in the biosphere, can interact in complex ways that affect life support systems. Then there is the threat of nuclear warfare, which would affect all four spheres simultaneously through explosions, radiation and a nuclear winter similar to that of super-volcanic eruptions.

In sum, we are on a molten bomb in a cosmic shooting gallery impacted by comets, meteorites, asteroids and gamma rays, alternating between deep fryer and deep freeze, deluge and desert. We have a window of opportunity for survival and realisation, in the equilibrium that led to our existence and sustains it, but, instead of preparing to reduce risks for threats we cannot avoid, we are accelerating disequilibrium that increase risks for threats to our existence of our own making. Do we really believe that the queue of species marching towards extinction, because of our impact on the environment, does not include our own?

The ethics of human security

Values

Like other species, *Homo sapiens sapiens* strives to survive, both at the species and individual levels. Life and the survival of life are values that are part of our nature as living beings, animals and human beings. Thus, life and survival are two values of our species that form part of the revolutions and evolutions of the universe and nature on Planet Earth. These values are not relative. They are absolute in the sense that they are all we have and can have. Derived from life and survival as human security values are safety (freedom from fear) and well-being (freedom from want).

As a social species individual *Homo sapiens sapiens* depend on each other for life and survival, as a species and as individuals. Sexual attraction and reproduction is one basis of our social life. Another is that our offspring are completely helpless at birth and require great care and affection for the first few years after birth. These relations form the deepest foundations of our social interaction. Care and affection (taken together, love and solidarity) are values directly linked to our life and survival. Not one of us would survive infanthood without solidarity.

We are also, with one notable exception, not a particularly well-endowed species. Many species can hear better, smell better, touch better and see better, while some also have highly developed radar and sonar. Some navigate the world with great precision. Many are better at fight and/or flight, while some are armed with impressive defensive mechanisms. We are not the biggest or the strongest, but we are able to transform our natural and social environments intentionally, but not necessarily wisely. Our social intelligence provides our comparative advantage. We have developed and accumulated the capacity to learn and create knowledge, as well as to produce, articulate, communicate, store and retrieve knowledge through language. Thus, closely linked to life and survival for our species are the values of learning and knowledge. They have been and are vital for life and survival for our species and ourselves.

This capacity to intentionally transform our natural and social environment, to learn and know, have allowed us to structure our societies and civilisations in social divisions of labour. Values, attitudes, beliefs, worldviews, customs and other patterns of behaviour, as well as their material manifestations, including tools, utensils, artefacts and art, form the culture of our societies and civilisations. Formal and informal rules, including laws, as well as incentive structures form the institutions that order social life. Culture and institutions allow our societies and civilisations to function and structure our interdependence for survival and realization.

Social life is based on inclusion and exclusion based on identities. The conflict that is inherent in all social life may be channelled peacefully or violently. Violence is human self-destruction or destruction of other beings and things. In addition to natural threats to our existence as a species and as individuals, there are also social threats due to exclusion, domination and violence. Therefore, peace and equity are social values highly related to life and survival. Closely related to peace and equity, as human security values, are dignity (freedom from humiliation) and human rights (freedom from injustice) that should be respected in all human beings and which institutionalise solidarity in social relations.

Human beings undertake goal-oriented actions in relation to life and survival, safety and well-being, care and affection, learning and knowledge, culture and institutions, peace and equity, dignity and human rights and the achievement of objectives. This intentional

behaviour produces collective social fulfilment and individual self-realisation, motivational elements that contribute to living life to the fullest and hence to the drive for survival.

In sum, human security values are life and survival, safety and well being, care and affection, learning and knowledge, culture and institutions, peace and equity, dignity and human rights and social fulfilment and self-realisation.

There are value conflicts at all levels from the individual and family to the national and international level. These are conflicts over belief including preferences, evaluations and obligations. At higher social levels, there are cultural and institutional conflicts. Processes of inclusion and exclusion create conflicts at any level and on almost any value. Violence is always latent in human social life. To attain the values of peace and equity, the violent part of our nature needs to be controlled and inevitable conflicts need to be channelled into peaceful, constructive channels. This is peace building, which is one of the highest achievements of human wisdom.

In current times characterised by declining resources, nuclear, biological and chemical weapons and new possibilities for havoc, we need global wisdom for peace-building to assure the survival of the species and most of life on the Planet Earth. What can completely overcome the division between "us" and "the others" is a species perspective. All human individuals, groups and nations are part of the species *Homo sapiens sapiens*. This is what unites us all. This is our common interest and should be our common value that sets our common objectives and goals.

Nor is this a matter of consequence only for *Homo sapiens sapiens*. The state of our current knowledge 65,000 years after our emergence allows us to appreciate the interconnections between all forms of life and all life support systems, biodiversity and basic ecological equilibrium. Life itself could depend on our building peace at the species level.

Ethics

Behaviour and interactions that contribute to the existence of the species and individuals in relation to life and survival are ethical. Behaviour and interactions that increase threats, vulnerabilities and risks in relation to the existence of the species and individual life, are unethical. Actions to remedy disequilibria in relation to life and survival are high-priority ethical actions. Actions that contribute to disequilibria are unethical actions that require remedial measures in the form of high-priority ethical actions.

Frequently, advances in our learning and knowledge show that actions and processes that were not previously seen to have ethical implications were highly unethical. For example, the excessive use of hydrocarbon energy that began with the Industrial Revolution has been proved to contribute to global warming and is threatening numerous species and billions, of human beings. High-levels of energy consumption are driven by a policy framework that is based on economic growth. Endless, unlimited, mindless growth could only be seen as a model for development for humankind if the earth had unlimited resources. Although alternative energy sources are available, unethical economic interests prevail over ecological necessities, thus increasing threats, vulnerabilities and risks.

Warnings from the scientific community as to the extinction level event underway due to human impact on the environment are overwhelming. Signs in daily life are also telling. In 2007 the major oil companies all achieved the highest corporate profits in the history of the world. The increase in human transformative capacity that was part of our adaptation for survival now contributes to our extinction. Even our science and technology now contribute to extinction. What makes science, technology and our productive capacities positive or negative is our individual behaviour and social processes. The institutions that guide our social processes and behaviour have become dysfunctional and now contribute to tendencies toward extinction and death. Greed is the predominant value of our time and growth the overriding goal.

Morality

As a species we have lost our moral compass and our ethical bearings. All we have is time, but currently we are reducing our species time, our quality of life for ourselves and our progeny and the earth's life support systems. This behaviour is immoral. We have a moral responsibility to contribute to existence and life and not to extinction and death. The ethical goal of human security policy is to contribute to the construction of harmonious relations between humans and nature, as well as between humans themselves, that contribute to species and individual survival and realisation. The immoral nature of prevailing economic and financial institutions, as well as of the political and cultural institutions that support them, becomes apparent when activities that tend toward extinction and death are justified for economic reasons, or when their discontinuation or replacement is delayed because the cost of alternatives is higher. Profit and growth are more valued than survival and realisation; greed has precedence over need.

Human security policy

Human security policy is based on the assumptions outlines above. Our concern for human security is as old as human society. With civilisation, state power and authority were placed on setting policy objectives and defining means to achieve them. Physical and food security were the overriding concern of early civilisations and they continue to be central to this day. With the advance of civilisations, the new opportunities for realising human potential bring with them new insecurities and our human security needs have become more complex with increasing complexity in civilisation (Goucha and Rojas Aravena 2003; UNESCO 2003).

The frequency and magnitude of revolutions and wars in the twentieth century led to the formation of international organisations with broader perspectives than the nation-state. The International Labour Organisation was the first, followed by the League of Nations and the United Nations. With the Universal Declaration of Human Rights (UN 1948) and successive covenants, the concept of rights contained in classical legislation, considered universal by philosophers in the Enlightenment and incorporated into the legal framework after the French and American Revolutions, became legally universal, as countries began to ratify the Declaration and successive covenants. Subsequent threats to human security have elicited attempts at global human security policies through international covenants. Implementation levels are generally low but are highly variable. Some of these agreements are discussed below.

The Montreal Protocol

The Montreal Protocol, an international treaty designed to protect the ozone layer by phasing out the production of a number of substances believed to be responsible for ozone depletion, entered into force in 1989. Due to its widespread adoption and adherence, it has been hailed as an example of exceptional international cooperation. The treaty provides a timetable for each group of hydrocarbons to be phased out and eventually eliminated, with a few exceptions for essential uses where no acceptable substitutes have been found. The catalyst for this treaty was the realisation that the depletion of the ozone layer by chlorofluorocarbons would lead to an in increase in UVB radiation the surface of the planet, resulting in an increase in skin cancer and other impacts such as damage to crops and to marine phytoplankton. The provisions of the Protocol include the requirement that the parties to the Protocol base their future decisions on information that is assessed through panels drawn from worldwide expert communities.

The Multilateral Fund for the Implementation of the Montreal Protocol provides resources to help developing countries to phase out their use of ozone-depleting substances. Australia, one of the countries most affected by ozone depletion contributes funding through AusAID and also undertakes bilateral projects in developing countries. At present 191 nations are parties to the Montreal Protocol. Only six, as of September 2007, have not signed.

Since the Montreal Protocol came into effect, the atmospheric concentrations of the most important chlorofluorocarbons and re lated hydrocarbons have either levelled off or decreased. Halon concentrations have continued to increase, but their rate of increase has slowed and they are expected to begin to decline by about 2020. The overall level of compliance has been high.

Kyoto Protocol

The Kyoto Protocol (UN 1997) is an agreement negotiated as an amendment to the United Nations Framework Convention on Climate Change (UNFCCC 1997), which was adopted at the Earth Summit in Rio de Janeiro in 1992. All parties to the UNFCCC can sign or ratify the Kyoto Protocol. The Kyoto Protocol was adopted in 1997 in Kyoto. As of June 2007, a total of 172 countries had ratified the agreement. The notable exception is the USA. Other countries, like India and China, that have ratified the Protocol, are not required to reduce carbon emissions under the present agreement. The objective of the Kyoto Protocol is to stabilise greenhouse gas concentrations in the atmosphere. According to a press release from the UNEP:

> The Kyoto Protocol is an agreement under which industrialised countries will reduce their collective emissions of greenhouse gases by 5.2 per cent compared to the year 1990. . . . The goal is to lower overall emissions from six greenhouse gases . . . over the five-year period of 2008–2012. National targets range from 8 per cent reductions for the European Union . . . [to] 0 per cent for Russia.

Most provisions of the Kyoto Protocol apply to developed countries, which have to pay and supply technology to other countries for climate-related studies and projects. Each ratifying country has agreed to limit emissions to the levels described in the Protocol, but many countries have limits that are set above their current production. These extra amounts can be purchased by other countries on the open market. So, for instance, Russia currently easily meets its targets and can sell off its credits for millions of dollars to countries that do not yet meet their targets, to Canada for instance. This rewards countries that meet their targets and provides financial incentives to others to do so as soon as possible. Countries also receive credits through various shared clean energy programmes and carbon dioxide sinks, in the form of forests and other systems that remove carbon dioxide from the atmosphere.

Some estimates indicate that, even if it is successfully and completely implemented, the Kyoto Protocol will not provide a significant reduction in temperature. Because of this, many critics and environmentalists question the value of the Kyoto Protocol. Proponents argue that Kyoto is a first step, as requirements to meet the UNFCCC will demand further action until the objective is met. They claim that reducing these emissions is crucially important. The governments of all of the countries whose parliaments have ratified the Protocol are supporting it. Most prominent among advocates of Kyoto have been the EU and many environmentalist organisations. Many US states and cities representing more than 40 million Americans supported Kyoto, despite the lack of Federal Government support.

Some public policy experts who are sceptical of global warming see Kyoto as a scheme either to slow down the growth of the world's industrial democracies, or to transfer wealth to the third world in what they claim is a global socialism initiative. Some environmental economists have been critical of the Kyoto Protocol. It should be noted, however, that this opposition is not unanimous and that the inclusion of emissions trading has led some environmental economists to embrace the treaty. The Bali Conference in December, 2007 confirmed the international impasse on the UNFCCC given continued US objections.

"Non-proliferation treaty" (NPT)

The 1968 NPT (UN 1968) seeks to limit the spread of nuclear weapons. Most sovereign states (188) are parties to the treaty. However, two out of seven confirmed nuclear powers (i.e., those that have openly tested nuclear weapons – India and Pakistan) and one undeclared nuclear power (Israel) have not ratified the treaty. In New York City in 1995 the parties to the treaty agreed to extend the treaty indefinitely and without conditions. It has three pillars: disarmament, non-proliferation and the right to peacefully use nuclear technology. At the time the treaty was being negotiated, NATO had a secret nuclear weapons-sharing agreement whereby the USA provided nuclear weapons to be deployed by and stored in, other NATO states. NATO states argued that the USA controlled the weapons in storage and that no transfer of the weapons or control over them was intended "unless and until a decision was made to go to war, at which time the treaty would no longer be controlling".

As of 2005, the USA still provided about 180 tactical B61 nuclear bombs for use in Europe under these NATO agreements. Many states and the Non-Aligned Movement now argue that this violates Articles I and II of the treaty and they are applying diplomatic pressure to terminate these agreements. Furthermore, even if the NATO argument is legally correct, such operations in peacetime contravene both the objective and the spirit of the NPT.

Three states – India, Pakistan and Israel – have declined to sign the treaty, arguing that the NPT creates a club of "nuclear haves" and a larger group of "nuclear have-nots", by restricting the legal possession of nuclear weapons to states that had tested them before 1967. India and Pakistan have publicly announced they have nuclear weapons and have detonated nuclear devices in tests. In March 2006 India and the USA finalised a controversial deal for the latter to provide India with US civil nuclear technology, and although India has not signed the NPT and the deal is widely seen as sending the wrong message to other non-NPT countries.

North Korea ratified the treaty, but withdrew from it in January 2003. On October, 2006 North Korea claimed to have conducted nuclear tests. In February 2005 it publicly declared that it possessed nuclear weapons. In September 2005 it announced that it would agree to a preliminary accord under which the country would scrap all its existing nuclear weapons and rejoin the NPT. On the following day North Korea reiterated its known view that, until it is supplied with a light water reactor, it will not dismantle its nuclear arsenal. In February 2007 North Korea announced an agreement brokered by the USA in which it would close its nuclear reactors by the end of 2007, but the negotiations with the USA have continued past that date with frequent ups and downs.

Iran is a signatory state of the NPT and, as of 2006, resumed development of its uranium enrichment programme, ostensibly for its civilian nuclear energy programme, as it is entitled to do under the terms of the NPT. Iran remains under investigation by the International Atomic Energy Agency, who at the time of writing have presented no evidence of any speculated nuclear weapons programme.

Convention on Biological Diversity

"The convention on biological diversity" was adopted at the Earth Summit in Rio de Janeiro (UN 1992). Its main goals are the conservation of biodiversity, the sustainable use of its components and fair and equitable sharing of benefits arising from genetic resources. It is often seen as the key document for sustainable development. It was opened for signature on

5 June 1992 and entered into force on 29 December 1993. The erosion of biodiversity, however, has been increasingly observed. In sum, the objectives of the Convention are not being advanced in the slightest.

Other international platforms

Other international platforms have been created to advance human security by identifying joint actions for conserving the environment. These include the Conference on the Human Environment (1972) in Stockholm, the World Commission on Environment and Development (1982) in Nairobi, and the Conference on Environment and Development (1992) in Rio de Janeiro. Great strides were made in relation to human security with the UN Charter in 1945 (UN 1945) and the Universal Declaration of Human Rights in 1948 (UN 1948). Since then, numerous covenants have further defined the civil, political, economic and social rights, as well as the rights of children, women, minorities and indigenous peoples. The latter involves cultural rights. UNESCO sponsored a convention on cultural diversity in October 2005 that declared that "Cultural diversity is as important for the human species as biodiversity is for all living things". This forms the edifice of the rights-based approach to development, including the right to development itself that forms a legal foundation for human security. This provides a legal and policy platform that defines human security at the individual level.

In academia and international organisations, the human security concept appeared in national security studies and Ken Booth's seminal work (Booth 1991, pp.313–326). This approach is based on the recognition that the state can at times be the greatest threat, not only to the citizens of other states, but also to its own citizens. In the policy context of multilateral governance, however, the concept emerged in the UNDP 1994 Human Development Report, in which human security was defined as the summation of seven distinct dimensions of security. Mahbub ul Haq in his seminal article, "New imperatives on human security", noted the "need to fashion a new concept of human security that is reflected in the lives of our people, not in the weapons of our country". The evolution of this concept is described by Brauch and Owen elsewhere in this volume.

In the context of measurement, Kanti Bajpai in 2000 suggested a human security index with qualitative and quantitative inputs (Bajpai 2000). The application of this index enables an identification of problem areas for each country. For the same purpose King and Murray propose a simple, rigorous and measurable definition of human security: the number of years of life spent outside a state of "generalised poverty".

Effective policy needs more than extra resources and greater political commitment: it also requires a better understanding of global and regional security trends. The first Human Security Report 2005 produced by the Human Security Centre at the University of British Columbia, presents "a comprehensive and evidence-based portrait of global security. ... It poses major challenges to conventional wisdom". To address these challenges when preparing this report, the Human Security Centre had drawn on a variety of data compiled by research institutions around the world and commissioned a major public opinion poll on popular attitudes to security in 11 countries. The Human Security Centre also commissioned a new dataset from Uppsala University's Conflict Data Programme. "The Uppsala/Human Security Centre dataset is the most comprehensive yet created on political violence around the world" (Human Security Report 2005).

Common assumptions

A common assumption of all of the approximations at forming a human security policy agenda, from whatever group or country, is that the old, well-known paradigms function less and less well. Several groups have contributed to the search from different dimensions. Four of them are now presented.

The first group consists of developmental analysts who have moved beyond the narrow national economic growth concepts of development to broader people-centred concepts such as "sustainable human development" and "human security". In the forefront of both interrelated concepts was the late Mahbub ul Haq, Special Advisor to the UNDP Administrator and Amartya Sen. In a 1993 address ul Haq stated "We cannot meet the new threats to human security through ideas and weapons of yesterday". The UNDP Human Development Report (UN 1990, 1993), which ranks countries on a variety of economic and social indicators, owes much to the contributions by Amartya Sen, among other social choice theorists, in economic measurement of poverty and inequality. Sen's contribution to development economics and social indicators is the concept of "capability", arguing that governments should be measured against the concrete capabilities of their citizens.

A second group consists of environmental analysts and activists, who emphasise the interrelations between global governance and the governance necessary to confront contemporary environmental challenges. This group identifies human insecurities that can be addressed by a human security policy framework that can bring it all together at different levels. Among these is the annual World Watch Report and work by Michael Renner (1996). They also find that the human security concern to "save our species" is a more productive call to action than "save our planet".

A third group consists of international relations analysts who have moved beyond the narrow national security concept based on territory to a broader human security concept that is people-centred. Ken Booth's work pioneers this approach. Countries like Mongolia and Japan recognise that they have no real military defence and that their only defence lies in networks of human security internally, subregionally, regionally and internationally.

Natural disaster and violent conflict prevention, mitigation, relief, recovery and reconstruction form a fourth line of human security studies. This includes the Institute for Environment and Human Security in the United Nations University that explores threats to human security arising from natural and human-induced hazards. The Institute spearheads research, capacity building and policy-relevant advisory activities relating to the broad interdisciplinary field of "risk and vulnerability" that are the consequence of complex – both acute and latent – environmental hazards. The Institute supports policy-makers and decision-makers with authoritative research and information.

The sixth group constitutes the integrationists like UNESCO, which has created platforms to advance integration in each region of the world as well as through high-level meetings of human security experts.

Japan and Canada have both adopted the concept of human security as part of their foreign policy, but not as national policy (Axworthy 1997, 2004). Canada's conflict-focused reformulation of human security sets aside poverty reduction goals, but defends this narrow interpretation "because we believe this is where the concept of human security has the greatest value added – where it complements existing international agendas already focused on promoting national security, human rights and human development" (Department of Foreign Affairs and International Trade of Canada 2002). Norway focuses on the freedom from fear aspects of human security and identifies a core agenda of preventive action, small arms and light weapons control and peace operations (Lodgaard 2001). Japan maintains a much broader definition of human security, which "comprehensively covers all the menaces that threaten human survival, daily life and dignity . . . and strengthens efforts to confront these threats". Japan does not prioritise freedom from fear over freedom from want, but holds them as dual objectives of human security. Japan's human security emphasis has found leadership in the highest levels of government in both development-related and peace-related activities. Human security has also been adopted as a basic policy framework of the Mongolian government and the Royal Government of Thailand has formed a Ministry of Social Development and Human Security. The Human Security Network (HSN) (Austria, Canada, Chile, Costa Rica, Greece, Ireland, Jordan, Mali, Norway, Slovenia, South Africa, Switzerland, Thailand) is formed by countries from all regions of the world and is discussed by Krause in this volume.

Another international forum, Friends of Human Security (FHS), is an unofficial, open-ended forum based in New York. The purpose of the FHS is to provide an informal forum for UN member states as well as relevant international organisations to discuss the concept of human security from different angles in order to seek a common understanding of human security and explore collaborative efforts for mainstreaming it in UN activities. Japan chaired the first FHS meeting in October 2006, represented by Yukio Takaso, Ambassador Extraordinary and Plenipotentiary of the Permanent Mission of Japan to the UN, one of the principal architects of human security theory and practice in Japan and the world. The second and third meetings were held in April and November 2007, respectively, co-chaired by Mexico. This group assures that human security as a policy framework as well as human security issues are considered in the agenda of different UN fora and entities.

An integrated, holistic human security policy framework analysis has the following advantages, compared with traditional policy frameworks:

- It strengthens policy, reduces risks and enhances opportunities across all policy spheres and at all levels from the species to the individual level.
- It allows for systematic comparisons by establishing an integrated prioritisation of human security policy across all policy spheres and potentially at different policy levels.
- It facilitates resource allocation through comprehensive analysis and prioritisation across all policy spheres and at different policy levels.
- It creates the possibility of integrated policy actions at different levels and in different spheres in the operational, as well as the planning, stages.
- It permits greater sensitivities to trade-offs between policy priorities.
- It focuses attention on how much to invest in low-risk policy contingencies that would have catastrophic consequences.
- It advances human security through establishing a network of interconnected formal and institutional networks to bring together key decision-makers.
- It reaffirms that "one size fits all" policies do not work and that the human security framework requires case-based analysis that includes policy, institutional and cultural dimensions.

A conceptual framework for policy-making

A conceptual framework employed in the policy framework is based on policy areas, which are analytical categories for grouping similar or highly inter-related threats. The threats are the factors that threaten species survival, individual life, and species and individual realisation. Proactive policies are actions to prevent or mitigate a threat. Reactive policies are actions that respond to a threat in the immediate, intermediate or long term. Vulnerabilities are the degree of exposure to a threat, taking into account the level of risk and the degree of probable or actual effectiveness of proactive and reactive policies. The potential consequences are the outcomes and impacts of a threat in different probable scenarios. A low probability of risk does not mean that a risk is small. One of the most difficult dilemmas in policy analysis is how much to invest in proactive and reactive policies in relation to very low risk threats whose potential consequences would be catastrophic.

The integrated, holistic human security policy framework can be applied equally to all levels. Policy areas and sub-areas of this framework must be identified in their cultural, historical and institutional context, as well as in relation to other ongoing policies. All policies are related to other policies. No policy stands alone. The framework of a new policy is iterative, in that relevant ongoing policies need to be factored into the analysis. The methodology for the application of the human security policy framework is culturally and historically based action research. The highest level of human security action research posits the species *Homo sapiens sapiens* as the unit of analysis and action. The end objective is to reinforce the factors that contribute to the equilibrium that maintains human existence and life on Earth and to discontinue human activities that strengthen tendencies leading to mass extinctions, including our own.

Notes

Core ideas of this chapter were presented in interventions at the UNESCO High Level Meeting on Human Security held at UNESCO in Paris, France (2–5 December 2005).

The uncertain future of human security in the UN

Taylor Owen

Introduction

The Westphalian contract between the state and its citizens has proved insufficient to fully protect citizens from the wide range of threats that vast numbers of people currently face. People are vulnerable to a far wider range of harms than those that threaten state integrity, and states are too often either unwilling or unable to adequately protect their citizens. This failure has led many to advocate a shift in security thinking and policy from a focus on the state to the individual. One concept, human security, makes the individual itself the referent of security. This chapter focuses on the discursive and policy debates surrounding this shift as articulated in the United Nations (UN) system.

The concept of human security has permeated virtually all aspects of the post-Cold War discourse on international peace and security. Whether through development studies, international relations theory, models of global governance, sustainable development policy or practices of military intervention, the notion that humans, rather than states, should be at the centre of security policy has entered, if not been entirely accepted, in contemporary scholarship and policy. Central in this discourse is the UN. The UN has in many ways served as an incubator for the concept of human security, pushing the referential shift at both the macro institutional level and in its

branches, and incorporating it into many aspects of its evolving post-Cold War mandate.

However, while it was widely used by UN branch organisations throughout the 1990s and the early twenty-first century, the concept of human security has yet to gain mainstream acceptance in either the field of international relations, or the international security policy-making discourse. This is in part due to the sheer dominance of the traditional security paradigm – any change will necessarily be slow but, as I argue, it is also due to a failure of proponents of human security to clearly articulate what human security is, and what mechanisms must be used to mitigate a new generation of security threats. This is particularly true in the UN system. The version of the concept introduced in the 1994 United Nations Development Programme (UNDP) Development Report raised interest, but failed to find a solid and workable place in the UN system. By the time of Kofi Annan's 2005 Secretary-General Report on UN reform, the term had all but dropped from the principal UN agenda (Annan 2005). In addition, the UN has not produced a universally accepted definition, and while some states, such as Canada and Norway have embraced the concept, there is considerable reluctance by many UN member states, including major Security Council powers as well as many developing nations, to endorse what some see as a challenge to the sovereign rights of states.

Taylor Owen is a doctoral candidate and Trudeau Scholar at the University of Oxford. He was a Post-Graduate Fellow in the Genocide Studies Programme at Yale University, has received a MA from the University of British Columbia and has worked at the International Peace Research Institute, the Liu Institute for Global Issues and the International Development Research Centre. His work is on the concept and operationalisation of human security and EU, Canadian and US foreign policy. Email: taylor.owen@jesus.ox.ac.uk

My intentions in this overview chapter are threefold. First, I document the post-Cold War history of the UN's use of human security using 12 major reports released over the past 15 years. Rather than grouping all uses of the concept into particular camps based on their perspective on human security, I attempt to articulate a linear, as opposed to dichotomous, map of human security's conceptual evolution within the UN.

Second, I outline what I believe are three challenges facing the concept of human security within the UN system: the ambiguity surrounding the concept and practice of development and of human security, the lack of clarity between human rights and human security and the potential conceptual overstretch of the UN's use of human security.

Third, I explore two alternative ways of conceptualising human security in order to address these three concerns. I first review what I believe to be the most sophisticated articulation of the narrow, or violence-based, definition of human security – Neil MacFarlane and Yuen Foong Khong's definition of human security as freedom from organised physical violence. I then present an alternative, in the form of the threshold-based definition of human security, and show how this conceptualisation helps to identify security threats as well as demonstrate how it can be used to counter the three concerns emerging from the UN analysis.

The UN has been at the centre of the debate over human security since its first substantive articulation in 1994. More than any other institution or state, it uniquely embodies the mechanisms necessary to operationalise this shift in the theory and practice of security. An assessment of the state of human security in the UN system therefore serves as a useful and necessary barometer of the concept at large.

Evolution of human security in the UN

In order to get a sense of the evolution of the concept of human security in the UN system, I first outline the use of the concept, as well as other broad security conceptualisations, in a series of major UN reports that have used the term. The overview addresses the following documents:

1992	Boutros Boutros-Ghali's *Agenda for peace*
1993	UNDP Human Development Report: *People's participation*
1994	UNDP Human Development Report: *New dimensions of human security*
1995	UN *The report of the world social summit for social development*
1995	Commission on Global Governance *Our global neighbourhood*
1997	UNHCR *State of the world's refugees: a humanitarian agenda*
1999	Kofi Annan *On the protection of civilians in armed conflict*. Report of the Secretary-General to the Security Council
2000	Kofi Annan *We the peoples*
2001	Commission on Human Security – *Human security now*
2004	Kofi Annan. *A more secure world: our shared responsibility*. Report of the Secretary General's High-level Panel on threats, challenges and change.
2005	Kofi Annan. *In larger freedom – towards security, development and human rights for all*
2005	UN World Summit *Outcome document*

The first major indication of where the UN fitted into the shifting post-Cold War security realignment came in Boutros Boutros-Ghali's 1992 report: *An agenda for peace* (Boutros-Ghali 1992). This report, followed by the more action oriented 1995 *Supplement to the Agenda for Peace*, (Boutros-Ghali 1995), is a good example of the UN grappling with the role they will play in the new security environment. While the term "human security" is not used in the report, this document represents the first important shift towards a much broader protection mandate for the UN.

The report was written in a period of significant re-assessment in the UN system. The largest ever environmental conference, the UN Conference on Environment and Development, had just been held in Rio de Janeiro, and the Second World Conference on Human Rights was about to take place. Both addressed individual protection in a very different light than at any time during the Cold War, and both put the UN at the centre of this quickly evolving global reconfiguration of security concepts.

Ostensibly to analyse and recommend "ways of strengthening and making more efficient ... the capacity of the UN for preventive diplomacy, for peacemaking and for peace-keeping", the *Agenda for peace* was a reaction to the removal of the ideological barrier to UN intervention that existed during the Cold War. In the early 1990s it became clear that the world remained rife with civil conflict. These conflicts required complex peace operations bringing together a much wider range of actors, including international organisations, non-governmental and regional organisations, states and the private sector. As Oliver Richmond states, "such coordinated action implies that there is a common, perhaps even universal, basis for such action" (Richmond 1991, p.42). *The Agenda for peace* consequently included with major sections covering preventative diplomacy, peacemaking and peacekeeping.

The concept of security articulated in this report, however, goes considerably further in its threat inclusion. The report states that the "new dimension of security" must include: "unchecked population growth, crushing debt burdens, barriers to trade, drugs and the growing disparity between rich and poor. Poverty, disease, famine, oppression" (Boutros-Ghali 1992, p.3). The report goes on to say that "a porous ozone shield could pose a greater threat to an exposed population than a hostile army. Drought and disease can decimate no less mercilessly than the weapons of war" (Boutros-Ghali 1992, p.3).

While articulate in much of its prognosis, the report struggles with some of the main operational challenges of the broadened security agenda. There is no clear articulation of the legitimacy of the use of force for humanitarian purposes, nor on the practical implications of the shift in sovereignty at the centre of the new security environment. These would become major themes of the discourse over the next 15 years.

While the 1994 UNDP *New dimensions of human security* report is cited as the first major UN articulation of human security, the conceptual shift to the protection of people, rather than states, was first made in the 1993 UNDP *Human development report – people's participation*. The report makes two claims that relate specifically to human security. The first is that people, more than ever, want to participate in

their destiny and that human development depends on this freedom to do so (UNDP 1993). The 1993 UNDP report also argues that this requires a re-conceptualisation of many of the core principles of international relations, including security:

Many old concepts must now be radically revised. Security should be reinterpreted as security for people, not security for land. . . . The concept of security must change – from an exclusive stress on national security to a much greater stress on people's security, from security through armaments, to security through human development, from territorial security to food, employment and environmental security (UNDP 1993, p.3).

Similar to other statements in the early 1990s, the report links this shift to new articulations of global governance and cooperation, focused on the UN. However, the articulation of this agenda for international change, based on the concept of human security, is left to Chapter 2 of the 1994 report. This report defined the general characteristics of what human security should be and how it could bring together the emerging, but in many ways disparate, post-Cold War UN themes. Second, it proposed means of framing threats to human security through freedom from fear and freedom from want, combined with threat categories. More than just bringing together themes, however, the concept of human security expressed here incorporated the actual activities that the UN was already undertaking: famine relief through the World Food Programme, development through the UNDP, cultural preservation through UNESCO; peacekeeping through the Department of Peacekeeping Operations, emergency assistance through United Nations Office for the Coordination of Humanitarian Affairs, and so on.

The 1994 UNDP report was also the first real attempt at providing a definition of human security. The authors did so using three different methods to categorise threats. The first was temporal. Human security means security from both long-term and short-term vulnerabilities. The second was a broad category that has become the basis for much of the human security debate: freedom from fear and freedom from want (UNDP 1994, p.24). The third and most important category was compartmentalising the potential threats to human security. The report proposed seven human security components: economic, food, health, environmental, personal, community and political security (UNDP 1994, pp.22–25). This categorisation set the "boundaries of the tent" very broadly, clearly separating itself from past security re-conceptualisations as well as forcing future definitions of human security to justify their narrowing from this very broad starting point.

What is most striking about the UNDP articulation of this concept is that it originated from policy-makers, rather than academics or analysts. Officials in the UN were seeking to capture the peace dividend that they saw emerging from the end of the Cold War and human security was quite pragmatically seen as a way of securing financial, logistical and political resources. "Right from the start", Krause writes, "the idea of human security was a practical one with clear strategic goals" (Krause 2004, p.44).

The 1995 *Report of the world social summit for social development* clearly articulated a people-centred view of international peace and security (UN 1995, p.5). What they add to this, however, is a focus on the interrelationship between violent threats and broader development-oriented vulnerabilities: "In turn, social development and social justice cannot be attained in the absence of peace and security or in the absence of respect for all human rights and fundamental freedoms" (UN 1995, p.5).

While the report includes a very wide range of harms in its discussion of prioritising social development in the UN system, it does acknowledge that some conditions may require particular attention, including chronic hunger, illicit drug problems, organised crime, corruption,armed conflicts, terrorism, incitement to racial, ethnic, religious and other hatreds and endemic, communicable and chronic diseases (UN, 1995, p.5). While the report does not label these "security threats" *per se*, it is clearly implying, as did the UNDP *Human development report* the previous year, that these threats must be considered within the framework of international peace and security (MacFarlane and Khong 2005, pp.149–150).

The 1995 report, *Our global neighbourhood* (Commission on Global Governance 1995) went a step further, by both identifying human security as an emerging conceptual framework and by addressing the issues of sovereignty and intervention.

The Commission called for a much-expanded UN, in both scope and power. While many of its recommendations fell on deaf ears at the time, others have regularly re-emerged as necessary elements of UN reform (such as global taxation, a standing UN army, and a new Court of Criminal Justice).

In defining relevant threats, however, the report specifically identifies the concept of human security and states that the right to "a secure life" means much more than freedom from the threat of war. The Commission's view of human security is firmly rooted in the discourse on sustainable development, and it sees the UN as the global authority responsible for protecting the global environment, and the security of individuals, to prevent conflict and war and to maintain the integrity of the planet's life-support systems (Lamb 1996, p.6). This report is a clear endorsement of a broad conception of human security.

The 1997 *State of the world's refugees* report uses the concept of human security to serve three purposes. It starts by making a clear effort to place the issue of internally displaced persons (IPDs) and forced displacement within the security, rather than development, discourse. By highlighting the issue as a consequence and tool of war, and linking it to the most egregious of war acts in many of the most troubling conflicts of the 1990s, the report makes a clear case for considering forced displacement as a narrow, or violence-based, human security threat.

Second, the report argues that IDPs present a particularly difficult situation in relief work, because the sovereign rights of their state take precedence over their own rights. As Sadako Ogata notes: "the international system of protection created for refugees at the end of the Second World War extended only to those who crossed borders" (Brookings Institution and Centre for Global Development, 2003) while "Historical experience has demonstrated that authoritarian and exploitative states are prone to treat their citizens as political and economic pawns" (UN High Commission for Refugees [UNCHR] 1997, p.3). Nevertheless, when the structure of the state disappears entirely, as was the case in Somalia, people are equally at risk. This theme would be taken up explicitly in the ICISS report. The difficult balance between these two extremes – a state being both the cause and cure for insecurity – has led many to argue that the UNHCR should shift away from legal asylum and towards a human security perspective on forced displacement within, or across, borders (Adelman 2001; Schmeidl 2002).

Third, the report argues that refugee and IDP movements are often an indicator of a region or group's wider state of insecurity. People do not leave their homes and communities unless they are faced with a serious threat (UNCHR 1997, p.2).

In 1999, at the request of the Security Council, the Secretary-General submitted a report on the multi-dimensional threats to civilians caught in war. While it is not as significant as some of the reports reviewed here, The Report of the Secretary-General to the Security Council *On the protection of civilians in armed conflict* does represent the first clear indication of a shift towards a narrow conceptualisation of human security in the UN system in general, but more importantly, in the Secretary-General's thinking.

The report lists quite specific recommendations on how the Security Council could address the plight of civilians, rather than nations, in war. It suggests that, in recognition of its duty to maintain peace and security, the Security Council must address the a range of threats including attacks against civilians, forced displacement, specific problems faced by children and by women, denial of humanitarian assistance and the continued use of anti-personnel landmines and the humanitarian impact of sanctions (Annan 1999, pp.2–4). In so far as it relates to the Security Council, this is a clear endorsement of the narrow, violence-based conceptualisation of human security. This shift is particularly important considering the nature of the Secretary-General's 2000 report to the Millennium Summit, *We the peoples*, that would follow the next year (Annan 2000).

At the heart of this report is the theme of people as the referent of international peace and security. It explicitly references the first article of the Charter as its mandate to urge wide-ranging UN action. In light of the human security discourse, however, the report makes a very interesting distinction between the two competing paradigms, with chapters on freedom from want and freedom from fear.

The freedom from want chapter highlights a wide range of development-oriented harms, many of which would be included in the Millennium Development Goals later in the year. While there is a focus on the most serious broad threats, such as extreme poverty and HIV/AIDS, they are often included in the same breath as a call for those in the developing world to be granted access to digital technology, debt relief and trade access, which are not threats, but mitigating mechanisms for potentially negative conditions. Notably, the term human security is not used to describe any of the threats in the freedom from want chapter.

The concept of human security, however, is used repeatedly in the freedom from fear chapter to describe what, as in the 1999 report, is a narrow security agenda. The chapter notes the changing nature of conflict and links both its causes and consequences to a broader range of threats. Alleviating human insecurity, however, is attached solely to "the protection of communities and individuals from internal violence" (Annan 2000, p.43). Areas prioritised include preventing deadly conflict, protecting vulnerable groups, strengthening peace operations, and addressing the dilemmas of intervention. Also central to this chapter is the idea that human security is linked to conflict prevention and peace operations, not development.

The Secretary-General's 2000 report is the first main example of the concept of human security having lost its way in the UN. It propagates a misguided dichotomy between broad and narrow security (Owen 2004) even using the fear and want terminology of the 1994 UNDP Human Development Report, and then goes on to attribute the concept of human security to "narrow" threats. This example of the policy consequence of conceptual ambiguity became particularly clear with the formation of the Commission on Human Security (CHS).

In 2001, as a response to UN Secretary-General's call for a world "free of want" and "free of fear". Under the leadership of Sadako Ogata and Amartya Sen, the CHS was asked: "to promote public understanding, engagement and support of human security and its underlying imperatives; to develop the concept of human security as an operational tool for policy

formulation and implementation; and to propose a specific programme of action to address
critical and pervasive threats to human security"
(Chourou 2005, p.16).

The resulting and much anticipated report,
Human security now, provides a detailed and
well-researched articulation of a conception of
human security that is very much rooted in the
discourse and theory of international development. However, whereas development is focused
on achieving equitable growth and sustainability, the report argues that human security goes
further to address the "conditions that menace
survival, the continuation of daily life and the
dignity of human beings" (Chourou 2005, p.19).
This conceptualisation also has a strong focus
on the protection of freedom, (Sen, 1999) and
places significant value on personal empowerment (Brookings Institution 2003).

The CHS definition of human security is
"to protect the vital core of all human lives in
ways that enhance human freedoms and human
fulfilment" (UN 2003, p.4). This articulation
had evolved considerably from earlier drafts
(Alkire 2002) and several aspects of it require
elaboration. First, the concept of the "vital
core" occupies a central place. This vital core is a
"set of elementary rights and freedoms people
enjoy. What people consider to be "vital" – what
they consider to be "of the essence of life" and
"crucially important" *varies across individuals
and societies*" (Ogata and Sen 2003). This
focuses human security not just on the individual, but on a specific aspect of individual
survival. To me this is far too broad an
interpretation of what the vital core entails.
Second, the definition found in the report
highlights both the critical (severe) and pervasive
(widespread) nature of the threats that should be
included under the rubric of human security.

The report goes to significant lengths to
stress that human security is a complementary,
rather than competing, paradigm to national
security. They are symbiotic in four ways:
human security's concern is the individual and
the community not the state, menaces to
people's security include threats and conditions
that have not always been classified as threats to
state security, the range of actors is expanded
beyond the state alone, and achieving human
security includes not just protecting people but
empowering them to fend for themselves (CHS

2003). While this is reasonable, it remains to be
seen whether this will convince the most
recalcitrant of states that human security,
particularly as articulated in this report, poses
little threat to their sovereign power.

While one commentator has characterised
the report as a document written "by idealists
and for idealists," (Brookings Institution 2003)
it does contain a significant pragmatic policy
prescription. Although the CHS lists 10 tasks
that should be undertaken to advance human
security, outside the framework of the Millennium Development Goals there is no mechanism
for assessing the progress of these tasks.

Perhaps the most valuable contribution of
Human security now has been the enthusiastic
endorsement it has received from several important donor nations and the action that this in
turn has generated. For example, the Japanese
government has all but adopted the CHS
definition as its guiding framework. Amongst
many other initiatives, Japan established the UN
Trust Fund for Human Security with $200
million of support for promoting human security-based development initiatives.

There has been much critique of the overly
broad nature of the Commission's definition of
human security. While this will be addressed in
the following section, one way to test its
relevance is to look briefly at the next major
UN document on international peace and
security – the report of the Secretary-General's
report to the High-level Panel on threats,
challenges and change: *A more secure world:
our shared responsibility.*

Similar to the Commission on Global
Governance and the CHS, the High-level Panel
on threats, challenges and change was established, at least in part, in response to a new
position taken in a major speech by the Secretary
General. This was Kofi Annan's "Fork in the
road" speech to the General Assembly in the
wake of the bombing of the UN headquarters in
Baghdad (Annan 2003). Following the speech, in
which he suggested the UN faced a decisive
moment in its ability to provide collective security
for member states, Kofi Annan asked the High-
level Panel to "assess current threats to international peace and security; to evaluate how our
existing policies and institutions have done in
addressing those threats; and to make recommendations for strengthening the United Nations

so that it can provide collective security for all" (Annan 2004, p.4.)

As the *Human security now* report had only recently been released, and as one of its principal authors, Sodako Ogata, was also on the High-level Panel, it would have been a significant endorsement for the Panel's report *More secure world: our shared responsibility* to use their definition. Instead of embracing the concept of human security, however, the report focuses on what it calls a "comprehensive system of collective security". While Annan provided conceptual flexibility in his instruction to the panel, they stayed within the confines of the traditional security paradigm. In order to bring new threats, such as HIV/AIDS and global warming, into the security mandate of the UN, however, they broadened the concept of collective security but without the deepening it to the individual level. The referent of security remains the state, and security threats are therefore defined as harms that threaten its integrity. This new articulation of collective security is therefore: any event or process that leads to large-scale death or lessening of life chances and undermines states is a threat to international security (UN 2004).

Like the UNDP definition, although incorporating a much narrower range of threats, all potential threats are grouped into six clusters: economic and social threats, including poverty, infectious disease and environmental degradation, inter-state conflict, internal conflict, genocide and other large-scale atrocities, nuclear, radiological, chemical and biological weapons, terrorism, and transnational organised crime.

Again, however, the concept of comprehensive collective security only gives these threats value insofar as they threaten the state, not the individual. Human security is not mentioned anywhere in the report. This could have been the result of a number of reasons. They could have been worried that the global South feared that the concept provided a rationale for intervention, that it was too broad and unmanageable, and that implementing it would overreach the UN's capacity, and remove their responsibility from states.

In March 2005 following the UN High-level Panel report Kofi Annan released a report in advance of the heads of state meeting for the five-year review of the Millennium Development Goals (Annan 2005). *In larger freedom* makes a particularly interesting case study, because it is a culmination of Annan's evolving thinking both on what role the UN should play in the world and, more specifically, on what select aspects of the sweeping High-level Panel report he believed were achievable.

As in *We the peoples* five years earlier, *In larger freedom* divides threats to security into freedom from want and freedom from fear. However, there is little use of the term "human security", even in the violent threat section. Instead, and in many ways remarkably, the High-level Panel report's notion of comprehensive collective security is used. The Secretary-General states that he embraces the "broad vision that the [High-level panel] report articulates and its case for a more comprehensive concept of collective security" (Annan 2000, p.25). Further, "this concept can bridge the gap between divergent views of security and give us the guidance we need to face today's dilemmas" (Annan 2000).

The ensuing description of comprehensive collective security has a striking resemblance to much of human security discourse. It recognises the broad nature of vulnerability, including environmental degradation and infectious disease, the inability of states to protect their citizens, that threats are fundamentally interconnected, and that in this "interconnectedness of threats we must found a new security consensus", and that the multilateral framework must adapt to this new reality" (Annan 2000, p.26). "Dignity" is treated as a separate section. This has implications for the definitional section below. What he is describing is essentially the UNDP's broad conceptualisation of human security.

Following the 2005 heads of state meeting for which Annan's *In larger freedom* was written, a joint memorandum, the World Summit *Outcome document*, was signed by all attendees. This document was the subject of much controversy as the US delegations made several hundred last-minute revisions. While it is a much more general and, many would argue, watered-down, document than either *A more secure world: our shared responsibility* or *In larger freedom*, the memorandum is important because it demonstrates what the member states of the UN are willing to collectively articulate as threats to international peace and security, as well as the UN's mandate to counter them.

Four areas are highlighted in the World Summit *Outcome document*: development, peace and collective security, human rights and the rule of law, and strengthening the UN. Notable are the separation of development from peace and security, the use but not explanation of the "comprehensive" qualifier to the concept of collective security, the inclusion of the "responsibility to protect", and the very limited mention of human security.

The *World Summit outcome* treats development as a separate field from security, and states that that "each country must take primary responsibility for its own development and that the role of national policies and development strategies cannot be overemphasised in the achievement of sustainable development" (UN 2000, p.4).

Second, the term "comprehensive collective security" is used, but the document does not mention what specific threats may fall under its purview: Member states are far more comfortable with the Security Council identifying a very limited range of threats to international peace and security, than either the Secretary-General, or the General Assembly doing so. The difficulty in broadening the list of threats to collective security, and in shifting the referent away from the state, does demonstrate the challenge facing advocates of the UN adoption of human security.

Third, after much lobbying by the Canadian delegation, the term the "Responsibility to protect" was included as the principle that should guide UN responses to genocide, war crimes, and crimes against humanity. This places a conditionality on state sovereignty with respect to the adequate protection of their citizens and represents a tangible shift away from the state as the sole unit of international peace and security in the UN.

Finally, the concept of human security is mentioned, and it is suggested that a debate on its proper definition should be held in the General Assembly.

Human security and the UN – three problems

Three themes emerge from the discourse on human security within the UN: the confusion between human security and development, the overlap between human security and human rights, and conceptual overstretch. Together,

these problems help to explain the reluctance of the Secretary-General and many UN member states to fully endorse the concept. If the UN is to adapt to most contemporary vulnerabilities it must be capable of operating outside the state as a unit of analysis. This means not only broadening the scope of threats that can threaten states, as suggested by the concept of comprehensive collective security, but also deepening the referent of security to groups and individuals. Consequently, for human security to be more fully streamlined into the UN system, these three areas of ambiguity must be addressed. This section will discuss these concerns, and the next will offer new ways of conceptualising human security in order to overcome these problems.

Development and human security

The principal ambiguity found in almost all UN treatments of human security is a lack of clear differentiation between human development and human security. Both in theory and in practice, the two are often used interchangeably, resulting in significant confusion regarding the value added offered by the human security discourse.

Possibly the biggest culprit is the CHS, which takes a decisively development-oriented approach to human security. The Commissioners state so many similarities between the two that it becomes difficult to grasp the differences. The CHS report argues that, human security "fruitfully supplements the expansionist perspective of human development by directly paying attention to what are sometimes called 'downside risks'". The concept of downside risks, is still tied the concept to the success, or lack thereof, of international development.

The 1994 *New dimensions of human security* report separates the two by arguing that, while development is about widening choices, security means that these choices can be exercised freely and safely (UNDP 1994). The report continues by describing the links between the two, and in so doing, loses some of this clarity: "Failed or limited human development leads to a backlog of human deprivation – poverty, hunger, disease or persisting disparities between ethnic communities or between regions [that] can lead to violence" (UNDP 1994).

Another attempt at distinguishing the concepts comes from Sabine Alkire, who was one of the principal authors of the CHS *report*. Alkire outlines four similarities and three differences between development and human security: both are people centred, multisectoral and multi-dimensional, both have long-term views on human fulfilment and both deal directly with chronic poverty (Alkire 2002). While the first two of these points seem correct, the latter two are questionable. The timeframe for human security depends very much on which concep-tualisation is used (whether on short-term emergencies or on a much longer term approach), and the connection with poverty is hardly a major confluence.

However, the differences between human security and human development provided by Alkire are quite useful. The first is the strictly delimited nature of human security. Its goal is limited to providing vital capabilities to all persons equally while human development includes concerns that are not basic (Alkire 2002). Human security looks directly at the threat outcomes, such as violence or economic downturns while development looks at the engendering process. Human development is more concerned with long-term institution building, whereas human security addresses emergency relief. The focus on emergencies is tremendously important, and will be ad-dressed below. However, the problem with all of these articulations is that they often contra-dict one another, depending on what concep-tualisation of human security is being used. If it is a very narrow, violence-based definition, then there is little overlap between the two but if a broad definition such as that of the CHS is used, then the conceptual ambiguity is more problematic.

Human rights and human security

The second problem is the relationship between human rights and human security. Because both concepts refer to the individual, their theories and mechanisms are often used interchangeably. This creates further ambiguity as to what human security is actually adding to the UN discourse. To address this challenge, it is valuable to look briefly at a series of academic distinctions between human rights and human security.

Greg Oberleitner argues that human rights provide a conceptual and normative framework for human security. Human rights violations often cause insecurity, and human rights institu-tions help to prevent human insecurity. Human security brings human rights closer to the debates about security, conflict-prevention and post-conflict peace-building. Finally, human security allows for a better explanation of the consequences of human rights violations by non-state actors (Oberleitner, 2002).

Sadoko Ogata builds on this idea of human security as a means of empowering human rights, both practically and conceptually. Con-ceptually, human security "gives equal impor-tance to civil and political, as well as to economic, cultural, and social rights, and thereby addresses the violations in a much more integrated and comprehensive way" (Brookings Institution 2003). Sabine Alkire makes a similar point. Human rights advocacy "is a coherent under-taking precisely because any rights violation *obliges* others to act" (Alkire 2002). Human security on the other hand, invokes a reciprocal duty, where primary responsibility for acting falls on the state, but if it is dysfunctional, then international organisations must step in, not just to pressure the state to respect human rights, but to replace the state's duty to protect. Thus, argues Alkire, "to some extent human rights provides a more basic framework of universal obligations; human security refers quite point-edly to a certain cross-section of such obliga-tions (Alkire 2002).

Finally, Oberleitner asks three questions regarding the relationships between human rights and human security that together provide useful guidance. First, is human security a human right itself? The answer, based on Article 3 of the Universal Declaration of Human Rights, is an unequivocal yes. Second, he asks whether human rights should be seen as the core, or normative foundation, for human security. Human rights, he argues, are part of human security. As basic needs have been reformulated and reframed as human rights issues, then if one takes the universality of human rights seriously, issues such as food, shelter, health and education must be seen as components of both rights and security. Basic needs in this sense are a precondition to human rights (Shue 1980). I would argue, however, that basic needs are one component of human security, which is a precondition for human rights.

Third, he asks what the relation is between human security and human rights in terms of mutual enrichment as well as potential mutual dilution of the respective concepts. The answer is threefold. As human rights are the "basis for a life in dignity, well-being and security", they "can provide a useful framework for the promotion of human security". There is a mutually benefiting relation between the two with respect to conflict – human rights violations are often the cause of conflict and, in turn, respect for human rights can help to prevent violence; and human rights foster the harmonious relations that can only benefit individual security. While these relations between the two are useful, a better base understanding of the two concepts is needed. Without this, correlative analysis of any kind, let alone empirical, would be non-substantive.

While these academic attempts at differentiation are helpful, if the distinction between human rights and human security is not explicitly made both in the definition of human security and in its use in the UN system, then the utility of both concepts is diluted. In addition, as the concept of human rights has a far more significant legal and normative history, the responsibility lies on proponents of human security to clearly define the difference between the two – something they have yet to do convincingly.

Conceptual overstretch

The third consistent problem with the use of human security in the UN system is what MacFarlane and Khong label "conceptual overstretch". The tendency to include every possible threat to the individual in various UN conceptualisations of human security has had a negative effect. This leads to false priorities and hopes, causal confusion and securitisation and military remedies. While aspects of their critique are problematic, as I will discuss later, they do provide a useful overview of the inherent risk in any broad conceptualisation of human security. If all issues are prioritised as threats to human security label, "What is not a security issue," MacFarlane and Khong ask, "And how does one prioritise among these dimensions?" (2003, p.237).

The second pitfall occurs when both development conditions and violent threats are

grouped together as threats to human security, so that identifying the causes of both becomes difficult. This dynamic is, of course, particularly poignant when looking at the relationship between conflict and development. Finally, by associating security so closely with military and defence infrastructures, securitisation may lead to militaristic remedies to problems best dealt with in other ways. The US use of the military to counter the problem of drug exportation in Columbia is a good example of this phenomenon. Further, as Krause and Williams (1996) argue: "Making the environment a national security issue may subvert the goal that proponents of this change seek to achieve.... placing [environmental issues] on the security agenda means subverting them within the concepts and institutions of state security (that is, military responses against a particular 'target').

Organised violence versus the threshold conceptualisation

If clearly and appropriately articulated, the concept of human security can uniquely capture the evolving nature, challenges and purpose of the post-Cold War UN system. However, the concept can remain true to its principles of shifting the referent of security to the individual in two possible ways: through the organised violence definition, and through the threshold-based conceptualisation.

Human security as organised violence

The most recent articulation of the narrow conceptualisation of human security by MacFarlane and Khong is of most relevance to this analysis. "Is there a way", they ask, "to mitigate the pitfalls [of human security] while retaining some of the more promising features of the concept?" (UN 2003, p.244). To do this, they argue that a definition must meet two challenges. It must achieve conceptual clarity by remaining true to its reference to the individual and it must analytically delineate and justify which threats are included and which are not (UN 2003).

The vertical and horizontal movement of the referents of security is similar to what both Rothschild and Paris see as the multi-directional extensions of security (Roland 2002, pp.87–102; Rothschild 2002, pp. 53–90). First, security can be extended vertically from the state up to the international system or down to the community, group or individual. Second, security can be extended horizontally to include a broader range of issues than simply those that threaten the integrity of the state. MacFarlane and Khong agree with the former but have concerns with the latter. Their organised violence articulation of human security, therefore, seeks to deepen security to focus on the individual, but to limit the broadening to a manageable list of threats.

The organised violence conceptualisation aims to limit the horizontal extension of legitimate human security threats to those that are physical and based on violence. This is not a new idea. However, MacFarlane and Khong build on these earlier narrow definitions by adding the source of the violence, a perpetrator. What makes violence particularly potent, they argue, is that it is organised. Targeting the perpetrator adds conceptual clarity and "analytic order" to what is potentially an unmanageable concept (UN 2003, p.246).

Using this definition, the threat to individuals has to be violent and has to come from other organised individuals. Therefore, a tsunami would not count as a threat to human security, but an Al Qaeda attack would. Also included would be genocide, internal, terrorist attacks, ethnic cleansing and torture. While MacFarlane and Khong state that environmental threats and disease are important, they argue that it is a mistake to treat them as security issues. They clearly believe that these "most deadly" threats are perpetrated by leaders of organised groups.

The problem, however, is that in order to gain conceptual clarity MacFarlane and Khong are forced to somewhat arbitrarily limit threat inclusion to one source, and in so doing they shut out most preventable threats to individuals from the mandate of security studies and policy. Communicable disease alone killed over 18 million people in 2000. Omitting these deaths from the security debate is a significant deviation from the original UNDP rationale for the concept and doing so for the sake of operational efficiency comes at a real cost.

Indeed, to argue that threats to the integrity of the individual can only come in the form of violence perpetrated in an organised fashion, and that all other threats to the lives of individuals should be addressed using different conceptual and operational frameworks, provides neither conceptual nor practical clarity. The former simply leaves out a wide range of harms that do in fact threaten the integrity of the individual, and the latter simply does not count the vast range of harms people face.

The question, therefore, is: can a definition be both conceptually accurate, in that it represents all major threats to the individual, and analytically coherent? Is there an alternative to narrowing the concept so far that only physical violent threats are included as threats to the individual? There must be a way to bring the vast number of preventable deaths from non-violent causes, into the human security rubric without making the term conceptually meaningless and practically unfeasible. Such an alternative will now be discussed.

The human security threshold

If the concept of human security is going to survive in the UN system it needs a definition that is both conceptually accurate and analytically coherent. If this cannot be accomplished, then the broad conceptualisation of human security will have to be abandoned and a narrow violence-based articulation, such as MacFarlane and Khong's, adopted to salvage at least one component of the concept the vertical shift to the individual.

To do this, I argue that the concept should be viewed as a threshold, surpassing which any threat in any location could become a security threat. Not all issues in all places would have to be addressed; only those that become severe enough to warrant the security label. What is needed is a dynamic conceptualisation that allows the space, scale and time frame of security to drive threat inclusion. Only when threat inclusion is defined by an objective assessment of what threatens individuals, rather than a subjective list (broad or narrow), will it be able to truly assist the UN system in identifying and acting against global insecurity.

First, human security must recognise that there is no difference between a death from a flood, a communicable disease, or a war: all preventable harms could potentially become threats to human security. However, people can be harmed by a vast array of threats and varying harms require dramatically different policy responses. The definition must be selective, without limiting any harms that affect large numbers of people. This aspect of the hybrid definition is derived from the Commission on Human Security: "Human security is the protection of the vital core of all human lives from critical and pervasive threats". The advantage of this wording is that it remains true to the broad nature of human security, while separating it from more general concepts of human well-being and development. Making the referent object "all human lives" puts the focus on the individual, while also indicating a universalism in its mandate.

As the highest level of human insecurity is likely to occur in the developing world, this is particularly important. Reference to "critical" attaches urgency to the concept and "pervasive" attaches scale. Threats must therefore be urgent and large-scale. The "vital core" can mean many things, and here it includes only survival. Threats to the vital core must therefore seriously threaten lives, not just well-being.

As there are an unlimited number of possible threats, only the most serious, those that take or seriously threaten lives, are included in this definition. The definition sets the parameters, and lets the conditions on the ground determine what is and is not included. Out of an infinite list of possible threats, some will surpass a threshold and become human security concerns, while others will be dealt with through existing mechanisms. This threshold echoes the contrast with human development highlighted in the 1994 UNDP report and a similar crisis-based approach is articulated by Thakur and the United Nations University (Thakur 1997).

The second part of the definition addresses the issue of conceptual clarity – a definition must be able to separate and categorise all possible threats for meaningful analytic study. Categories are therefore established under which all human security threats are ordered. These categories are not threats themselves, but rather are conceptual groupings, providing a degree of disciplinary alignment to what is an overarching concept. Therefore, human security is the

protection of the vital core of all human lives from critical and pervasive … environmental, economic, food, health, personal and political threats.

Human security thresholds and the three UN problems

For any definition of human security to be of use to the UN system, it must be able to address the three concerns raised above. It must be able to clearly differentiate itself from the concepts of development and human rights. If this definition seeks to challenge the narrow, violence-based definition, then it must also address the three pitfalls of conceptual overstretch outlined by MacFarlane and Khong and discussed above.

First, there is a clear need in the UN system to distinguish between the development and human security. They simply cannot be conflated. Using the threshold conceptualisation the distinction between the two is the point at which a development issue crosses the threshold of severity and becomes a threat to human security. Determining this line entails a subjective decision, but in any country or region, the development concerns that fundamentally threaten the lives of large numbers of people are, for experts, relatively easy to identify. For example, in some countries in Africa, HIV/AIDS is such a large-scale and imminently destructive menace that it must be tackled with all the resources and prescience afforded to a security concern. In other countries, HIV/AIDS may not be as significant a problem and traditional development mechanisms may be more appropriate.

In short, not all development concerns should be labelled threats to human security. Under a threshold definition, issues such as education, for example, would most likely not be considered threats to human security. Certain environmental, health, economic and human rights abuses would, however, in some cases cross the threshold and become human security threats. Human security is therefore a precondition for human development, but not vice versa.

Second, human rights and human security are very different concepts. While rights signify the basic legal entitlements of individuals, security involves personal safety. Rights generally depict conditions to which all people are entitled; security addresses their very survival.

Finally, a right is a claim against someone or something. Security, on the other hand, is a condition, or state, of someone or something.

As outlined in the threshold definition, using the term "security" has certain requirements. Security carries a level of urgency that should only be used to address imminent disasters. Certainly, some human rights abuses would qualify as human security threats, but not all. Mass human rights abuses against a particular group of society are also a threat to human security. Suppression of religious freedom, while a concern, would not in most cases qualify as a human security threat.

The Universal Declaration of Human Rights, for example, lists many conditions that, while certainly harmful, do not surpass the threshold of severity to be treated as security threats rather than criminal, political or legal issues (UN 1948). What is most important is the recognition that protection from the abuse of human rights is one component of ensuring human security. Individuals also need protection from poverty, disasters, conflict and disease. Put another way, protection from gross violations of human rights is a necessary, but not sufficient, condition of human security.

The legal system, whether national or international, is the appropriate mechanism for addressing most human rights abuses, and international environmental organisations and treaties are the appropriate institutions to deal with most environmental problems. Some, however, surpass the threshold and become human security concerns. When they do, we must have both a monitoring system that can identify them and a security infrastructure that can effectively mitigate the threat. As Oberleitner states well, "human security is thus a broader concept, comprising fundamental rights as well as basic capabilities and absolute needs ... Human rights are part of human security" (Oberleitner 2002, p.14).

Finally, the threshold conceptualisation can also help us address the three potential pitfalls of conceptual overstretch outlined by MacFarlane and Khong and discussed above. By limiting threat inclusion by severity it avoids the potential false priorities and hopes of making all "bad things" human security issues. This threshold is, of course, to a certain degree subjective, although it can be informed by a wide

range of data. But it is worth remembering that national security threat identification is also subjective. A state decides what constitutes a threat to its integrity.

Second, regarding causal and analytic confusion, I am not convinced that the relationship between conflict and underdevelopment is either dichotomous, or necessarily sequential. Complex issues are often fundamentally interconnected. Isolating the very worst, as the threshold conceptualisation does, allows for the modelling of just those very worst conditions. This is a different exercise from simply modelling violence in all cases, regardless of threat level. It may be that there are certain underlying attributes found in all cases of human insecurity, whatever the cause, violent or not. We would not know this by only isolating violent threats as dependent variables. This simply suggests that there is value in studying multiple threats as outcomes of various models of insecurity. I see no reason why other threats should not be singled out as dependent variables. On a qualitative level, by bringing the wide range of human security issues together we are able to better facilitate the very type of interdisciplinary analysis needed in order both to understand the various threat types, and to decipher the complex relations between them. The study of violence is an important exercise; however, it is incapable, on its own, of capturing all meaningful (critical and pervasive) threats to individuals. It therefore should be treated as one of many potential causes of human insecurity – and studied as such.

Third, securitisation does not necessarily mean militarisation. It is exactly the association between security and the military that human security was first instigated to oppose. To many, the peace dividend was seen as a means of reallocating resources to non-militaristic, but still deadly, threats. Further, by deepening human security but not broadening it, as the organised physical violence definition does, are we not simply propagating this association? While all violence is not militarised, the policy prescriptions for most violence-related threats falling under the "organised violence" definition (small arms, gang violence, landmines, etc) are generally based in the security sector. By both deepening *and* broadening the concept of security to include any threat that surpasses the security threshold, no matter what the cause of origin, the threshold conceptualisation necessarily forces non-military, or non-traditional security sector, response mechanisms into the discourse and practice of international peace and security.

Conclusions

The relationship between the UN and the concept of human security is a complex one. The organisation has responded to the widely felt inadequacies of the traditional security paradigm by naming and defining a fairly broad version of the concept in 1994. However, if the concept fails to take root within the welcoming environment of the UN system, what hope does it have in other venues fixated on the national security paradigm? Understanding the state and future of human security within the UN is therefore critical for proponents of the concept.

Overall, while the idea that security should be broadened to include a wider range of threats is present at all levels of the UN system, member states should still be viewed as reluctant to adopt a concept that so explicitly challenges the traditional security mandate. This is in part due to the failure of human security proponents to clearly define the concept. In particular, three principal ambiguities are of significant concern.

There has simply not been a clear enough articulation of the difference between human development and human security by proponents of human security and there has been almost no attempt in the UN system to articulate the differences between human security and human rights. Had the early UNDP and CHS reports provided a clear and workable definition, then the concept would have stood a far better chance of being used in the three major reports on the changing UN conception of security to follow. The third problem is the conceptual overstretch of the term leading to the three potential pitfalls discussed by MacFarlane and Khong.

In addressing address these concerns, MacFarlane and Khong have proposed the adoption of a narrow, violence-based definition. While pragmatically they may be correct, they deviate too far from the core principle for human security – to match the theory and practice of

security to the realities of contemporary vulnerability.

A compromise can potentially be found in a threshold-based conceptualisation of human security. This definition limits the threat inclusion of threats by their severity rather than their cause. Only the worst threats in any region, whatever their cause, are prioritised with the label of security. All others remain within their constituent disciplines and institutional structures. The conditions that are seen as crossing the threshold of human insecurity, whereby they become something qualitatively different – an emergency requiring the prescience and resources attributed to the security label. This may or may not affect the response mechanisms used to address the security threat – which could range from development tools, to humanitarian relief, to Security Council-authorised interventions.

This articulation recognises that human security is a precondition for human development, but not vice versa. People must first be secure from critical and pervasive threats to their vital core, whatever the cause, before the mechanisms of development can take root. The two are not synonymous. Second, using the threshold definition, the protection from gross abuses to human rights – those that cross the threshold – should be seen as a necessary but not sufficient condition for human security. Human rights abuses are only one category of potential human security threats. As with environmental and health issues, most human rights abuses should be dealt with outside the security mandate but in some locations, come simply must be prioritised with the security label. Third, a threshold approach deals with conceptual overstretch by not allowing all threats in all places under every potential category of security to be prioritised. While there are infinite possible harms that could threaten an individual, there are only so many that critically and pervasively threaten the vital core of large numbers of people.

The UN is in the ideal position to promote and instigate the threshold conceptualisation of human security. As nearly all major reports since 1992 have recognised, the UN system must adapt to the evolving nature of insecurity. The balance of power between states is incapable of ensuring international peace and security, and in the Security Council's Chapter VII, power, even if broadened to include "comprehensive collective security", still refers solely to threats to the state. Despite this limitation the UN remains uniquely suited to tackling human insecurity. However, to do so, phenomena that may not threaten the integrity of the state, but that do kill large numbers of people, must be considered within the security mandate that the UN was established to protect.

Some argue that a universal definition is not necessary and that human security can in fact thrive on its ambiguity, interpreted in different ways for various purposes in various contexts. Human security, like sustainable and human development, would be understood via the successes and failures of its varying advocates. I am sceptical of this *laissez-faire* approach. The very purpose of human security is to re-evaluate current security theory and policy and to rally the world's thinkers, leaders and resources to the issues actually affecting people, rather than to those the military establishment deems important. Advocates of the narrow conceptualisation are aware of this reality and think we should cut our losses and focus on one harm: organised violence. This will, however, do little to protect the millions who will die from non-violent, yet preventable, human security threats.

The conception and apparatus of security should not be used to address each and every possible threat to the individual. It should, however, be capable of protecting people from the most serious harms they face. Until we can ensure that people are safe not just from inter-state war and nuclear proliferation, but also from preventable disease, starvation, civil conflict and terrorism, then we have failed in the primary objective of security – to protect.

References

ABDO, N. 1999. "Gender and politics under the Palestinian authority", *Journal of Palestine Studies*, 18 (2), 38–51.

ABDUS SABUR, A. K. M. 2003. "Evolving a theoretical perspective of human security: the south Asian context", *In:* Chari, P. R. and Gupta, S., eds. *Human security in south Asia*. New Delhi: Social Science Press, 35–51.

ABRAMOVITZ, J. N. 2001. *Unnatural disasters*. Worldwatch Paper 158. Washington: Worldwatch Institute.

ACHARYA, A. 2004. "A holistic paradigm", *International Security*, 35 (3), 355–356.

ADELMAN, H. 2001. "From refugees to forced migration: the UNHCR and human security", *International Migration Review*, 35 (1), 7–32.

AGNES, F. 1988. "Violence in the family: wife beating", *In:* Ghadially, R., ed. *Women in Indian society: a reader*. New Delhi: Sage, xxx–xxx.

AL FA'OURY, N. 2004. "Gender and democratization in the Arab region: an Islamic perspective", *In:* Odaibat, A. and Bahou, R. F., eds. *Gender and democratization in the Arab Region*. Jordan: Regional Human Security Center.

ALCAMO, J. AND ENDEJAN, M. 2002. "The security diagram – an approach to quantifying global environmental security", *In:* Petzold-Bradley, E., Carius, A. and Vinvze, A., eds. *Responding to environmental conflicts – implications for theory and practice*. NATO ASI Series. Dordrecht: Kluwer Academic Publishers, 133–147.

ALKIRE, S. 2002. *A conceptual framework for human security*. Working paper 2. Harvard: CRISE available online at: http://www.humansecurity-chs.org/activities/outreach/frame.pdf [accessed 20 April 2008].

ALSTON, P., ed. 2005. *Non-state actors and human rights*. Oxford: Oxford University Press.

AMIN, A. 2004. "Multi-ethnicity and the idea of Europe", *Theory Culture & Society*, 21 (2), 1–24.

ANDERSON-GOLD, S. 2005. "Kantian fundamentals of contemporary cosmopolitanism", *Deutsche Zeitschrift Fur Philosophie*, 53 (1), 97–109.

ANNAN, K. 1999. *On the protection of civilians in armed conflict*. Report of the Secretary-General to the Security Council, UN Doc. S/1999/957. UN.

ANNAN, K. 2000. "We the people" Report of the Secretary General. New York: UN available online at http://www.un.org/millennium/sg/report/full.htm [accessed 20 April 2008].

ANNAN, K. 2000. *Millenium report: we the peoples, the role of the United Nations in the 21st century*. New York: UN available online at http://www.un.org/ millennium/sg/report/.

ANNAN, K. 2001. "Foreword", *In:* McRae, R. and Hubert, D., eds. *Human security and the new diplomacy. Protecting people, promoting peace*. Montreal, Kingston and London: Queen's University Press, xix.

ANNAN, K. 2003. *Interim report of the secretary general on the prevention of armed conflict* available online at http://www.un.org/webcast/ga/58/statements/sg2eng030923.htm [accessed 20 April 2008].

ANNAN, K. 2004. *A more secure world: our shared responsibility*. Report of the High-level panel on threats, challenges and change UN Doc. A/59/565 of 2 December 2004.

ANNAN, K. 2005. *In larger freedom: towards development, security and human rights for all*. Report of the Secretary General. New York: UN. Available at: http://www.un.org/largerfreedom/contents.htm [accessed 20 April 2008].

ARBOUR, L. 2005. The right to life and the responsibility to protect in the modern world. Lecture, Boston, 9 December available online at http://www.unhchr.ch/huricane/huricane.nsf/0/5342933E5E9D7D67C12570D6002F7D57?opendocument [accessed 20 April 2008].

ARCHIBUGI, D. 2004. "Cosmopolitan democracy and its critics: a review", *European Journal of International Relations*, 10 (3), 437–473.

ASHWOTH, G., ed. 1995. *A diplomacy of the oppressed: new direction in international feminism*. London: Zed Books.

ATWOOD, D., GLATZ, A-K. AND MUGGAH, M. 2006. *Demanding attention: addressing the dynamics of small arms demand*. Occasional Paper 18. Geneva: Small Arms Survey.

AXWORTHY, L. 1997. "Canada and human security: the need for leadership", *International Journal*, 52 (2), 183–196. Available online at http://www.dfait-maeci.ge.ca/canada-magazine/wv_se1/selt3-e.htm

AXWORTHY, L. 2004. "A new scientific and policy lens", *International Security*, 35 (3), 348–349.

BANNON, I. AND COLLIER, P. 2003. *Natural resources and violent conflict. options and actions*. Washington, DC: World Bank.

BARNETT, J. 2001. *The meaning of environmental security ecological politics and policy in the new security era*. London and New York: Zed.

BASUT, A. 1995. *The challenge of local feminisms*. Boulder, CO: Westview Press.

BECK, U. 2002. "The cosmopolitan society and its enemies", *Theory Culture & Society*, 19 (1–2), 17–44.

BELLAMY, R. AND CASTIGLIONE, D. 1997. "Building the union: the nature of sovereignty in the political architecture of Europe", *Law and Philosophy*, 16 (4), 421–445.

BELLAMY, R. AND WARLEIGH, A. 1998. "From an ethics of integration to an ethics of participation: citizenship and the future of the European Union", *Millennium-Journal of International Studies*, 27 (3), 447–468.

BENEDEK, W. 2004. "Human security and prevention of terrorism", *In:* Benedek, W. and Yotopoulos-Marangopoulos, A., ed. *Anti-terrorist measures and human rights*. Leiden and Boston, MA: Martinus Nijhoff, 171–184.

BENEDEK, W. 2005. "Der Beitrag des Konzeptes der menschlichen Sicherheit zur Friedenssicherung", *In:* Dicke, K., Hobe, S., Meyn, K-U., Peters, A., Riedel, E., Schütz, H-J. and Tietje, C., eds. *Weltinnenrecht*. Delbrück: Liber Amicorum Jost and Berlin: Duncker & Humblot, 25–36.

BENEDEK, W. 2006a. "Human rights and human security: challenges and prospects", *In:* Yotopoulos-Marangopoulos, A. ed. *L'Etat actuel des droits de l'homme dans le monde – Défis et perspectives*. Paris: Ed. A. Pedone, 95–109.

BENEDEK, W. AND NIKOLOVA-KREES, M., eds. 2003. *Understanding human rights. Manual on human rights education*. Vienna: Manz.

BENEDEK, W., NIKOLOVA, M. AND OBERLEITNER, G. 2002. *Human security and human rights education. pilot study*. Graz: European Training and Research Center for Human Rights and Democracy.

BLACK, R. 1998. *Refugees, environment and development*. Harlow: Longman.

BLACK, R. 2001. *Environmental refugees: myth or reality?* New issues in refugee research, working paper No. 34. Falmer: University of Sussex.

BOGARDI, J. 2004. "Hazards, risks and vulnerabilities in a changing environment: the unexpected onslaught on human security?", *Global Environmental Change*, 14 (4), 361–365.

BOGARDI, J. AND BRAUCH, H. G. 2005. "Global environmental change: a challenge for human security – defining and conceptualising the environmental dimension of human security", *In:* Rechkemmer, A., ed. *UNEO – towards an international environment organization – approaches to a sustainable reform of global environmental governance*. Baden-Baden: Nomos, 85–109.

BOHLE, H.-G. 2002. "Land degradation and human security", *In:* Plate, E., ed. *Environment and human security, contributions to a workshop in Bonn*: 3/1:3/6.

BOOTH, K. 1991. *New thinking about strategy and international security*. London: HarperCollins.

BOSERUP, E. 1970. *Woman's role in economic development*. New York: St Martin's Press.

BOSOLD, D. AND WERTHES, S. 2005. "Human security in practice: Canadian and Japanese experiences", *International Politics and Society*, 1, 84–101.

BOUTROS-GHALI, B. 1992. *Agenda for peace*. A/47/-S/24111 available online at http://www.globalpolicy.org/reform/initiatives/ghali/1992/0617peace.htm [accessed 20 April 2008].

BOUTROS-GHALI, B. 1992. *An agenda for peace: preventive diplomacy, peacemaking and peace-keeping*. Report of the Secretary-General pursuant to the statement adopted by the Summit Meeting of the Security Council. New York: United Nations, 1992.

BOUTRUCHE, T. 2000. "Le statut de l'eau en droit international humanitaire", *Revue internationale de la Croix Rouge*, 840, 887–916.

BRAUCH, H. G. 1997a. "Migration von Nordafrika nach Europa", *Spektrum der Wissenschaft*, August, 56–61.

BRAUCH, H. G. 1997b. "La emigración como desafío para las relaciones internacionales y como área de cooperación Norte-Sur en el proceso de Barcelona", *In:* Marquina, A., ed. *Flujos Migratorios Norteafricanos Hacia La Union Europea. Asociacion y Diplomacia Preventiva*. Madrid: Agencia Española de Cooperación Internacional, 17–90.

BRAUCH, H. G. 1997c. "Causas a largo plazo de las migraciones desde el Norte de Africa a los países de la Unión Europea. El Factor Demográfico", *In:* Marquina, A., ed. *Flujos Migratorios Norteafricanos Hacia La Union Europea. Asociacion y Diplomacia Preventiva*. Madrid: Agencia Española de Cooperación Internacional, 241–333.

BRAUCH, H. G. 1998. "Long-term security challenges to the survival of the North African countries: population growth, urbanisation, soil erosion, water scarcity, food production deficits and impact of climate change (2000–2050)", *In:* Marquina, A., ed. *Perceptions mutuelles dans la Méditerranée – Unité et Diversité. Mutual perceptions in the Mediterranean – unity and diversity*. Collection Strademed 6. Madrid: UNISCI and Marcial Pons and Paris: Publisud, 35–123.

BRAUCH, H. G. 2000–2001. "Environmental degradation as root causes of migration: desertification and climate change. Long-term causes of migration from North Africa to Europe", *In:* Friedrich, P. and Jutila, S., eds. *Policies of regional competition. Schriften zur öffentlichen Verwaltung und öffentlichen Wirtschaft*. vol. 161, Baden-Baden: Nomos, 102–138.

BRAUCH, H. G. 2002a. "Climate change, environmental stress and conflict – AFES-PRESS report for the Federal Ministry for the Environment, Nature Conservation and Nuclear Safety", *In:* Federal Ministry for the Environment, Nature Conservation and Nuclear Safety ed *Climate change and* conflict. *Can climate change impacts increase conflict potentials? What is the relevance of this issue for the international process on climate change?* Berlin: Federal Ministry for the Environment, Nature Conservation and Nuclear Safety, 9–112.

BRAUCH, H. G. 2002b. "A survival pact for the Mediterranean: linking 'virtual water' and 'virtual sun'", *In:* Pachauri, R. K. and Vasudeva, G., eds. *Johannesburg and beyond. Towards concrete action. Proceedings of the Colloquium held on 24 March 2002 in New York, U.S.A.* New Delhi: Teri, 151–190.

BRAUCH, H. G. 2003a. "Security and environment linkages in the Mediterranean: Three phases of research on human and environmental security and peace", *In:* Brauch, H. G., Liotta, P. H., Marquina, A. R.s. P. and Selim, M. E-S., eds. *Security and environment in the Mediterranean. Conceptualising security and environmental conflicts.* Berlin, Heidelberg: Springer, 35–143.

BRAUCH, H. G. 2003b. "Towards a fourth phase of research on human and environmental security and peace: conceptual conclusions", *In:* Brauch, H. G., Liotta, P. H., Marquina, A. R.s. P. and Selim, M. E-S., eds. *Security and environment in the Mediterranean. Conceptualising security and environmental conflicts.* Berlin and Heidelberg: Springer, 919–954.

BRAUCH, H. G. 2003c. "Natural disasters in the Mediterranean (1900–2001): from disaster response to disaster preparedness", *In:* Brauch, H. G., Liotta, P. H., Marquina, A. R.s. P. and Selim, M. E-S., eds. *Security and environment in the Mediterranean. Conceptualising security and environmental conflicts.* Berlin and Heidelberg: Springer, 863–906.

BRAUCH, H. G. 2003d. "Urbanization and natural disasters in the Mediterranean – population growth and climate change in the 21st century", *In:* Kreimer, A., Arnold, M. and Carlin, A., eds. *The future of disaster risk: building safer cities.* Conference papers. Washington, DC: World Bank.

BRAUCH, H. G. 2004. "From a Hobbesian security to a Grotian survival dilemma", 40th Anniversary Conference of IPRA, Peace and Conflict in a Time of Globalisation, Sopron, Hungary, 5–9 July available online at http://www.afes-press.de/pdf/Sopron_Survival%20Dilemma.pdf [accessed 20 April 2008].

BRAUCH, H. G. 2005a. *Environment and human security, Intersections,* 2/2005. Bonn: UNU-EHS.

BRAUCH, H. G. 2005b. "Environmental threats, challenges, vulnerabilities and risks", *In: Encyclopedia of life support systems.* Paris: UNESCO; Oxford: Encyclopedia of life support systems.

BRAUCH, H. G. 2006a. Four pillars of human security: freedom from fear, freedom from want, freedom from hazards impacts and freedom to live in dignity". Presentation at the invitation of El Colegio de Tlaxcala, Tlaxcala, State Tlaxcala, México, 8 March available online at http://www.afes-press.de/pdf/Brauch_%20Tlaxcala.pdf.

BRAUCH, H. G. 2006b. "Towards a fourth pillar of human security: "freedom from hazard impacts", Addressing global environmental change, environmental stress and natural hazards". Presentation at the International Symposium On Building and Synergizing Partnership for Global Human Security and Development, Bangkok, Thailand, 30–31 May available online at http://www.afes-press.de/pdf/Brauch_Bangkok_HSN.pdf.

BRAUCH, H. G., GRIN, J., MESJASZ, C., KRUMMENACHER, P., BEHERA, N., CHOUROU, B., OSWALD SPRING, U. AND KAMERI-MBOTE, P., eds. 2007. *Facing global environmental change: environmental, human, energy, food, health and water security concepts.* Berlin, Heidelberg, New York: Springer-Verlag.

BRENNAN, T. 2001. "Cosmo-theory (cosmopolitanism)", *South Atlantic Quarterly,* 100 (3), 659–691.

BROCK, L. 1991. "Peace through parks. The environment on the peace research agenda", *Journal of Peace Research,* 28 (4), 407–423.

BROOKINGS INSTITUTE 2003. *The policy implication of the Commission on Human Security report,* Transcript of a Brookings Institution and Center for Global Development Event, 13. Available online at http://www.brookings.edu/events/2003/0612global-economics.aspx [accessed 23 July 2008].

BROWN, C. 2002. "The construction of a 'realistic utopia': John Rawls and international political theory", *Review of International Studies,* 28 (1), 5–21.

BROWN, G. W. 2005. "State sovereignty, federation and Kantian cosmopolitanism", *European Journal of International Relations,* 11 (4), 495–522.

BURGESS, J. P. AND OWEN, T. 2004. "Special section – what is 'human security'?", *Security Dialogue,* 35 (3), 345–372.

BURGESS, J. P. AND OWEN, T. 2004. "Special section – what is 'human security'?", *Security Dialogue,* 35 (3), 345–372.

BUZAN, B., WÆVER, O. AND WILDE, J. D. 1998. *Security. A new framework for analysis.* Boulder, CO and London: Lynne Rienner.

BUZAN, B., KELSTRUP, M., LEMAITRE, P., TOMER, E. AND WÆVER, O. 1990. *The European security order recast – scenarios for the post-Cold War era.* London: Pinter.

CASTLES, S. 2002. "Environmental change and forced migration", Refugee Studies Centre University of Oxford available online at http://www3.hants.gov.uk/forced_migration.pdf [accessed 20 April 2008].

CHAESUNG, C. 2003. Human security and women's insecurity: debating women's security in East Asia. Paper read to the *International Conference on Human Security in East Asia,* Seoul, 16–17 June.

CHÉLINI, J. AND RICHÉ, P. 1991. *L'aube du Moyen Age : naissance de la chrétienté occidentale : la vie religieuse des laïcs dans l'Europe carolingienne (750–900).* Paris: Picard.

CHOUROU, B. 2005. *Promoting human security: ethical, normative and educational frameworks in the Arab states.* Paris: UNESCO.

COCHRAN, M. 1996. "The liberal ironist, ethics and international relations theory", *Millennium-Journal of International Studies,* 25 (1), 29–52.

COCK, J. 1998. "Light weapons proliferation: the link between security and development", *In:* Cock, J. and Mckenzie, P., eds. *From defence to development: redirecting military resources in South Africa* available online at http://www.idrc.ca/en/ev-68073-201-1-DO_TOPIC.html [accessed 20 April 2008].

COLLIER, P. 2000. *Economic causes of civil conflict and their implications for policy.* Washington, DC: World Bank.

COLLIER, P., ELLIOTT, V. L., HEGRE, H., HOEFFLER, A., REYNAL_QUEROL, M. AND SAMBANIS, N. 2003. *Breaking the conflict trap: civil war and development policy.* Washington, DC: World Bank.

COMMISSION ON GLOBAL GOVERNANCE 1995. *Our global neighbourhood. Report of the commission on global governance.* Oxford: Oxford University Press.

COMMISSION ON HUMAN SECURITY 2001. *Human security now.* New York: United Nations Publications.

COMMISSION ON HUMAN SECURITY 2003. *Human security now.* New York: CHS available online at http://www.humansecurity-chs.org/finalreport/index.html.

CONCA, K. AND DABELKO, G. D., eds. 2002. *Environmental peacemaking.*

Baltimore, NJ: Johns Hopkins University Press and Woodrow Wilson Center Press.

COOK, E. 1993. *The generation of feminism: outsiders or insiders.* Upper Saddle River, NJ: Prentice Hall.

DALBY, S. 2002a. "Security and ecology in the age of globalization", *Woodrow Wilson International Center for Scholars ed. Environmental change & security project report,* 8 (Summer), 95–108.

DALBY, S. 2002b. *Environmental security.* Minneapolis: University of Minnesota Press.

DALLMAYR, F. 2003. "Cosmopolitanism – moral and political", *Political Theory,* 31 (3), 421–442.

DEDRING, J. 2008. "Human security and the UN Security Council", *In:* Brauch, H. G., Oswald Spring, U., Mesjasz, C., Grin, J., Dunay, P., Behera, N. C., Chourou, B., Kameri-Mbote, P. and Liotta, P. H., eds. *Globalization and environmental challenges: reconceptualizing security in the 21st century.* Hexagon Series on Human and Environmental Security and Peace, 3. Berlin, Heidelberg and New York: Springer-Verlag, 605–620.

DFID, EU, UNDP, AND WORLD BANK 2002. *Linking poverty reduction and environmental management: policy challenges and opportunities a contribution to the world summit on sustainable development processes.* London: DFID.

DIEHL, P. F. AND GLEDITSCH, N. P., eds 2001. *Environmental conflict* Boulder, CO and Oxford: Westview.

DOBSON, A. 2006. "Thick cosmopolitanism", *Political Studies,* 54 (1), 165–184.

DOWER, N. 1998. *World ethics: the new agenda.* Edinburgh: Edinburgh University Press.

DUBY, G. AND DALARUN, J. 1996. *Féodalité.* Paris: Gallimard.

DYER, H. C. 2002. "Theoretical aspects of environmental security", *In:* Petzold-Bradley, E., Carius, A.

and Vinvze, A., eds. *Responding to environmental conflicts – implications for theory and practice.* NATO ASI Series. Dordrecht: Kluwer Academic, 67–81.

EL-HINNAWI, E. 1985. *Environmental refugees.* Nairobi: UNEP.

FAO (FOOD AND AGRICULTURE ORGANIZATION) 1996. *The state of food insecurity in the world.* Rome: FAO available online at http://www.fao.org/wfs/index_en.htm [accessed 20 April 2008].

FAO 2005. *The state of food insecurity in the world 2005.* Rome: FAO available online at http://www.fao.org/docrep/008/a0200e/a0200e00.htm.

FARR, V. A. 2004. "Voices from the margins: a response to security sector reform in developing and transitional countries", Berghof Research Center for Constructive Conflict Management available online at http://www.berghofhandbook.net/articles/ssr.farr.pdf.

FELDMAN, S., ed. 1992. *Unequal burden: economic crisis, persistent poverty, and women's work.* Oxford: Westview Press.

FINE, R. 2003. "Cosmopolitanism and social theory", *Filosoficky Casopis,* 51 (3), 407–429.

FINE, R. 2006. "Cosmopolitanism and violence: difficulties of judgment", *British Journal of Sociology,* 57 (1), 49–67.

FODHA, H. 2002. "Keynote address on the promotion of human security within the United Nations", *In:* UNESCO, What agenda for human security in the twenty-first century? Proceedings of the First International Meeting of Directors of Peace Research and Training Institutions available online at http://www.unesco.org/securipax/whatagenda.pdf [accessed 20 April 2008].

FOSTER, S. W. 2003. "Cosmopolitanism", *American Ethnologist,* 30 (3), 457–458.

FOUCAULT, M. 1994. "Le retour de la moral", *In:* Defert, D. and Ewald,

F., eds. *Dits et écrits*. Paris: Gallimard, 696–707.

FUENTES, C. AND ROJAS ARAVENA, F. 2005. *Promoting human security: ethical, normative and educational frameworks in Latin America and the Caribbean*. Paris: UNESCO.

GAMBLE, S., ed. 2001. *The Routledge companion to feminism and postfeminism*. London: Routledge.

GEORGE, A. 1979. "The causal nexus between cognitive beliefs and decision-making behaviour: the "operational code"", *In:* Falkowski, L., ed. *Psychological models in international politics*. Boulder, CO: Westview, 95–124.

GLEDITSCH, N. P. 2003. "Environmental conflict: Neomalthusians vs. Cornucopians", *In:* Brauch, H. G., Liotta, P. H., Marquina, A. R.s. P. and Selim, M. E.-S., eds. *Security and Environment in the Mediterranean. concep-tualising security and environmental conflicts*. Berlin and Heidelberg: Springer, 477–486.

GLEDITSCH, N. P., WALLENSTEHEN, P., ERIKSSON, M., SOLLENBERG, M. AND STRAND, H. 2002. "Armed Conflict 1946–99: a new dataset", *Journal for Peace Research*, 39 (5), 615–637.

GLEICK, P. H. 1991. "Environment and security: the clear connections", *Bulletin of the Atomic Scientists*, 47 (3), 16–21.

GLEICK, P. H. 1993a. "Water and conflict: fresh water resources and international security", *Inter-national Security*, 18 (1), 79–112.

GLEICK, P. H. 1993b. *Water in crisis: a guide to the world's fresh water resources*. New York: Oxford University Press.

GLEICK, P. H. 1993c. "Water and security", *International Security*, 18 (1), 79–112.

GLEICK, P. H. 1994. "Water, war and peace in the Middle East", *Environment*, 36 (3), 6–15.

GLEICK, P. H. 1998. *The world's water 1998–99: the biannual report on fresh water resources*.

Washington, DC and Covelo, CA: Island Press.

GLEICK, P. H. 2000. *The world's water 2000–2001*. Washington, DC: Island Press.

GLEICK, P. H. 2004. "Water conflict chronology". Pacific Institute for Studies in Development, Environment and Security available online at http://www.worldwater.org/conflictchronology.html.

GLOBAL ENVIRONMENTAL CHANGE AND HUMAN SECURITY (GECHS) 1999. GECHS Science Plan. IHDP Report No. 11 Bonn: IHDP.

GOOSE, S. D. AND SMYTH, F. 1994. "Arming genocide in Rwanda", *Foreign Affairs*, 73 (5), 86–96.

GREENWOOD, C. 1999. "Historical development and legal basis", *In:* Fleck, D., ed. *The handbook of humanitarian law in armed conflicts*. Oxford: Oxford University Press, 1–38.

GUTIERREZ, E. 1999. *Boiling point. Issues and problems in water security and sanitation*. A Water Aid Briefing paper. London: Water Aid.

HAAVISTO, P. 2003. "Environmental post-conflict assessments: a new UN tool developed by UNEP", *In:* Brauch, H. G., Liotta, P. H., Marquina, A., R.s. P. and Selim, M. E.-S., eds. *Security and environment in the Mediterranean. Conceptual-ising security and environmental conflicts*. Berlin and Heidelberg: Springer, 535–562.

HAMPSON, F. O. 2004. "A concept in need of a global policy response", *International Security*, 35 (3), 349–350.

HANNAN, C. 2004. "Gender equality and women's empowerment in the new millennium". An address to the Interfaith Institute for Women available online at http://www.un.org/womenwatch/daw/news/speech2004/CH-InterfaithInstitute-Oct2004.pdf [accessed 20 April 2008].

HAYDEN, P. 2005. *Cosmopolitan global politics*. Aldershot and Burlington, VT: Ashgate.

HERZ, J. 1950. "Idealist internationalism and the security dilemma", *World Politics*, 2 (2), 157–180.

HEWITT, K. 2002a. "Natural hazards", *In:* Munn, T., ed. *Encyclopedia of global environmental change*, vol. 3: Douglas, I. ed. *Social and economic dimensions of global environmental change*. Chichester: John Wiley, 479–493.

HEWITT, K. 2002b. "Hazards in global environment change", *In:* Munn, T., ed. *Encyclopedia of global environmental change*, vol. 5: Timmerman, P. ed. *Social and economic dimensions of global environmental change*. Chichester: John Wiley, 297–303.

HOLST, J. J. 1989. "Security and the environment: a preliminary exploration", *Bulletin of Peace Proposals*, 20 (2), 123–128.

HOLZGREFE, J. AND KEOHANE, R., eds. 2003. *Humanitarian intervention: ethical, legal and political dilemmas*. Cambridge: Cambridge University Press.

HOMER-DIXON, T. F. 1991. "On the threshold: environmental changes as causes of acute conflict", *International Security*, 16 (2), 76–116.

HOMER-DIXON, T. F. 1994. "Environmental scarcities and violent conflict: evidence from cases", *International Security*, 19 (1), 5–40.

HOMER-DIXON, T. F. 1999. *Environment, scarcity, and violence*. Princeton, NJ: Princeton University Press.

HOMER-DIXON, T. F. 2000. *The ingenuity gap*. New York and Toronto: Alfred A. Knopf.

HSN 1999. Chairman's summary, Human Security Network First Ministerial Meeting, Lysøen 20 May available online at http://www.humansecuritynetwork.org/docs/Chairman_sumM.May99-e.php.

HSN 2003. *Graz declaration on principles of human rights education and human security*. Graz, 8.10 May

2003 available online at http://www.humansecuritynetwork.org/docs/8may2003-e.php [accessed 20 April 2008].

HUMAN RIGHTS WATCH 1995. *Rearming with impunity: international support for the perpetrators of the Rwandan genocide*. Project Report A704 (1995).

HUMAN SECURITY CENTRE 2005. *The human security report 2005. War and peace in the 21ˢᵗ century*. New York: Oxford University Press.

HUTCHINGS, K. 1999b. *International political theory: rethinking ethics in a global era*. London and Thousand Oaks: Sage.

HUTCHINGS, K. AND DANNREUTHER, R. 1999. *Cosmopolitan citizenship*. Houndmills and New York: Macmillan and St Martin's Press.

IFRC 2001. *World disasters report 2001. Focus on recovery*. Bloomfield, CT: Kumarian and London: Eurospan.

IFRC 2002. *World disasters report 2002. Focus on reducing risk*. Bloomfield, CT: Kumarian and London: Eurospan.

IFRC 2005. *World disasters report 2005. Focus on information in disasters*. Bloomfield, CT: Kumarian and London: Eurospan.

INSTITUTO DEL TERCER MUNDO 2004. *Social watch report: Fear and want, obstacles to human security*. Montevideo available online at http://www.socwatch.org/en/informeImpreso/pdfs/SW-ENG-2004.pdf [accessed 20 April 2008],

INTERNATIONAL COMMISSION ON INTERVENTION AND STATE SOVEREIGNTY 2001. *The responsibility to protect* available online at http://www.iciss.ca/pdf/Commission-Report.pdf [accessed 20 April 2008].

INTERNATIONAL RESCUE COMMITTEE 2006. "The Lancet publishes IRC mortality study from DR Congo; 3.9 Million Have Died: 38,000 Die per Month" available online at http://www.theirc.org/news/page.jsp?

itemID = 27819067 [accessed 20 April 2008].

IPCC 1996a. *Climate change 1995. Impacts, adaptations and mitigation of climate change*. Contributions of Working Group II to the Second Assessment Report of the Intergovernmental Panel on Climate Change. Cambridge: Cambridge University Press.

IPCC 1996b. *Climate change 1995. Economic and social dimensions of climate change*. Contributions of Working Group III to the Second Assessment Report of the Intergovernmental Panel on Climate Change. Cambridge: Cambridge University Press.

IPCC 1998. *The regional impacts of climate change: an assessment of vulnerability*. Cambridge and New York: Cambridge University Press.

IPCC 2001a. *Climate change 2001. The scientific basis*. Cambridge and New York: Cambridge University Press.

IPCC 2001b. *Climate change 2001. Impacts, adaptation and vulnerability. mitigation*. Cambridge and New York: Cambridge University Press.

IPCC/TEAP 2005. *Safeguarding the ozone layer and the global climate sustem*. IPCC/TEAP special report Bonn, IPCC.

IRWIN, R. 2001. *Ethics and security in Canadian foreign policy*. Vancouver: UBC Press.

JACKMAN, D. AND O'BRIEN, M. 2006. *A clear step forward: attention to demand issues at the prepcom on small arms*. Geneva: Quaker UN Office.

JAD, I., JOHNSON, P. AND GIACAMAN, R. 2000. "Transit citizens", *In:* Suad, J., ed. *Gender and citizenship in the Middle East*. New York: Syracuse University Press.

KABEER, N., 2003. *Gender mainstreaming in poverty eradication and the millennium development goals A handbook for policy-makers and other stakeholders*. London:

Commonwealth Secretariat, IDRC and CIDA.

KALDOR, M. 1999. *New and old wars: organized violence in a global era*. Cambridge: Polity.

KALDOR, M. AND VASHEE, B., eds. 1997. *New wars*. London: Pinter.

KANT, I. 1991[1795]. "Zum ewigen Frieden", *In:* Werkausgabe, W., ed. *Collected works*. vol 11, Frankfurt am Main: Suhrkamp.

KASPERSON, J. X., KASPERSON, R. E. AND DOW, K. 2001. "Introduction: global environmental risk and society", *In:* Kasperson, J. X. and Kasperson, R. E., eds. *Global environmental risk*. Tokyo, New York and Paris: UN University Press, London: Earthscan, 1–48.

KASPERSON, J. X., KASPERSON, R. E., TURNER, B. L., DOW, K. AND MEYER, W. B. 1995. "Critical environmental regions: concepts, distinctions, and issues", *In:* Kasperson, J. X., Kasperson, R. E. and Turner, B. L., eds. *Regions at risk. Comparisons of threatened environments*. Tokyo, New York and Paris: UN University Press, 1–41.

KAUFMANN, E. 2000. "Liberal ethnicity: beyond liberal nationalism and minority rights", *Ethnic and Racial Studies*, 23 (6), 1086–1119.

KAUL, I. 2002. "Development cooperation of the UN system", *In:* Volger, H., ed. *A concise encyclopedia of the United Nations*. The Hague, London and New York: Kluwer Law International, 70–81.

KENNEDY, P. 2000. "Global issues and the new security agenda", *In:* Kennedy, P. and Hitchcock, W. I., eds. *From war to peace. Altered strategic landscapes in the twentieth century*. New Haven, CT and London: Yale, 231–245.

KETTEMANN, M. C. 2007. "Towards a Human Security Council?," *Human Security Journal/Révue de la Sécurité Humaine* 3 98–101 available online at http://www.peacecenter.sciences-po.fr/journal/issue3pdf/issue3_BL_Matthias-

Kettemann.pdf [accessed 20 April 2008].

KLARE, M. T. 2001. *Resource wars: the new landscape of global conflict.* New York: Henry Holt and Metropolitan Books.

KRAUSE, K. 2004. "Is human security 'more than just a good idea'?" Brief 30: Promoting security: but how and for whom? Bonn: BICC: 43–46.

KRAUSE, K. AND WILLIAMS, M. 1996. "Broadening the agenda of security studies: politics and methods", *Mershon International Studies Review*, 40 suppl. 2, 229–254.

LACROIX, J. 2002. "For a European constitutional patriotism", *Political Studies*, 50 (5), 944–958.

LAMB, H. 1996. "Our global neighbourhood, Report of the Commission on Global Governance. A summary analysis", *Eco-Logic*, January/February 4.

LATOUR, B. AND BIEZUNSKI, M. 2005. *La science en action. Introduction to La sociologie des sciences.* Paris: la Découverte.

LATOUR, B. AND GUILHOT, N. 2006. *Changer de société, refaire de la sociologie.* Paris: la Découverte.

LAVAUDEN, L. 1927a. "Les forêts du Sahara", *Revue des Eaux et Forêts*, 65 (6), 265–277.

LAVAUDEN, L. 1927b. "Les forêts du Sahara", *Revue des Eaux et Forêts*, 65 (7), 329–341.

LEE, S.-W. 2001. *Environment matters: conflict, refugee and international relations.* Seoul and Tokyo: World Human Development Institute Press.

LEE, S.-W. 2004. *Promoting human security: ethical, normative and educational frameworks in East Asia.* Paris: UNESCO.

LODGAARD, S. 2001. "Human security: concept and operationali-zation" available online at http://www.hsph.harvard.edulhpcrlevents lhsworkshopllodgaard.pdf

LONERGAN, S. 2002. "Environmental security", *In:* Munn, T., ed. *Encyclopedia of global environmental change.* vol. 5 Timmerman, P., ed. *Social and economic dimensions of global environmental change.* Chichester: John Wiley, 269–278.

LONERGAN, S. et al. 1999. *Global environmental change and human security.* IHDP Report Series No. 11. GECHS: Paris and Tokyo: Springer.

LONERGAN, S., GUSTAVSON, K. AND CARTER, B. 2000. The index of human insecurity. *AVISO* 6 available online at http://www.gechs.org/aviso/06/index.html [accessed 20 April 2008].

M'BAREK, R. 1996. "Aspects de mutation dans la societe Maroccaine: le cas de la famille et des valeurs" *Journee d'etude et de reflexion sur les petites filles "bonnes" travaillant dans les familles.* Royaume Du Maroc, Ligue Marocaine pour la Protection de l'Enfance.

MACFARLANE, N. AND KHONG, Y. F. 2005. *Human security and the UN.* Bloomington, IN: Indiana University Press, 149–150.

MACK, A. 2004. "A signifier of shared values", *International Security*, 35 (3), 366–367.

MACK, A. 2005. *Human security report 2005: War and peace in the 21st century.* New York: Oxford University Press.

MAINGUET, M. 1994. *Desertification. Natural background and human mismanagement.* 2nd edn. Berlin and Heidelberg: Springer Verlag.

MAINGUET, M. 2003. "Desertification: global degradation of drylands", *In:* Brauch, H. G., Liotta, P. H., Marquina, A. R.s. P. and Selim, M. E.-S., eds. *Security and environment in the Mediterranean. Conceptualising security and environmental conflicts.* Berlin and Heidelberg: Springer, 645–654.

MAKINDA, S. M. 2005. "Security in international society: a comment on Alex J. Bellamy and Matt

McDonald", *Australian Journal of Political Science*, 40 (2), 275–287.

MASON, A. D. AND KING 2001. *Engendering development: through gender equality in rights, resources and voice.* Washington, DC: World Bank.

MATHEWS, J. T. 1989. "Redefining security", *Foreign Affairs*, 68 (2), 162–177.

MATTHEW, R. A. 1997. "Rethinking environmental security", *In:* Gleditsch, N. P., ed. *Conflicts and the environment.* Dordrecht, Boston and London: Kluwer Academic, 71–90.

MATTHEW, R. A. 2000. "Integrating environmental factors into conventional strategy", *In:* Lowi, M. R. and Shaw, B. R., eds. *Environment and security. discourses and practices.* Houndsmills and London: Macmillan; New York: St Martin's Press, 33–48.

MEADOWS, D. H., MEADOWS, D. L. AND RANDERS, J. 1992. *Beyond the limits.* Post Mills, VT: Chelsea Green Publishing.

MEADOWS, D. H., MEADOWS, D., RANDERS, J. AND BEHRENS, W. W. III 1972. *The limits to growth: a report for the Club of Rome's project on the predicament of mankind.* New York: Universe.

MELCHIOR, J. 1999. "Democratic theory and globalization. Stimuli for discussion", *Osterreichische Zeitschrift Fur Politikwissenschaft*, 28 (2), 201–212.

MØLLER, B. 2001. "National, societal and human security: general discussion with a case study from the Balkans", *In:* UNESCO (ed.): *First international meeting of directors of peace research and training institutions. What agenda for human security in the twenty-first century.* Paris: UNESCO, 41–62.

MØLLER, B. 2002. "National, societal and human security: general discussion with a case study from the Balkans", *In:* UNESCO ed. What agenda for human security in the twenty-first century? Proceedings of the First International Meeting of

Directors of Peace Research and Training Institutions. Available online at http://www.unesco.org/securipax/whatagenda.pdf, pp. 48–49 [accessed 20 April 2008].

MØLLER, B. 2003. "National, societal and human security: discussion – a case study of the Israeli-Palestine conflict", *In:* Brauch, H. G., Liotta, P. H., Marquina, A. R. s. P. and Selim, M. E-S., eds. *Security and environment in the Mediterranean. Conceptualising security and environmental conflicts.* Berlin and Heidelberg: Springer, 277–288.

MORGENTHAU, H. J. 1948. *Politics among nations; the struggle for power and peace.* New York: A. A. Knopf.

MORGENTHAU, H. J. 1951. *In defense of the national interest; a critical examination of American foreign policy.* New York: Knopf.

MUKHOPADHYAY, S. S. AND SUDARSHAN, R. M. 2003. *Tracking gender equity under economic reforms, continuity and change in south Asia.* Ottawa: International Development Research Centre.

MUNICH RE 2006. Selected slides from talk by Peter Hoeppe: "Worldwide Natural disasters – effects and trends" available online at http://www.munichre-foundation.org/NR/rdonlyres/E7ED6B1D-2D9F-4E64–9FB3–5C8A4539AD9B/0/20051116_Hoeppe_Hohenkammer_short_WEB.pdf.

MÜNKLER, H. 2002. *Über den Krieg. Stationen der Kriegsgeschichte im Spiegel ihrer theoretischen Reflexion.* Weilerswist: Velbrück Wissenschaft.

MÜNKLER, H. 2005. *The new wars.* Cambridge: Polity.

MUNN, T., ed. 2002. *Encyclopedia of global environmental change.* 5 vols. Chichester: John Wiley.

MUSAH, A. F. AND CASTLE, R. 1998. Eastern Europe's arsenal on the loose: managing light weans flows to conflict zones. British-American Security Council (BASIC)

Occasional papers on international security issues, 26 May.

MYERS, N. 1989a. "Environment and security", *Foreign Policy,* 74, 23–41.

MYERS, N. 1989b. "Environmental security: the case of south Asia", *International Environmental Affairs,* 1 (2), 138–154.

MYERS, N. 1994. *Ultimate security. The environmental basis of political stability.* New York: W.W. Norton.

MYERS, N. 1995. *Environmental exodus. An emergent crisis in the global arena.* Washington, DC: Climate Institute.

MYERS, N. 1996. *Ultimate security. The environmental basis of political stability.* Washington, DC and Covelo, CA: Island Press.

MYERS, N. 2002. "Environmental refugees: a growing phenomenon of the 21st century", *The Philosophical Transactions of the Royal Society (Biological Sciences),* 357 (1420), 609–613.

NAGEL, T. 2006. "Cosmopolitanism: ethics in a world of strangers", *New Republic,* 234 (7), 30–33.

NAJAM, A. 2003a. "The human dimensions of environmental insecurity: some insights from south Asia." Washington, DC: Woodrow Wilson International Centre for Scholars available online at http://wwics.si.edu/topics/pubs/najam.pdf [accessed 20 April 2008].

NAJAM, A. 2003b. "Environment and security: exploring the links", *In:* Najam, A., ed. *Environment. Development and human security. perspectives from south Asia.* Lanham, New York and Oxford: University Press of America, 1–24.

NARAYAN, D. AND PETESCH, P. 2002. *Voices of the poor: from many lands.* New York: Oxford University Press.

NARAYAN, D., CHAMBERS, R., SHAH, M. K. AND PETESCH, P. 2000b. *Voices of the poor: crying out for change.* New York: Oxford University Press.

NARAYAN, D. WITH PATEL, R., SCHAFFT, K., RADEMACHER, A. AND

KOCH-SCHULTE, S. 2000a. *Voices of the poor: can anyone hear us?* New York: Oxford University Press.

NEWMAN, E. 2004. "A normatively attractive but analytically weak concept", *International Security,* 35 (3), 358–359.

NOWAK, M. 2003. *Introduction to the International human rights regime.* Leiden and Boston, MA: Martinus Nijhoff.

OBERLEITNER, G. 2002. Human security and human rights. ETC Occasional Paper Series 8 available online at http://www.etc-graz.at/cms/index.php?id = 74

OBERLEITNER, G. 2005a. "Human security: a challenge to international law?", *Global Governance,* 11, 185–203.

OBERLEITNER, G. 2005b. "Porcupines in love: the intricate convergence of human rights and human security", *European Human Rights Law Review,* 6, 588–606.

OECD 1993. *Core set of indicators for environmental performance reviews: a synthesis report by the Group on the State of the Environment* OECD. Paris: OECD.

OECD 1994. *Environmental indicators: OECD core set.* Paris: OECD.

OECD 1997. *Trends in international migration. SOPEMI 1997.* Paris: OECD.

OECD 1998. *Towards sustainable development: environmental indicators.* Paris: OECD.

OECD 1999. *OECD Environment monograph.* Paris: OECD.

OECD 2000. *Towards sustainable development – indicators to measure progress – Rome Conference.* Paris: OECD.

OECD 2001a. *Environmental indicators – towards sustainable development.* Paris: OECD.

OECD 2001b. *Key environmental indicators.* OECD. Paris: OECD.

OGATA, S. AND SEN, A. 2001. *Human security now. Commission on Human Security*. Newyork: UN.

OSWALD SPRING, U. 2001. "Sustainable development with peace building and human security", *In:* Tolba, M. K., eds. *Our fragile world. challenges and opportunities for sustainable development.* Forerunner to the *Encyclopedia of life support systems.* Oxford: EOLSS, 873–916.

OSWALD SPRING, U. 2004. Peace, environment and security: a gender perspective from the third world – IPRA 40 years after Groningen available online at http://www.afes-press.de/pdf/Hague/Oswald_Peace_Environment.pdf [accessed 20 April 2008].

OSWALD SPRING, U. AND BRAUCH, H. G. 2005. "Desertification and migration: case study on Mexico", Presentation at the Global Interactive Dialogue, UNCCD Third Session of the Committee for the Review of the Implementation of the Convention (CRIC 3), 10 May 2005, Bonn, Bundestag Conference Centre available online at http://www.afes-press.de/pdf/Oswald_Brauch_kurz.pdf

OSWALD SPRING, U. AND DE LOURDES HERNANDEZ RODRIGUEZ, M. 2005b. *El Valor del Agua: Una Vision Scioeconomica de un Conflicto Ambiental.* Tlaxcala: El Cologio de Tlaxcala.

OWEN, T. 2004. "Human security – conflict, critique and consensus: colloquium remarks and a proposal for threshold-based definition", *Security Dialogue*, 35 (3), 373–387.

PACHAURI, R. K. 2000. "Environmental security: a developing country perspective". Meeting report of the Wilson Center, Environmental Change and Security Project, Current Events, 17 October 2000 available online at http://ecsp.si.edu/archive/rk-pauchari.htm

PAPANEK, H. 1989. *Socialization for inequality. entitlements, the value of women and domestic hierarchies.* Boston, MA: Boston University.

PARIS, R. 2002. "Human security: paradigm shift or hot air", *International Security*, 26 (2), 87–102.

PARKER, O. AND BRASSETT, J. 2005. "Contingent borders, ambiguous ethics: migrants in (international) political theory", *International Studies Quarterly*, 49 (2), 233–253.

PHOCA, S. 1997. "Feminism and gender", *In:* Brooks, A., ed. *Postfeminism: feminism and cultural norms.* London: Routledge.

POGGE, T. 1992. "Cosmopolitianism and sovereignty", *Ethics*, 103, 48–73.

PORTNOV, B. A. AND HARE, A. P., eds., 1999. *Desert regions. Population. migration and environment.* Berlin: Springer.

PUIGDEFÁBREGAS, J. AND MENDIZABAL, T., eds. 1995. *Desertification and migrations – desertificacion y Migraciones. International symposium on desertification and migrations.* Madrid: Ministerio de Asuntos Exteriores and Logroño: Geoforma Ediciones.

RAMCHARAN, B.G. 2002. *Human security and human rights.* The Hague: Martinus Nijhoff.

RENNER, M. 1996. *Fighting for survival: environmental decline, social conflict and the new age of insecurity.* Washington, DC: Worldwatch Institute.

RICHMOND, O. P. 1991. "The limits of multidimensional UN peace operations", *In:* Newman, E. and Richmond, O. P., eds. *Human security and the UN.* New York: Palgrave.

ROBBINS, B. 2003. "Cosmopolitanism", *Journal of Asian Studies*, 62 (1), 192–194.

ROTHSCHILD, E. 2002. "What is security?", *Daedalus*, 124 (43), 53–90.

RUGGIE, J. G. 1998. *Constructing the world polity. Essays on international institutionalization.* London and New York: Routledge.

SCHMEIDL, S. 2002. "(Human) security dilemmas: long-term implications of the Afghan refugee crisis", *Third World Quarterly*, 23 (1), 7–29.

SCHNABEL, A. 2001. "Playing with fire: humanitarian interventions post-Kosovo", *In:* Newman, E. and Richmond, O. P., eds. *The United Nations and human security.* Houndmills: Palgrave, 137–150.

SCHOTT, M. 2009. "Human security: international discourses and local reality – case of Mali", *In:* Brauch, H. G., Grin, J., Mesjasz, C., Krummenacher, H., Chadha Behera, N., Chourou, B., Oswald Spring, U. and Kameri-Mbote, P., eds. *Facing global environmental change: environmental, human, energy, food, health and water security concepts.* Hexagon Series on Human and Environmental Security and Peace, vol. 4. Berlin, Heidelberg and New York: Springer-Verlag.

SCHWARTZ, P. AND RANDALL, D. 2003. *An abrupt climate change scenario and its implications for United States national security* available online at http://www.gbn.com/GBNDocumentDisplayServlet.srv?aid=26231&url=/UploadDocumentDisplayServlet.srv?id=28566 [accessed 20 April 2008].

SECURITY DIALOGUE 2004. passim

SEN, A. 1999. *Development as freedom.* Oxford: Oxford University Press.

SEN, A. 2000. Why human security? presentation at the International Symposium on Human Security, Tokyo. Available online at http://www.humansecurity-chs.org/doc/Sen2000html.

SHALABI, A. 1997. *Islam between truth and false allegations.* Morocco, Islamic Educational, Scientific and Cultural Organizations, ISESCO.

SHINODA, H. 2007. "Human security initiatives of Japan", *In:* Brauch, H. G., Oswald Spring, U., Grin, J., Mesjasz, C., Kameri-Mbote, P.,

Chadha Behera, N., Chourou, B. and Krummenacher, H., eds. *Facing global environmental change: environmental, human, energy, food, health and water security concepts.* Hexagon Series on Human and Environmental Security and Peace, vol. 4. Berlin, Heidelberg and New York: Springer-Verlag.

SHIVA, V. 2002. *Water wars: privatization, pollution, and profit.* Cambridge, MA: Southend Press.

SHUE, H. 1980. *Basic rights: subsistence, affluence, and U.S. foreign policy.* Princeton, NJ: Princeton University Press.

SIAKEU, G. 2000. "Peace and human security in Africa", in *What agenda for human security in the twenty first century.* Proceedings of First International Meeting of the Directors of Peace Research and Training 27 November 2000. Paris: UNESCO.

SIVARAMAKRISHNAN, K. 2005. "Cosmopolitanism", *Journal of the Royal Anthropological Institute*, 11 (3), 606–607.

SMITH, K. 1996. *Environmental hazards. Assessing risk and reducing disaster.* 3rd edn. London and New York: Routledge.

STEFFEN, W., SANDERSON, A., TYSON, P. D., JÄGER, J., MATSON, P. A., MOORE III, B., OLDFIELD, F., RICHARDSON, K., SCHELLNHUBER, H. J., TURNER II,, B. L. AND WASSON, R. J. 2004. *Global change and the earth system. A planet under pressure.* The IGBP series. Berlin, Heidelberg and New York: Springer-Verlag.

STICHICK, T. AND BRUDERLEIN, Č. 2001. *Children facing insecurity: new strategies for survival in a global era.* Harvard Program on Humanitarian Policy and Conflict Research available online at http://www.hpcr.org/pdfs/ChildrenFacingInsecurity.pdf [accessed 20 April 2008].

STYCHIN, C. F. 2000. "A stranger to its laws: sovereign bodies. global sexualities, and transnational citizens", *Journal of Law and Society*, 27 (4), 601–625.

TAKUR, R. 2004. "A political worldview", *Security Dialogue*, 35 (3), 347–348.

TELHAMI, S. 2002. "Kenneth Waltz, neorealism, and foreign policy", *Security Studies*, 11 (3), 158–170.

THAA, W. 2001. "'Lean citizenship' the fading away of the political in transnational democracy", *European Journal of International Relations*, 7 (4), 503–523.

THAKUR, R. 1997. "From national to human security", *In:* Harris, S. and Mack, A., eds. *Asia-Pacific security: the economics-politics nexus.* Sydney: Allen & Unwin, 52–80.

TIGNINO, M. 2007. "Water security in times of armed conflicts", *In:* Brauch, H. G., Grin, J., Mesjasz, C., Krummenacher, H., Chadha Behera, N., Chourou, B., Oswald Spring, U. and Kameri-Mbote, P., eds. *Facing global environmental change: environmental, human, energy, food, health and water security concepts.* Hexagon Series on Human and Environmental Security and Peace, vol. 4. Berlin, Heidelberg and New York: Springer-Verlag.

TOSET, H., PETTER, W., GLEDITSCH, N. P. AND HEGRE, H. 2000. "Shared rivers and interstate conflict", *Political Geography*, 19 (8), 971–996.

ULLMAN, R. 1983. "Redefining security", *International Security*, 8 (1), 129–153.

UN 1945. "Charter of the United Nations" available online at http://www.un.org/aboutun/charter/ [accessed 20 April 2008].

UN 1948. "Universal declaration of human rights" available online at http://www.un.org/Overview/rights.html [accessed 20 April 2008].

UN 1968. "Non-proliferation treaty" available online at http://www.state.gov/www/global/arms/treaties/npt1.html [accessed 20 April 2008].

UN 1979. "The convention on the elimination of all forms of discrimination against women" available online at http://

www.un.org/womenwatch/daw/cedaw/ Accessed 20 April 2008.

UN 1992. "The convention on biological diversity". Earth Summit, Rio de Janeiro.

UN 1995. *Report of the world social summit for social development* A/CONF.166/9 available online at http://www.un.org/documents/ga/conf166/aconf166-9.htm [accessed 20 April 2008].

UN 1997. *Kyoto protocol UN framework convention on climate change* (UNFCCC) UNEP.

UN 2000. Millennium declaration United Nations General Assembly. 55/2 of 2000 available online http://www.un.org/millennium/declaration/ares552e.pdf [accessed 20 April 2008].

UN 2001. *Report of the United Nations Conference on the illicit trade in small arms and light weapons in all its aspects*, New York, 9–20 July 2001 (A/CONF.192/15).

UN 2002. Millennium development goals (MDGs). United Nations General Assembly 55/2.

UN 2003. *United Nations Convention to combat desertification in those countries experiencing serious drought and/or desertification, particularly in Africa.* Bonn: UNCCD and Geneva: WMO.

UN 2004. *Implementation of the United Nations Millennium Declaration. Report of the Secretary-General.* UN General Assembly. New York: UN.

UN 2005. *World Summit outcome.* 15 September. Resolution adopted by the General Assembly, 24 October, Agenda items 46 and 120,4. Available online at http//www.refomtheun.org/index.php/united_nations/1433 [accessed 223 July 2008].

UN FRAMEWORK CONVENTION ON CLIMATE CHANGE (UNFCC) 1992. Framework Convention on Climate Change available online at http://unfccc.int/resource/docs/convkp/

conveng.pdf [accessed 20 April 2008].

UNDP 1990. *First Human development report* available online at http://hdr.undp.org/en/reports/global/hdr1990/ Accessed 20 April 2008.

UNDP 1993. *Human development report: people's participation.* New York: Oxford University Press.

UNDP 1994. *Human development report: new dimensions of human security* available online at http://hdr.undp.org/reports/global/1994/en.

UNDP 2004. *Reducing disaster risk: a challenge for development.* A global report UNDP Bureau for Crisis Prevention and Recovery. New York: UNDP.

UNEP 1987. *Montreal protocol on substances that deplete the ozone layer.* UNEP available online at http://www.unep.org/OZONE/pdfs/Montreal-Protocol2000.pdf [accessed 21 April 2008].

UNEP 1996. *Status of desertification and implementation of the UN plan of action to combat desertification, UNCED Part I.* Nairobi: UNEP.

UNESCO 1997. *From partial insecurity to global security* available online at http://unesdoc.unesco.org/images/0011/001106/110639e.pdf.

UNESCO 1998a. *What kind of security?* available online at http://unesdoc.unesco.org/images/0010/001096/109626eo.pdf.

UNESCO 1998b. *Proceedings, cooperative peace in southern Asia: regional symposium.* ASEAN Secretariat – Jakarta, 11–12 September 1998. Paris: UNESCO.

UNESCO 2000. *What agenda for human security in the twenty-first century?* Proceedings of the First International Meeting of Directors of Peace Research and Training Institutions available online at http://www.unesco.org/securipax/whatagenda.pdf [accessed 209 April 2008].

UNESCO 2001. *What agenda for human security in the twenty-first century?* Paris: UNESCO.

UNESCO 2002. *Proceedings of the Expert Meeting on peace, human security and conflict prevention in Latin America and the Caribbean.* UNESCO-FLACSO-Chile, Chile available online at http://www.unesco.org/securipax/flacsoeboletin.pdf [accessed 20 April 2008].

UNESCO 2003a. *Consequences for human security in Latin America, Santiago, Chile.* International Conference on Contemporary International Security available online at http://www.flacso.cl/flacso/biblos.php?code=642 [accessed 20 April 2008].

UNESCO 2003b. *Proceedings of the International Conference on "Human security in East Asia.* Seoul available online at http://unesdoc.unesco.org/images/0013/001365/136506e.pdf [accessed 20 April 2008].

UNESCO 2003c. *Human security, conflict prevention and peace.* Goucha, M. and Rojas Aravenna, F., eds. Paris: UNESCO.

UNESCO 2004a. *International conference on human security in east Asia.* Seoul. Paris: UNESCO.

UNESCO 2004b. *Promoting human security: ethical, normative and educational frameworks in East Asia.* Paris: UNESCO.

UNESCO 2004c. *Proceedings of the international conference on "human security in east Asia"* with Korean Commission on UNESCO; Ilmin International Relations Institute of Korea University: Seoul, and Paris: UNESCO.

UNESCO 2005. *Promoting human security: ethical, normative and educational frameworks in the Arab states.* Available online at http://unesdoc.unesco.org/images/0014/001405/140513E.pdf [accessed 20 April 2008].

UNESCO ed. 2001. *First international meeting of directors of peace research and training institutions. What agenda for human security in the twenty-first century.* Paris: UNESCO.

UNISDR 2004. *Living with risk. A global review of disaster reduction activities.* 2 vols. Geneva: UNISDR.

UNITED NATIONS HIGH COMMISSION FOR REFUGEES (UNHCR) 1997. *State of the world's refugees: a humanitarian agenda.* Oxford: UNHCR and Oxford University Press.

UNU 2000. *UNU strategic plan 2000 – advancing knowledge for human security and development.* Tokyo: UNU.

UNU 2002. *Advancing knowledge for human security and development – The UNU strategic plan 2002.* Tokyo: UNU.

UNU 2003. *United Nations University. Annual report 2003.* Tokyo: UNU.

UNU-EHS 2004. *Human security in a changing environment, strategic directions 2005–2008.* Bonn: UNU-EHS.

UNU-EHS 2005. *Human security in a changing environment, strategic directions 2005–2008.* Bonn: UNU-EHS.

UVIN, PETER 2004. "A field of overlaps and interactions", *Security Dialogue*, 35 (3), 352–353.

WAEVER, O. 2007. "Societal security", *In:* Brauch, H. G., Grin, J., Mesjasz, C., Dunay, P., Behera, N., Chourou, B., Oswald Spring, U. and Kameri-Mbote, P., eds. *Globalisation and environmental challenges: reconceptualising security in the 21st century.* Berlin, Heidelberg and New York: Springer-Verlag.

WÆVER, O., BUZAN, B., KELSTRUP, M. AND LEMAITRE, P. 1993. *Identity, migration, and the new security agenda in Europe.* New York: St Martin's Press.

WALKER, R. B. J. 1994. "Norms in a teacup: surveying the 'new normative approaches'", *Mershon International Studies Review*, 38, 265–270.

WALTZ, K. M. 1959. *Man, the state and war.* New York: Columbia University Press.

WATSON, R. T. 2001. *IPCC Third assessment report.* Geneva: IPPC.

WELSH, J. 2004. *Humanitarian intervention and international relations.* Oxford: Oxford University Press.

WENDT, A. 1992. "Anarchy is what states make of it: the social construction of power politics", *International Organization*, 46 (2), 391–425.

WEST, D. 2002. "Global justice: defending cosmopolitanism", *Ethics*, 112 (3), 618–621.

WESTING, A. H., ed. 1988. *Cultural norms, war and the environment. Military activities and the human environment.* Oxford: Oxford University Press.

WHEELER, N. J. 2003. *Saving strangers: humanitarian intervention in international society.* Oxford: Oxford University Press.

WHO 2002. *Consultation on health and human security.* Cairo, 15–17 April available online at http://data.unaids.org/Topics/Security/Cairo_intervention_en.doc [accessed 20 April 2008].

WILLIAMS, M A. J. AND BALLING, R. C. JR. 1996. *Interactions of desertification and climate.* London, New York and Sydney: Arnold.

WILLIAMS, M. A. J. AND BALLING, R. C. JR. 1996. *Interactions of desertification and climate.* London, New York and Sydney: Arnold.

WOLF, A. T. 1998. "Conflict and cooperation along international waterways", *Water Policy*, 1 (2), 251–265.

WOLFERS, A. 1962. "National security as an ambiguous symbol", *In:* Wolfers, A., ed. *Discord and collaboration. Essays on international politics.* Baltimore, NJ: Johns Hopkins University Press, 147–165.

WOLFRUM, R. 1994. "Chapter 1. Purposes and principles, Art. 1", *In:* Simma, B., ed. *The Charter of the United Nations. A commentary.* Oxford: Oxford University Press, 49–56.

WOODHOUSE, TOM AND OLIVER, RAMSBOTHAM 2005. "Cosmopolitan peacekeeping and the globalization of security", *International Peacekeeping*, 12 (2), 139–156.

WORLD BANK 2000. *World development report: attacking poverty* available online at http://web.worldbank.org/WBSITE/EXTERNAL/TOPICS/EXTPOVERTY/0,,content MDK:20195989~isCURL:Y~pagePK:148956~piPK:216618~theSitePK:336992,00.html Accessed 20 April 2008.

WOUTERS, P. 2005. "Water security: what role for international water law?", *In:* Dodds, F. and Pippard, T., eds. *Human and environmental security. An agenda or change.* London and Steling VA: Earthscan, 166–181.

YERGIN, D. 1977. *Shattered peace. The origins of the Cold War and the national security state.* Boston, MA: Houghton Mifflin Co.

YOFFE, S. B. AND WOLF, A. T. 1999. "Water, conflict and cooperation: geographical perspectives", *In: Cambridge Review of International Affairs*, 12 (2), 197–213.

YOFFE, S., WARD, B. AND WOLF, A. T. 2000. "The transboundary freshwater dispute database project: tools and data for evaluating international water conflict", TFFD Publications.

YOFFE, S. B., FISKE, G., GIORDANO, M., GIORDANO, M., LARSON, K., STAHL, K. AND WOLF, A. T. 2004. "Geography of international water conflict and cooperation: data sets and applications", *Water Resources Research*, 40 (5), 1–12.

INDEX

Abdo, N. 95–6
Abdus Sabur, A. K. M. 22
Abramovitz, J. N. 46
Acharya, A. 10
Action Aid International 11
Adelman, H. 117
Africa 39–40, 41, 43, 88, 89, 90, 96, 102, 124
African Human Security Initiative 11
Aga Khan Development Network 11
Agenda 21, 28
Agnes, F. 89
Alcamo, J. 43
Al Fa'oury, N. 86
Algeria 87
Alkire, S. 118, 120–1
Almería Statement 42
Alston, P. 10
Amin, A. 62
ancient Greece 53
Anderson-Gold, S. 62
Annan, Kofi 8, 22, 23, 29, 44
    A more secure world (2004) 14, 75, 114, 118–19
    High-level panel 9, 20, 73, 75, 114, 118, 119
    In larger freedom (2005) 9–10, 21, 23, 75, 113, 114, 119
    On the protection of civilians in armed conflict (1999) 17, 117
    UN's key goals 19, 20–1
    We the peoples (2000) 114, 117, 119
anti-personnel landmines (APLMs) 65, 67, 69–70, 75, 77
Aptekar, L. 46
Arab states 14, 96
Arbour, Louise 8
Archibugi, D. 62
armed groups 67
Ashworth, G. 81
Asia 43, 90, 93
    see also individual countries
Atwood, D. 72
AusAID 108
Austin, J. L. 57
Australia 87, 108
Austria 12
    and HSN 15–16, 65, 70, 111
    European Training Centre for Human Rights and Democracy 76
Axworthy, L. 8, 9, 11, 66, 73, 111

Bächler, G. 31, 45
Baghdad 118
Bajpai, K. 110
Bali Conference 109
Bamako 68, 69
Bangkok 68
Bangladesh 38, 42, 47, 87, 104
Bannon, I. 331
Barcelona European Council 29
Barnett, J. 32
Basut, A. 96
Beck, U. 62
Beckett, M. 28
Beijing Platform for Action 85
Bellamy, R. 62
Benedek, W. 7, 9, 10, 12, 13, 14, 15, 16
Bern-Zürich Group 28
best practices 16
Biezunski, M. 49
biodiversity 19
Black, R. 42
Bogardi, J. 20, 22, 23, 33
Bohle, H.-G. 27
Booth, K. 110, 111
Boserup, E. 88
Bosold, D. 8
Boutros-Ghali, B. 71, 114, 115
Boutruche, T. 44
Brassett, J. 62
Brauch, H. G. 20, 21, 22, 23, 24, 25, 27, 28, 30, 33, 34, 36, 37, 45, 47
Brazil 68
Brennan, T. 62
British Columbia, University of 11, 67, 74, 76, 110, 113
Brock, L. 30
Brookings Institution 116, 118, 121
Brown, C. 62
Brown, G. W. 62
Bruderlein, C. 68
Burgess, J. P. 8, 50
Bush Administration 31
Buzan, B. 20, 22, 24, 57

Canada 44, 108, 113, 120
    and HSN 12, 23, 65, 66, 70, 71, 76, 111
    Canadian Consortium on Human Security 76
    Human Security Centre 76

Human Security Report 69, 72, 74, 76, 110, 115,
    120
human trafficking 83, 89, 90
Hutchings, K. 60, 61, 62

ICISS (International Commission on Inter-
    vention and State Sovereignty) 72, 73, 117
idealism 60
index of human insecurity 41
IHDP (International Human Dimensions
    Programme) 23, 28, 33, 43, 44, 45
India 38, 69, 90, 95, 96, 102, 109
individuality 55
Indonesia 28
industrialisation 90, 104
Instituto del Tercer Mundo 13
internally displaced persons (IDPs) 116–17
    see also migration
International Action Network on Small Arms 71
International Atomic Energy Agency 109
International Campaign to Ban Landmines
    (ICBL) 11, 69, 70, 76
International Commission on Intervention and
    State Sovereignty 17
International Committee of the Red Cross 72, 75
International Conference on Population and
    Development 93
International Council for Science 25
International Criminal Court 8, 38, 65, 76, 77
International Criminal Tribunals 8
International Decade on Natural Disasters 47
International Development Research Centre 97
International Federation of Red Cross Red
    Crescent Societies (IFRC) 47, 75
International Fund for Agricultural
    Development 41
International Geosphere-Biosphere Programme
    43
international humanitarian law (IHL) 67, 72
International Labour Organisation 90, 92–3,
    107
international law 9–11, 17
International Peace Academy 11
International Peace Research Institute 76
international relations theory 55
International Rescue Committee 13
International Security 83
International Social Science Council 25
International Women's Year 84
IPCC (Intergovernmental Panel on Climate
    Change) 24, 26, 36, 37, 38, 40, 104
    Working Group II 36, 44

Iran 109
Iraq 74
Ireland 111
Irwin, R. 62
Islam 86, 88
Israel 109
IUCN (International Union for Conservation
    of Nature) 105

Jackman, D. 72
Jad, I. 96
Japan 23, 72, 77, 111, 118
    Ministry of Foreign Affairs 11
Johannesburg Plan of Action 28
Johannesburg summit 28, 29
Jordan 67–8, 111
    Regional Human Security Centre 76
Journal of Peace Research 12
Judaism 86

Kabeer, N. 90
Kaldor, M. 28
Kant, I. 19, 60
Kasperson, J. X. 46, 47
Kaufmann, E. 62
Kaul, I. 21
Kennedy, P. 32
Keohane, R. 73
Ketteman, M. C. 9, 13, 17
Khong, Y. F. 114, 116, 122, 122–3, 125, 126
Kiev Ministerial Conference 29
King, A. 92
kinship 88–9
Klare, M. T. 27
Korean National Commission for UNESCO
    82
Kosovo 72, 74
Krause, K. 22, 116, 122
Kyoto Protocol 20, 29, 39, 108–9

Lacroix, J. 62
Lamb, H. 116
Latin America 88, 90, 96
Latour, B. 49
Lavauden, L. 39
League of Arab States (LAS) 5
League of Nations 19, 107
Lee, S.-W. 42, 78
liberalisation 52–3
Lodgaard, S. 111
Lonergan, S. 31, 33, 41
Lysøen Agenda 14, 66

Potsdam Institute for Climate Impact Research 44
poverty 53, 82, 89, 90–1
Programme of Action of the World Summit for Social Development 66
Puigdefabregas, J. 40

Qatar, 28

Ramcharan, B. G. 9, 13, 15
Ramsbotham, O. 62
Randall, D. 37
realism 55, 56, 60–1
refugees 116–17
    see also migration
reform of security sector 97–8
Renner, M. 111
research institutions 11
responsibility 59
Retreat on Human Security 66
Riché, P. 54
Richmond, O. 115
Rio de Janeiro 21, 28, 39, 109, 110
risk 46, 47, 112
Robbins, B. 62
Rojas Aravena, F. 78, 89, 95, 107
Roosevelt, Franklin 7, 17
Rothschild, E. 123
Ruggie, J. G. 32
Russia 28, 69, 103, 108
Rwanda 70, 72, 74

Sahel 39, 41, 43
    see also Africa
Sahnoun, M. 73
Santiago 67, 68, 73, 74
Saudi Arabia 87
Save the Children Alliance 76
Scandinavia 86
Schmeidl, S. 117
Schnabel, A. 15
Schnellnhuber, H.-J. 44
Schwartz, P. 37
securitas 53–4
securitisation 22, 28, 31, 34, 57, 122, 125
security 21–2
    and human security 57–9
    and politics 54
    and the nation 53–4
    in international relations theory 55
Security Dialogue 11, 22
Sen, A. 8, 42, 110, 111, 117, 118

Sevilla European Council 29
Shalabi, A. 86
Shinoda, H. 23
Shiva, V. 45
Shue, H. 121
Siakeu, G. 93
Sierra Leone 16
Sivaramakrishnan, K. 62
Slovenia 111
small arms 67, 68, 70–2, 75, 77
Small Arms Survey 67, 71, 76
small island states 37–8
Smith, K. 46
Smyth, F. 70
Social Watch report 13
Somalia 71, 72, 74, 116
South Africa 28, 87, 111
    see also Africa
South America 102, 104
South Asia 88, 93, 104
    see also Asia
South East Asia 102
    see also Asia
southern Africa 43, 89
    see also Africa
South America 88
    see also individual countries
south-eastern Europe 29
Spillmann, K. 31, 45
Steffen, W. 25, 44
Stichick, T. 68
Stockholm Conference on the Human Environment 110
Stychin, C. F. 62
subjectivity 59
sub-Saharan Africa 88, 90, 93
    see also Africa
Sudan 41
Sweden 78
Switzerland 65, 67, 70, 71, 72, 75, 76, 77, 111
    Centre for Democratic Control of Armed Forces 76
    CHD 67, 76
    Geneva International Centre for Humanitarian Demining 76
    Small Arms Survey 76

Takaso, Y. 111
Takur, R. 10
Tata Energy and Resources Institute 30
TEAP (Technology and Economic Assessment Panel) 104